MID-CENTURY MODERN
GLASS IN AMERICA

MID-CENTURY MODERN
glass
in America

DEAN SIX
with Paul Eastwood

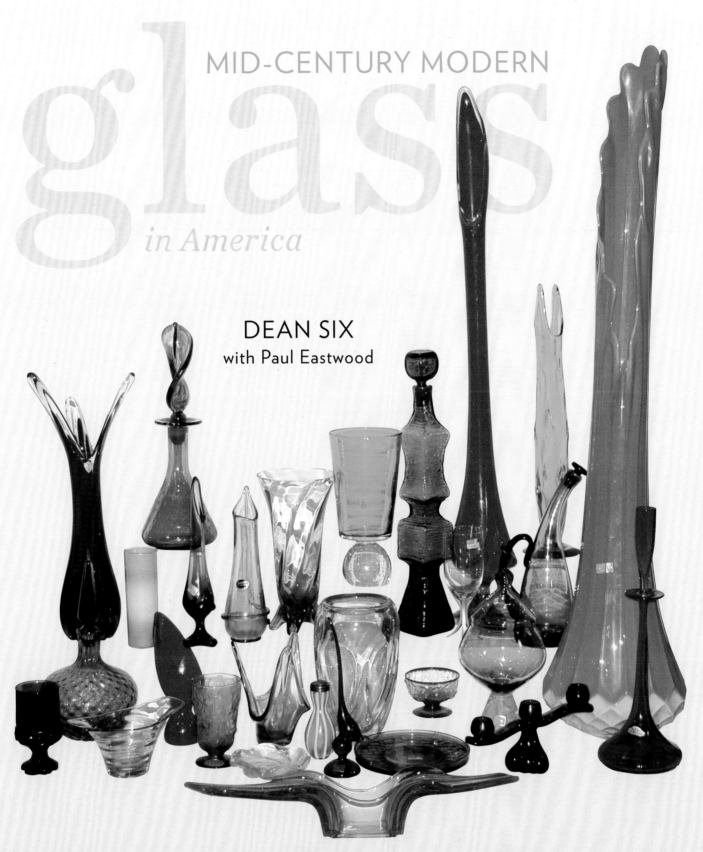

Schiffer Publishing Ltd

4880 Lower Valley Road • Atglen, PA 19310

Other Schiffer Books by the Author:

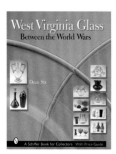

West Virginia Glass Between the World Wars. $29.95
978-0-7643-1546-6

Viking Glass: 1944–1970. $29.95
978-0-7643-1859-7

Lotus: Depression Glass and Far Beyond. $29.95
978-0-7643-2163-4

American Machine-made Marbles. $29.95
978-0-7643-2464-2

Popular American Marbles. $14.95
978-0-7643-2640-0

Library of Congress Control Number: 2014945623

Designed by Matt Goodman
Type set in Coronet, ZaphHumnst & ITC Clearface

ISBN: 978-0-7643-4744-3
Printed in China
6 5 4 3

Published by Schiffer Publishing, Ltd.
4880 Lower Valley Road
Atglen, PA 19310
Phone: (610) 593-1777;
Fax: (610) 593-2002
E-mail: Info@schifferbooks.com

For our complete selection of fine books on this and related subjects, please visit our website at www.schifferbooks.com. You may also write for a free catalog.

This book may be purchased from the publisher. Please try your bookstore first.

We are always looking for people to write books on new and related subjects. If you have an idea for a book, please contact us at proposals@schifferbooks.com.

Schiffer Publishing's titles are available at special discounts for bulk purchases for sales promotions or premiums. Special editions, including personalized covers, corporate imprints, and excerpts can be created in large quantities for special needs. For more information, contact the publisher.

FSC
www.fsc.org
MIX
Paper from responsible sources
FSC® C167893

Contents

Foreword

This timely and important book adds to the very limited material in print on American Mid-century Modern glass. While the style has seen attention from historians and curators of architecture and home furnishings, it is just now attracting attention from scholars and collectors of 20th century American glass. As with any pioneer, Dean Six is forced to make choices about his subject which may later be disputed—what constitutes "modern" glass objects, what is the date range in which production should fall—but he is right to forge ahead and begin the discourse on this topic.

The period after World War II became a time of great change in the social and cultural landscape of America. The GI Bill provided access to education and lifted a generation into the middle class. Mills and factories boomed, filling orders to satisfy consumer demand pent up by wartime restrictions. The automobile made suburban living feasible and opened the door to not just a new place to call home, but also a new style of living. Colleges and universities formalized the training of industrial designers who created a fresh visual language. All this gave manufacturers of consumer goods a clientele—post-war brides, new home owners, white collar workers—interested in and able to buy new, modern furnishings to fill their homes.

Only now, a little more than a generation after this change, are we beginning to save and treasure the pieces of that past. American Mid-century Modern glass is the stuff of our parents and grandparents, the objects we grew up around, but replaced with the new styles of our lifetime. Now we must chase it and study it, search for it and save it. Dean Six's book provides an important first step in knowing, understanding, and appreciating that glass.

Anne Madarasz
Museum Division Director, Senator John Heinz History Center
Pittsburgh, Pennsylvania

Acknowledgments

No book or creative process is accomplished in a vacuum. The following kind people helped me accomplish what is presented in this volume. Any shortcomings are fully my responsibility. These folk provided me with critical building blocks. I thank them.

Gail Bardhan, Rakow Library
Walter Blenko
Blenko Glass
Tom and Neila Bredehoft
The late J. Stanley Brothers
Hanna Burch
Dave Bush
Debbie and Randy Coe
Sandi Connally
Tom and Sherry Cooper
Millie Coty
Mary Ann and Clark Emch
Tom Felt
George Fenton
Fenton Art Glass
Amy Fisher
Dale Frederiksen
Terry Gartman
Kathy Grant
Todd Hall
Randy Harris

John Houze
Wayne Husted
Helen Jones
Bob Page
Kelsey Murphy
National Duncan Glass Society
National Fenton Glass Society
National Imperial Glass Museum
Bob O'Grady for photos shared
Kelly O'Kane
Fred Ottoson
Deborah Patterson, Chalet Vintage
     Art Glass Gallery
Sharon Pickens
Robert Porath
The Imaging Department of
     Replacements, Ltd.
Jaime Robinson
Harley Trice
Katie Trippe
Rock Wilson

About This Book's Organization—and a Word About Price Guidelines

In creating the architecture for this book, several ideas were explored. I first organized it by pattern. Then I tried to break it into tableware and other forms. I believe that organization by manufacturer is labor intensive, as it requires looking through the entire book to identify a possible object. However, I could not convince myself that any other manner of ordering the information worked better.

This book has two divisions—the first is American Mid-century Modern (AMCM) hot glass, organized by the glass makers. It is followed by a shorter section on decorators and designers who applied "cold decoration" to the glass made by others. Cold decoration is the industry term for decoration or embellishment to a glass object long after it has been produced. This includes painting, decals, cutting, etching and all surface decoration. To apply cold decoration, the once liquid hot glass

having is allowed to turn cold and sit, days or months perhaps, before the decoration is applied. The decoration might be done at the factory where the hot glass was produced or shipped far away to a second firm.

The entries for hot glass manufacturers have brief histories of the glass manufacturers in America that made Mid-century Modern. This section is the "who" part of the AMCM story including the brief historical sketch and short bibliographies titled "To learn more."

What follows are AMCM glass products divided into two predominate categories: giftware and accessories, and stemware and tableware. Giftware and accessories includes vases, candy dishes, smoking items and all of the glass that is not intended for tabletop use. Stemware and tableware includes all of the pieces that would be used on a dining table to serve food and beverage.

Textured tumblers and drink ware that became popular in the AMCM era are a significant part of the glass of this style and period and are addressed, however briefly, within tableware.

"Good, Better, Best" Visual Shorthand for AMCM Manufacturers

Within the section of this book that addresses the individual manufacturers of Mid-century Modern American glass, is inserted a small visual clue about the range of ware in the AMCM manner for that manufacturer. Having seen another author use a sampling of "Good, Better, Best" to illustrate the hierarchy of quality and desirability, I have sought to create such a shorthand visual for this book so that one can glimpse an example or two or three of diverse products from each firm.

There are one to three examples and they are captioned Good, Better, or Best. In all events, that same object appears in a larger image and with a more detailed caption later in that specific manufacturers section.

The intent of this shorthand is to give an at-glance idea of the scope of a company's production. For some manufacturers, there is only one example (or two). Those may be titled only good, or best. In those circumstances, it may

be that a manufacturer produced only one line that qualifies as AMCM (like Canton Glass) or it may reflect my belief that only one line merits mention and that it is indeed of the "best" caliber of Mid-century design. These are not intended as definitive examples of a makers best ware, they are only quick, visual clues and overviews. I do hope they prove useful to readers.

Price Guidelines

Comments on the pricing guidelines offered in this work should be noted by readers. Prices for any piece of glass varies greatly at different places and times. Prices vary by region across the continent. They vary by things as specific as single events and venues. What is high priced at a Mid-century show in an urban area might be offered at a very low cost in a rural community. Or the reverse might be true. Some colors bring more at various times of the year, and on the list of pricing variances goes.

The numbers suggested as pricing guidelines are only that—guidelines and suggestions. In no way are they intended to reflect absolute values or to suggest your object has that exact value. Like any price guide these numbers suggest some consideration of supply and demand and are to be used, along with other market indicators, in your consideration to determine a reasonable market value for your object in your specific market. Please use the indicated guidelines wisely.

We have endeavored to provide price range suggestions for all of the objects in the photographs, but have declined to attempt prices on items shown on catalog pages. Having never held the object or seen it in person, we simply lack the expertise to provide a meaningful suggestion as to value.

An Introduction to American Mid-century Modern Glass

Popular culture aficionados have dubbed the products of striking new design sensibilities produced in the "mid-twentieth century" as Mid-century Modern (MCM). The use of the phrase "Mid-century Modern" was coined as recently as 1983 by author Cara Greenberg, in her book *Mid-century Modern: Furniture of the 1950s.* In the intervening thirty years, the term has been accepted and used around the globe. Terms like atomic, futuristic, space-age, organic, Jetson, and others have surfaced. I find some of them more descriptive and fun as potential tags for the style of objects addressed here. However, it is the phrase "Mid-century Modern" that seems to prevail in use when describing the designs of this period and movement. Writing on mid-century architecture has been prolific, furniture designs have been widely explored, even ceramic tableware much touted. American glass from mid-twentieth century and the emerging glass aesthetics has, to date, been little written about and, arguably, under-appreciated.

Looking to the time before the mid-century we find collecting American glass was popularized for the affluent in the early twentieth century. The DuPonts were some of the first to purchase early examples, or what they then believed to be early examples, of American glass, for what would become a core of the glass collection at Winterthur in Delaware. At The Metropolitan Museum of Art in New York, a pioneering step was taken with the gift from a wealthy patron in 1909 of objects from the Hudson-Fulton exposition, including American glass. The Rockefellers' interest in decorative arts fueled Colonial Williamsburg and colonial glass, furniture and designs were popularized. Other wealthy families became collectors and patrons as collections, private and public, grew.

Books on American glass began to appear and kindled (or responded to) a thirst for information about the glass. Some influential volumes include *Early American Pressed Glass* by Ruth Webb Lee (1931); *American Glass* by George S and Helen McKearin (1941); *American Glass Cup Plates* by Ruth Webb Lee and James H. Rose (1948); and *Milk Glass* by E. McCamly Belknap (1949). The topics covered in these books parallel the popular glass collecting trends though the 1950s. The focus was largely on nineteenth century American glass.

Three significant occurrences worked in tandem to move glass collecting beyond Early American and Victorian objects. These were the launching by Nora Koch of *The Depression Glass Daze*, a newspaper of articles and secondary market sales ads in 1970; the publication by Hazel Marie Weatherman of her influential *Colored Glassware of the Depression Era* in 1970; and the highly popular sequel, *Colored Glassware of the Depression Era 2*, in 1974; and the perennial *Collector's Encyclopedia of Depression Glass* by Gene Florence in 1972 and annually thereafter. These three leaders as well as other books, events, and periodicals to a lesser degree launched glass collecting and "Depression glass" in particular onto a new, higher plane.

As I write this, some forty plus years ahead in time from those early depression glass publications, the phrase "depression glass" remains the most commonly evoked glass catch-phrase for glass books, shows, club names, and almost anything trying to catch public interest related to glass. However, as the events outlined above suggest, glass collecting moves forward with time: early blown glass, flint glass, early American pattern glass, and Depression glass all had and retain appeal.

For today's new collectors, and some young collectors, the meaning of the "depression" is not even understood. I have heard the question of the difference between pressed and depressed glass. I offer the evolution and history of our collecting as the unmistakable story that we will move forward. I further suggest that the movement forward in glass collecting has been ongoing for some years but lacks a clear identity and a concentrated voice (like those formative and focused depression projects of Koch, Weatherman, and Florence).

It is time. This is far from a revolution and more an adoption. Collectors of ceramic American tableware have long adopted the decorative arts term Mid-century Modern to describe their mid-century interests. Books on mid-century ceramics have been written for several years: chronicling, illustrating, naming, and expounded on our sister product, the clay crafts, for both decoration and table accessories.

It is time to get serious about America Mid-century Glass. It is time to add the chapter to glass collecting and to the scholarship that follows "Depression Glass."

Goblet forms across time. Early American Pattern Glass, circa 1880s; American Rich (or Brilliant Cut) circa 1890–1915; Depression era machine-pressed glass, circa 1930s; Elegant handmade, circa 1940s; and Tiffin heavy pressed, circa 1970.

In this book I advocate an even narrower slice of that mid-century production. First, the topic is narrowed to include only American glass. Please note that "American" is not just the United States but includes Canada, i.e., North American, producers as well. I have struggled to delineate not just the products from the mid-century time period and further defined by geography, but specifically objects of glass that aspire to being "Modern."

By "Mid-century" I choose to accept two definite moments in time as the parameters. A study group at the Museum of American Glass in West Virginia struggled with this at the first Mid-century Modern Symposium in the fall of 2012. We largely agreed to define mid-century as beginning with the end of World War II (in the European Theatre that was April–May 1945 and in the Pacific before year's end 1945) which we shall accept as 1945. It was then proposed that the era ran until the "end" of the 1960s. The 1960s were a period of unique social upheaval and consequence in America that did not end, in mind-set or cultural consequence, until the early 1970s when the Vietnam War was winding down. The Vietnam War officially ended with the fall of

Saigon in early 1975, but for our purposes we shall define the end of the "1960s era" as the end of the year 1974. This book largely looks at glass produced, designed, and marketed in between 1945 and the 1974-ish time frame. We are ready to explore glass produced in the true "middle years" of the 20th century.

The term "modern" is much more difficult. For the purposes of this book, we shall accept that it means "design that consciously and intentionally breaks with the design traditions that came before." Modern, as used in this book, is denouncing and rebelling against the form, embellishment, and visual appeal that came before. Modern is the adoption of alternatives in design to the historical visual language. In the simplest and purest perspective, modern design must look like nothing that came before it.

Some have written that modern is synonymous with timeless. They suggest that prehistoric cave paintings or some Native American designs are in fact modern. I reject that notion and suggest that those are in fact classic and timeless designs, but they are not modern. This issue of modernity is the second litmus test to be considered after the time period of production for objects, lines and patterns to be included in this book.

Objects to be considered AMCM must be both produced mid-twentieth century and address modern design as defined above.

It might come as no surprise to readers that, when crafting this book, some designs or patterns, indeed some entire companies, were deemed appropriate for inclusion in this book. They were later removed when arguably decided to not be "modern," and then replaced in the book outline with further debate and consideration only to be removed again later.

The question of how much, or to what degree, this breaking with the past must be apparent in a specific object or design is far from a clear line for this author or for the many to whom I have spoken. Arguments to include objects not shown here and to exclude some that are included here can be well reasoned and sustained with justification. The extent to which I buy into those arguments changes almost daily. It is a slippery slope of inclusions and exclusion indeed.

Is it critical to introduce the concept of a designer into any equation or discussion of what modern is? Forms of objects have often been dictated by intended use, practicality, and function.

In the name of art, creations have often been layered with embellishment and imposed decoration. From buildings to vessels, we have subjected design to superficially imposed surface decoration. As a hard rule, modernity defies embellishment for its own sake. Yet much of what is defined as "Mid-century Modern" is so placed due to the graphics and decoration on an otherwise purely functional object. Examples are decorated tumblers, the designs of Fred Press, and the ware commonly referred to as "signed and designed."

Historically, we do find occasional artisans who added their embellishments and modifications to practical and traditional forms. However, it is the entry of "outside" designers, those we call industrial designers, who introduced a dedicated awareness of the aesthetic to the act of glass creation and production. Design was no longer a byproduct or end result, but a factor in the conceptualization—an integral component from the very beginning. While the involvement of a designer was not a new concept, it was to become a standard of practice in much of the mid-century aesthetic. And their most common mantra was that "form follows function."

With the element of the American Mid-century glass time period resolved, (1945–1970-ish), I continue to struggle with defining what modern glass is. Simply being made between those two dates does not evoke modernity. Is it modern if a very contemporary design or decoration, one that indeed breaks with tradition, is applied to an old form? If a simple bowl, tumbler or platter has Mid-century Modern decoration on it, is it in fact an example of American Mid-century Modern glass? Where do we draw the line in regards to the point where a design "breaks with tradition?" Can it be a little modern or must it scream? The mid-century Scandinavian glass is heavy and bold. If glass has heft, weight, and largeness, is it modern per sei? Italian mid-century often featured biomorphic shapes and liquid, amoebic forms. If a piece of American glass is shaped in a flowing, fluid, asymmetrical form, is it considered modern? Then, there are issues of texture and color to contend with. If it is bright orange glass, an uncommon color in American glass until the post World War II era, or if it has a heavily textured, abstract, or

Discussion are ongoing about the degree of modernity a piece embraces. Shown here are two additional hot beverage servers, both with metal and plastic components. The handles and base on these examples suggest a mid–century design concern. Left server $8–12 and right $10–18.

organic surface decoration (breaking with the geometric or realistic surfaces of prior glass decoration), are those objects modern, *per se*? It quickly becomes apparent that there are more questions than answers.

I was led to look at two additional themes. I revisited the working definition of Depression glass while searching for guidance in how collectors as well as time dealt with categories of glass. Secondly, I wanted to delve into the complex topic of glass made by a hot glass manufacturer that was purchased and decorated later by a firm that applied post-market decorations. Were these decorating firms "glass companies" of a sort, or is this a different beast altogether? Should decorators of glass be treated the same as those who designed the forms and crafted the blank glass canvas? Did they belong in the same book, or were their stories so divergent as to merit distinct treatments?

Looking at and understanding "Depression" glass as popular glass and

how to define it is a daunting task. The Great Depression in the U.S. began with the stock market crash of October 1929 and generally is viewed as ending in 1939. Though the Depression's duration was one decade, what the collectable and antique markets have dubbed "Depression glass" is generally a style of light colored, transparent glass that began perhaps as early as the late 1910s. The styles, colors and patterns that get lumped into Depression glass texts often were produced as far as the early 1950s. Four decades plus of production is grouped into the style labeled Depression glass. We have accepted a very loose definition of Depression glass and have allowed numerous related themes all to be bundled and remarketed under that single banner. The producers of both Depression glass and Mid-century Modern glass were manufacturing a product. It happened to be glass. It is today's collectors, dealers, and authors who have come along later in time and who strive to impose names, order, categories and styles onto those glass products. We seek to create an orderly world from a random one, a world we can chronicle, catalogue, and reduce to organized lists. It is a daunting task, one never meant to be undertaken.

The names and labels we apply to glass periods and styles are yet an additional set of riddles. The term Depression glass did not come into use until three or four decades after the Depression era ended. It was similar for Mid-century Modern, which became an identified term years after the period so named had passed. Those who made, marketed, and retailed both Depression glass and Mid-century Modern glass had never heard of either of these terms used today to describe the products. As glass giant Frank Fenton often reminded us, for the producers at the time it was a business and they could not foresee or imagine the world of collectors that would emerge years later, seeking to understand and impose order onto a body of products that were driven by one and only one goal: sales. In Mr. Fenton's words, "Remember that to us this was a business. First, foremost and always a business."

As a business in America, the ideas and visual vocabulary of Mid-century Modern never fully took root. Granted, American furniture makers produced Swedish modern furniture, and there were other pockets of interest, but there was never a major acceptance of the modern aesthetic into the broad American lifestyle.

Rarely does a single event launch a new design infatuation. It is true that some designs incorporating our concept of an orbiting atom were prevalent in post-World War II design. It was the Russian satellite, Sputnik, and the vision of it creeping across the world's night sky that sparked an interest in design and other cultural phenomena with space-age related themes. Added to the AMCM vocabulary of form, a concern for minimal superficial surface decoration became important. Other themes paid homage to the atomic and space age. These were largely American infatuations.

The extremes of modern design were beyond the desire of middle-American housewives, who were then the main consumers and decision makers concerning domestic goods.

Numerous advertising campaigns of the mid-century note that a certain

The centerfold, double page illustration from the Brasillia line of furniture catalog by Broyhill. Note how the sweeping vertical points and curves, described in the catalog as the "upward" look, so closely echo the architecture of the city Brasilia. The same catalog has numerous photos of the city and its architecture to drive home the point of similarity. The glass of this era might share the same description of Broyhill gave the furniture: It is the dynamic embodiment of a new way of life. And with it, style–conscious American families everywhere can bask in the positive assurance that their furniture (or glass) is the last word in contemporary elegance. Broyhill catalog from the collection of Jaime Robinson.

pattern or design are indeed modern, but in a nice and "acceptable" way. The best example of this middle-America approach to modern was expressed in a jewelry store pamphlet created by Redwing pottery. For the Redwing pattern Fantasy, the literature reads, "this pattern is our answer to those who 'love' modern but simply cannot live with it." Perhaps that says everything about why the very edgy modern designs never really took hold in homes across America. They loved the idea of modern, but simply could not live with it?

Fred Press, a significant name in signed and designed glassware at mid-century, and a vice-president of Rubel & Co. of NYC (as of June 1951) wrote in *The Gift and Art Buyer* of May 1953, "For a period in the market there has been a strong trend toward producing gifts in the modern and extreme modern design. The 'bizarre' period is past, and recently we have observed a softening of the modern, to obtain coordination of modern with traditional. This trend is most interesting and in the long run, produces the most 'livable' products. Firms will continue to strive toward

modern designs, yet try at the same time to please the customers by means of this coordination. This particular turn has proved of value to the industry, as well as to the customer. If any loss in popularity of certain items is forthcoming, it will most likely to found [sic] in the characteristically novelty items which have only a short lived-appeal."

Press continued, "Among other new developments which should continue strong in the future is the turning of wire-crafted merchandise into practically a staple in the industry. These articles are more important now than ever."

While Press's writing style is a bit challenging to follow, his points seem to be that cutting edge modern, that which he calls "bizarre," is too challenging and too modern for "livable" middle America. He observes a moderate, customer-pleasing coordination of modern and livable. He also notes the use of wire with glass. Noteworthy is that designs by Press and designs marketed by Rubel are very much involved with glass, wood, and wire combinations in the 1950s. Is he

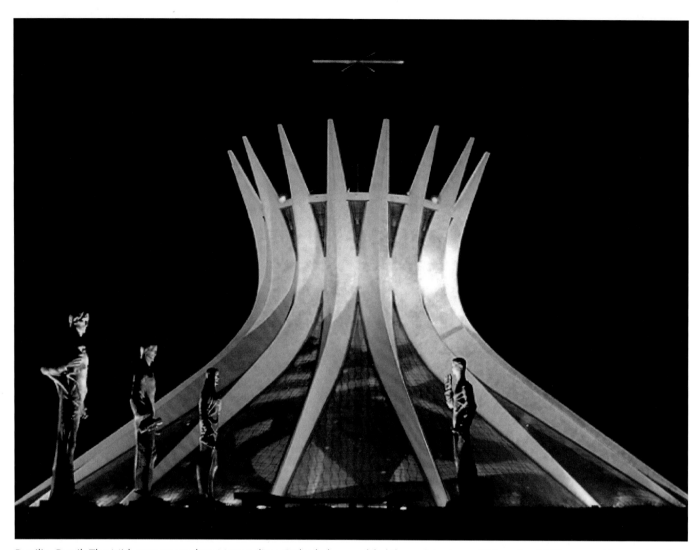

Brasilia, Brazil. The Mid–century modern Metropolitan Cathedral exemplifies the architecture of this entire 1960s created international city. This photograph was produced by Agência Brasil, a public Brazilian news agency. The image is published under the Creative Commons License Attribution 3.0 Brazil

observing, predicting, or promoting the glass and wood "coordination"?

It is indeed true that wire became one of the visual hallmarks of 1950s modern designs. Dunbar Glass introduced their Contrast pattern in 1953. It is colorless crystal in black wire frames bent to "atomic age" points reminiscent of illustrations of orbiting particles in an atom. In a world of Swedish Modern furniture of lightly colored polished wood came glass that incorporated wood and metal. Duncan and Miller's wood, brass and glass line, Festive, introduced in July of 1954, utilized wood lids and brassy metal components. Firms like Libbey marketed mass-produced glass in wood and wire holders, racks, carriers, and much more.

In Europe, the rebellion against traditional forms sprang forth and soared. Scandinavian firms like Orrefors utilized heavy, colorless crystal to craft

bold, massive, enduring looking modern designs. The same enthusiasm for modern flared to new heights with Italian glass. In the hands of Italian glass workers, modern became color, abstractions, and organic forms, all part of a newly expanded visual lexicon.

A select number of international events occurred in this the mid-century time frame that influenced design and advanced Modernism in major ways.

Beginning in 1956, a bold plan began with the construction of a new federal capital for the country of Brazil. Between then and April 21, 1960, a city was planned, developed, and built to present modernist architecture on a grand scale based on a utopian plan. The new city, built in forty-one months, caught the imagination of the world. Designs emerged echoing visual elements employed in the city's buildings. American popular culture items from

furniture (Broyhill of Lenoir, North Carolina, introduced Brasilia in 1962) to music (Herb Alpert Presents Sergio Mendes and Brasil '66) were touched by the charisma of the new Brazilian city.

Planned with Lucio Costa as the lead urban planner, Oscar Niemeyer as the principal architect, and landscaping created by Roberto Marx, Brasilia was the world's newest and most modern city. Three main architectural icons model the source of the visual elements that infiltrated other designs. These were the Cathedral of Brazil, the National Congress of Brazil, and the presidential home. Half a century later, all remain international symbols of modernism.

America's answer to the city of Brasilia was the 1962 World's Fair, held in Seattle, Washington. President John F. Kennedy opened the fair April 21,

Examples of metal, plastic and glass that embrace the Mid–Century Modern aesthetic. Designs like these were utilized in the 1950s and forward, both forms for coffee. Left is server $10–14 and right is server with candle warmer base $14–22. Makers unknown.

This cocktail glass, colorless with an Amber stem captured the shape of the Space Needle at the Seattle World's Fair and was produced by Bryce Glass. It was for exclusive use and sale at the revolving restaurant atop the Space Needle. China, Glass & Tableware. June 1962.

1962, via a telephone call by stating, "I am honored to open the Seattle World's Fair today. What we show is achieved with great effort in the fields of science, technology and industry. These accomplishments are a bridge which carry us confidently towards the 21st century." The mascot of the fair was, again, inspired by architecture. The building that became iconic and a symbol for modern at mid-century is the Seattle World's Fair Space Needle.

One reflection on American Mid-century glass must address color. There are perhaps a few paths through the color pallet of AMCM glass. Bold colors like orange, a relatively scarce color in glass until this period, bright yellows, deep greens, and vibrant reds, are all used in varying manners to craft AMCM glass. By the 1960s, trends in home interiors were shifting to avocado green and harvest Gold. From shag carpets to kitchen appliances, variations on those

two "earth tone" colors were common well into the 1970s. Glass of the period did not escape these two popular new tones. Called by numerous names, the dusty greens and Amber yellows invaded glass for almost two decades. One largely unique MCM color appeared under a number of names. It was cleverly named gray glass. Smoke, Charcoal, steel blue— and so go the names for the mid-century gray-toned glass.

Across time, glass has been largely utilitarian. Crafting and creating glass has long been regarded as a revered craft, and only recently attained recognition as an art form. Due to its utilitarian and craft nature, objects made of glass have rarely been signed by their maker. Signatures are the work of artists, a creative claim to an individual creation. Most historical glass bears no mark or identification. When glass has been marked, and since the nineteenth century it often was, it had a paper label

attached to the surface. Paper labels are and were intended to fall away or be removed. This lack of maker's identification has been a stumbling block for glass collectors. Turn over a porcelain, pottery, or ceramic creation as well as objects made of metal and it often and, for centuries, has had a maker's mark stamped or imprinted there. Glass has not been commonly identified by maker, leaving the question of who made it unknown.

Through writing, shared images, and documentation, we learn about glass. Here is a body of stories and objects that, to date, beg for further study.

Welcome to the brave new world of what was American Mid-century Glass.

Brief Histories of AMCM Hot Glass Manufacturers

Anchor Hocking

Lancaster, Ohio
1905–Present

Good   *Better*

Anchor Hocking Glass began with Isaac J. Collins and six friends in 1905. Collins had been working in the decorating department of Ohio Flint Glass Company, saw opportunities, and acted to acquire a carbon factory and convert it to a glasshouse. After a disastrous fire the Lancaster, Ohio, factory was rebuilt in 1924. Hocking subsequently purchased a controlling interest in the Lancaster Glass Company and the nearby Standard Glass Manufacturing Company. Anchor Hocking Glass Corporation came to be in 1937 when the Anchor Cap and Closure Corporation merged with the Hocking Glass Company, and used the name, Anchor Hocking Glass Corp., during the Mid-century era. The firm was a large corporation that produced inexpensive, machine-made glass wares in vast numbers.

During the 1945–1970s era Anchor Hocking utilized mechanized glass manufacturing to produce immense volumes of glassware intended for everyday use. The intended use did not negate the inclusion of modern design. Perhaps the olive green and Amber toned glass of Anchor Hocking at mid-century are their most recognized and distributed production. While Anchor incorporated textured glass and gave recognition to "Swedish Modern" influences it never moved beyond a conservative and safe utilization of Mid-century Modern.

In 1969 "Glass" was dropped from the corporate name because the company had evolved into an international company with an infinite product list. The Newell Corporation acquired the Anchor Hocking Corporation in 1987 and Hocking filed for chapter 11 bankruptcy protection in 2006. At the time of writing glass continues to be produced in America by the Anchor Hocking Company which is owned by the private equity firm Monomoy Capital Partners.

Anchor Hocking
AMCM Tableware
Anchor Hocking was a giant mid-century producer of machine-made, affordable tableware. An early line appealing to modern taste was attractively named Swedish Modern and was produced in colorless crystal and a deep green, called Forest Green. It is a 1940-50s era product. The 1960s saw Forest Green tableware replaced by the trendy Avocado Green, colorless glass remained in production, and added to the Anchor pallet was Honey Gold. The textured patterns with abstracted tactile surfaces were popularized at Anchor by lines like Sorento and Milano, lines that resembled the handmade textured glass of Bryce, Seneca, Fostoria, and others.

Swedish Modern (left front) #522 square dish, 6⅝″, $2–5; (back left) #523 relish tray 9″ l. $2–4; #521 deep square dish, 6½″, $3–6.

SWEDISH MODERN PIECES

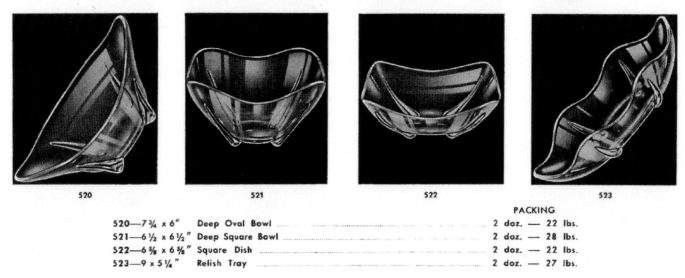

520 521 522 523

		PACKING	
520—7 ¾ x 6″	Deep Oval Bowl	2 doz. — 22 lbs.	
521—6 ½ x 6 ½″	Deep Square Bowl	2 doz. — 28 lbs.	
522—6 ⅝ x 6 ⅝″	Square Dish	2 doz. — 22 lbs.	
523—9 x 5 ¼″	Relish Tray	2 doz. — 27 lbs.	

Anchor Hocking catalog illustration for the short line Swedish Modern.

Anchor Hocking "rocket" vase. Forest Green, $12–20.

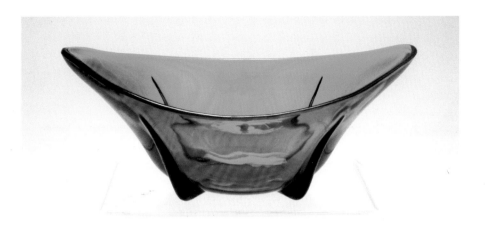

Swedish Modern #520 deep oval bowl, 7¾" x 6", Green, $6–10.

Colored Glass Sets

Six piece Soreno colored glass sets, in attractive gold and white gift boxes.

		Sets Ctn.	Lbs. Ctn.	Price Set
T4000/139	Avocado 6 pc. 12 oz. beverage set	4	20	$ .90
N4000/138	Honey Gold 6 pc. 12 oz. beverage set	4	20	.90
B4000/140	Aquamarine 6 pc. 12 oz. beverage set	4	20	.90
T4000/136	Avocado 6 pc. 9 oz. On-the-Rocks set	4	17	.80
N4000/135	Honey Gold 6 pc. 9 oz. On-the-Rocks set	4	17	.80
B4000/137	Aquamarine 6 pc. 9 oz. On-the-Rocks set	4	17	.80
B4000/90	Aquamarine 3 pc. ash tray set, 4¼", 6¼" and 8"	4	22	1.10
T4000/88	Avocado 3 pc. ash tray set, 4¼", 6¼" and 8"	4	22	1.10
N4000/89	Honey Gold 3 pc. Ash tray set, 4¼", 6¼" and 8"	4	22	1.10

17

Anchor Hocking Glass catalog featuring the pattern Soreno in Avocado, Honey Gold, and Aquamarine. The pattern was a very successful pattern for premium glass in the 1960s when it was given with detergent powders, gasoline and other products.

Milano textured iced tea, 16 oz., in Avocado, $1–4.

Soreno pattern (l to r) Honey Gold tumbler, $2–4, Crystal handled mug, $2–6; Avocado footed vase, $5–8; Avocado shaker (salt or pepper), $2–3 each; Crystal iridescent handled mug, $2–4, Honey Gold pitcher, $7–10, shaker, $2–3 each; and Honey Gold tumbler, $1–3.

MILANO TUMBLERS — "CRYSTAL ICE"

| 4005 — 4010 | 4007 — 4014 | 4012 — 4015 | 4087 |

PACKING		
4005 — 5 oz. Tumbler		3 doz. — 12 lbs.
4007 — 7 oz. Old Fashioned		3 doz. — 15 lbs.
4010 — 10 oz. Tumbler		3 doz. — 22 lbs.
4012 — 12 oz. Tumbler		3 doz. — 23 lbs.
4014 — 14 oz. Double Old Fashioned		3 doz. — 25 lbs.
4015 — 15 oz. Tumbler		3 doz. — 25 lbs.
4087 — 3 qt. Ice Lip Pitcher		½ doz. — 20 lbs.

PILLAR PACK CARRIERS

THREE SIZES IN SETS OF FOUR

4005-D	4007-D	4012-D
4005-D — 4 Pce. Set (5 oz. Fruit Juice)		12 sets — 18 lbs.
4007-D — 4 Pce. Set (7 oz. Old Fashioned)		12 sets — 23 lbs.
4012-D — 4 Pce. Set (12 oz. Tall Tumbler)		12 sets — 35 lbs.

REFRESHMENT SETS

4000/41 — 9 Pce. Refreshment Set
Each Set in C/D Ctn. — 4 Sets to Shipper — 32 lbs.
COMPOSITION: Eight 4012 Tumblers
One 4087 Pitcher

4000/45 — 24 Pce. Refreshment Set (Not Illustrated)
Each Set in Shipping Carton — 12 lbs.
COMPOSITION: Eight 4005 Juice Glasses
Eight 4012 Tumblers
Eight 4015 Iced Teas

4000/46 — 25 Pce. Refreshment Set (Not Illustrated)
Each Set in Shipping Carton — 17 lbs.
COMPOSITION: Eight 4005 Juice Glasses
Eight 4012 Tumblers
Eight 4015 Iced Teas
One 4087 Pitcher

4000/41

PROMOTE SETS

Anchor Hocking catalog page, Milano pattern. Milano, a second popular textured glass by Anchor Hocking, was available in colorless "crystal ice" as well as avocado. Both Milano and Sorento, products mass produced made by machine, were similar in appearance to more expensive handmade patterns from Seneca, Bryce and others.

Colored Glass Sets

T4000/132

T4000/133

Attractively packaged in printed parchment cartons.

	Sets Ctn.	lbs. Ctn.	Price Set
T4000 132 Avocado — 20 pc. Soreno luncheon set, four 10" plates, four 7 oz. cups, four 5¾" saucers, four 5⅝" salad or soup bowls, four 12 oz. beverages	2	29	$2.60
T4000 133 Avocado — 9 pc. Soreno salad set, 4 qt. salad bowl, six 5⅝" bowls, plastic fork and spoon	2	20	2.00

Bulk Packaged	Doz. Ctn.	lbs. Ctn.	Price Doz.
T4079 Avocado Soreno 7 oz. cup	3	16	$1.20
T4029 Avocado Soreno 5¾" saucer.	3	16	1.20
T4066 Avocado Soreno 5⅝" bowl	3	23	1.45
T4041 Avocado Soreno 10" plate	3	38	2.40
T4042 Avocado Soreno 12 oz. tumbler	3	22	1.25

Anchor Hocking Glass catalog illustrating Soreno pattern, Avocado luncheon and salad sets.

Altaglass

Medicine Hat, Alberta, Canada
1950–1981

Altaglass founder John Furch was born in Czechoslovakia in 1896. Prior to immigrating to Canada in 1949, he worked at English glass factories and others in Europe. In Canada he worked at Glass Guild in Stratford, Ontario (where only glass buttons were produced) and at Chalet in Cornwall. By 1950 he had established Altaglass in a former aircraft hangar at the Medicine Hat, Alberta, airport. In 1961 Altaglass relocated to 16th Street in Medicine Hat. S.W. Furch retired in 1971. The firm continued producing hot glass until December 1981. For some time after 1981, Altaglass produced borosilicate glass lamp-worked figurines and decorative objects, but not hot glass.

To Learn More:
McNaney, Dereak & Ann. *Swan Song: The Story of Altaglass with a Guide to Identification and Sales.* Privately published. 2005. www. altaglass.ca

Altaglass Amber/Brown air-trap three point vase/ bowl with ground and polished base. $14–22. Museum of American Glass in West Virginia collection.

Altaglass paper label as it appears on the base of the vase/bowl above.

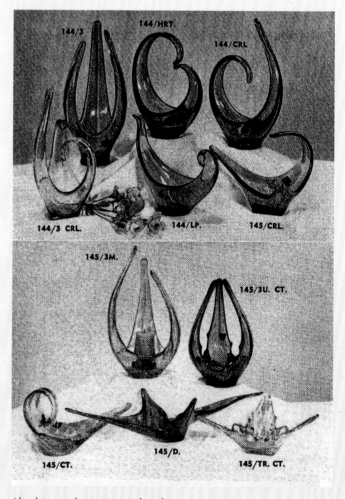

Altaglass catalog page, undated.

Bischoff

Culloden, West Virginia
1921–1964

Good   *Better*   *Best*

Bischoff glass was produced at two sites, by three different closely related family firms. The earliest was Bischoff Sons & Co., in Huntington, West Virginia, operating from 1921 until 1935 when it relocated to Culloden, West Virginia. In the Culloden factory they began using the name A. F. Bischoff Glass, Inc., which operated in Culloden from 1935 until 1963 and produced a number of forms that today are readily recognized as Mid-century Modern.

Members of the Bischoff family told an audience, at the West Virginia Glass gathering held at Huntington Museum of Art in 1993, about their design process. The tale was that during the two week shut down in the summer glass workers were allowed to make objects from the company tanks at their leisure. These glass creations were later set on boards atop sawhorses in the parking lot and the Bischoff brothers and their mother circulated, selecting pieces they liked, to be included in the next year's

catalogued offering. The extreme design difference between nearby Blenko (there was a short five miles distancing the two factories), with academically schooled designers, and Bischoff, with hot glass trained artisans, is apparent in the two companies wares. Bischoff designs often address the fluid nature of glass as an adaptation of an existing form or mould.

The Culloden factory was purchased by Indiana Glass in 1963, which operated the factory making forms identical to what Bischoff had produced as well as other shapes and other colors. The factory quickly became Sloan Glass Company (1964–1986) when Indiana relocated their hand-produced modern work to their existing large factory in Indiana. Sloan Glass continued the use of the name Bischoff to market the glass that Sloan produced. Sloan paper labels, colors, and forms were often identical to those used, pre-1963, by the Bischoff family.

Bischoff produced no dinnerware or tableware lines. They were prolific in manufacturing decanters, both practical and purely ornamental. Pitchers, tumblers, and cream and sugar sets largely round out the limited tableware and practical offerings from Bischoff.

Bischoff crackle decanter with pinched sides and colorless teardrop & air-trap stopper. Lime Green, pontiled, #478, 12" h., lip has pouring spouts, $32–40.

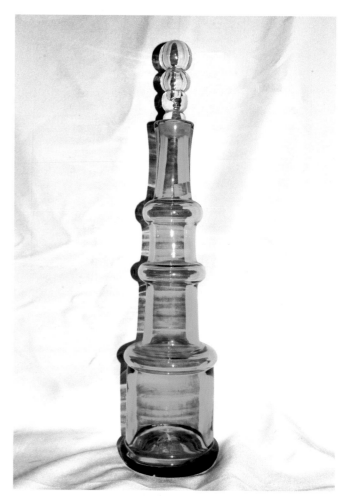

Bischoff tall floor vase, Peacock Blue with colorless stopper. 19½" h., pontiled, $85–125

Bischoff pinch pitchers, all with colorless applied handles. Small Brown or Green, $18–22; Ruby, half gallon, $35–55

Bischoff Peakock Blue pitcher with colorless, hand-applied handle and pontil, 8" h. $24–30; Amber with Amber applied handle and pontil, 5½" h., $18–26.

Bischoff Barracuda vases. So referenced by the author for the elongated vase form with fish–like lips; both pontiled. Ruby with Crystal foot, $35–48; Amber with Crystal foot, $30–45.

Bischoff Barracuda vase, exceptionally tall, Peacock Blue with pontil, $80–115. Small Peacock Blue bottle vase, rimmed top, pontiled, $18–24 (add 10% with original label).

Bischoff air-trap forms with pontil. Goblet vase form, Amethyst $30–40; crimped vase (possibly not Bischoff but another nearby Teays Valley manufacturer?) $35–45; and goblet vase in Peacock Blue $30–40.

Bischoff bent-neck decanters. Left, Emerald Green, pontiled with colorless handle and air-trap teardrop stopper, $40–55; Blenko crackle version, shown for similarities/differences; Ruby bent-neck form/vase. Neck not ground. Pontiled with colorless handle and folded neck (by design or accident?). As shown, $40–50.

Bischoff Amethyst and colorless stoppered bottle/
decanter, $65–75.

Bischoff stoppered bottles/decanter diversity. Poinsettia Red (Ruby) and Crystal
16" h., pontiled, $75–90; Orange with Crystal, 15½", t. $65–75 (note red has
colorless stem and orange has colored stem); Peacock Blue decanter with
colorless handle and stopper 15½" h., $40–55.

Bischoff Poinsettia, Red, hand-sheared edge bowl, pontiled, $30–45 (original
tag add 10%).

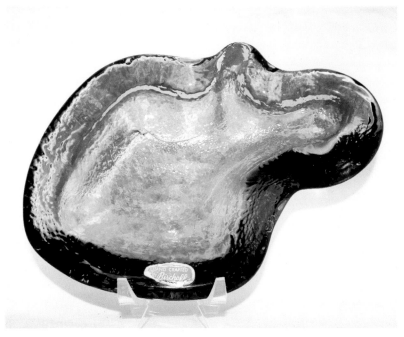

Bischoff Lime dump mould "amoeba" ash tray. (original Bischoff label add 10%). Note that most mid–century glass manufacturers made their version of a similar ash tray. $12–18 as shown.

Bischoff Gold (Amber) sheared edge and twist stem compote or simply "bowl" in Bischoff terms. Pontiled, $24–32.

Base showing Lefton label in the Italian form strikingly similar to Bischoff shown above.

Not Bischoff, but very similar in form, Red and Amber-footed bowl. Paper label reads "Lefton's Made in Italy."

Bischoff Brown/Charcoal footed and crimped-rim bowl $30–40 with matching #236 candlesticks. $30–38 pair. Circa 1950s.

Bischoff catalog cover, undated.

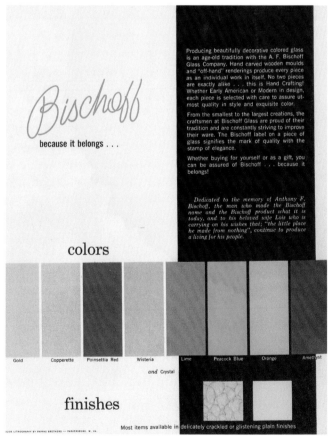

Bischoff catalog page listing colors made and noting available as crackled or "glistening plain finishes."

Bischoff catalog page, undated. Note the tall #287 bottle with stopper.

Peacock Blue pitcher with colorless handle, pontiled. Note the beginning mould blown base is identical to the "bowl" #948 shown on the preceding catalog page. 13¼" h., $40–55.

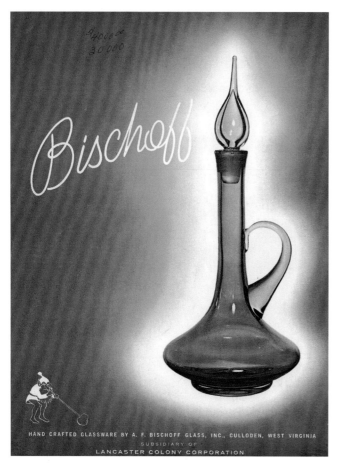

Bischoff catalog, undated. Note there appears on this catalog the additional line "subsidiary of Lancaster Colony Corporation."

Bischoff catalog page when owned by Lancaster Colony.

Bischoff catalog page when owned by Lancaster Colony.

Bischoff catalog page when a owned by Lancaster Colony.

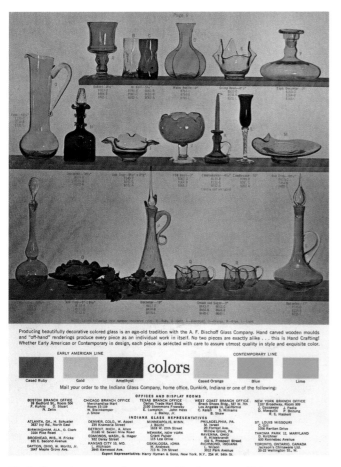

Bischoff catalog page when owned by Lancaster Colony.

Bischoff decanter. Designer Wayne Husted wrote the authors that "the design (shown here) which I named 'Kingston' was made in two sizes. One is 16.5 inches tall and the other is 21.5 inches tall. All of the designs on the three pages from the first catalog I designed before Tom Conally took over designing." Kingston, 21.5" Honey decanter with stopper, $60–85.

Bischoff decanter shown in the nearby company catalog with the unique "jesters cap" colorless stopper. Pontiled and air-traps, hand applied ornate handle, 19" h., $75–95.

Blenko

Milton, West Virginia
1921–Present

Good   *Better*   *Best*

Blenko Glass Company began operation in Milton, West Virginia, in 1921 as Eureka Glass. English glassmaker William John Blenko was a determined and competent glass man and his persistence paid off. The original company product line was limited to richly colored flat glass for church windows and architectural uses. The Great Depression had a dramatic impact on building construction and a quest for supplemental products led to the introduction of tableware and giftware in 1930. The earliest shapes and forms were heavily influenced by two Swedish brothers who had previously worked at nearby Huntington Tumbler, Axel Muller and Louis Miller. Their role in the production of heavier, pontiled, handmade production for the Blenko line is likely one influence in the presence of American Mid-century Modern glass in the glass area today defined as the Teays Valley of West Virginia.

In 1937, another Swede, Carl Erikson, joined the Blenko team and brought with him additional skills and influences rooted in the Swedish glass tradition. Erikson contributed by crafting heavy, thick forms and introducing controlled air-trap bubbles into pieces made at Blenko. His influences are readily visible in the 1940 Blenko catalog. Erikson left Blenko in 1942 and established his own factory in Ohio. See Erikson Glass later in this book.

Blenko introduced designers to their factory in 1947 with the arrival of Winslow Anderson, then newly graduated from Alfred University. Anderson was the first of several prominent designers to serve at Blenko and he remained there until 1953. His glass designs were widely acclaimed as modern and won several prestigious awards. He was followed by an impressive list of successors.

Wayne Husted was hired by Blenko in 1952. Time was required to create and put into production his designs so, according to Husted's interviews with collectors at Blenko Collector Conventions, his first four designs did not appear until 1953. In 1953, designs 5313, 5318, 5320, and 5321 were by Husted. He moved on to other design work in 1963, landing at nearby Bischoff glass for a time.

Joel Myers came in 1963, and remained the designer until 1970. John Nickerson was the last modernist designer retained by Blenko in the mid-century era. Nickerson served 1970 until 1974.

Blenko has often been deemed the forefront of American glass in Mid-century Modern designs. The four designers cited created designs in glass that embodied the essence of bold rebellion against pre-existing forms. Blenko pieces, often monumental in size, bold in color, and striking in form, reflect some of the best use of American modernism.

Blenko produced tableware in the early years (1930–40s), but by the early 1950s had largely shifted production to accessories and decorative objects, often more sculptural than functional.

Today, Blenko Glass continues to operate, making several of their classic mid-century designs as well as evolving new designs.

To Learn More:

Pina, Leslie. *Blenko Glass: 1962–1971 Catalogs.* Atglen, Pennsylvania: Schiffer Publishing, Ltd. 2000.

Pina, Leslie. *Blenko: Cool '50s & '60s Glass.* Atglen, Pennsylvania: Schiffer Publishing, Ltd. 2007.

Wonderful stylized AMCM cover for the
Blenko 1953 catalog.

986—Rosette Vase, 11 inches high.
963—Optic Pitcher, 14 inches high.
979—Optic Vase, 10¼ inches high.
404S—Fluted Vase, 9 inches high.
404M—Fluted Vase, 11½ inches high. (Not Shown)
404L—Fluted Vase, 15 inches high. (Not Shown)

963—Optic Vase, 11 inches high.
439M—Flared Beaker, 9½ inches high.
439S—Flared Beaker, 7½ inches high. (Not Shown)
439L—Flared Beaker, 12½ inches high. (Not Shown)
536—3-Legged Bowl, 11 inches diameter.
981—Optic Vase 10½ inches high.

16

Blenko company catalog 1953. While pre–designer forms like the
#986 Rosette Vase remain in the line (it is based on a centuries-
old European drinking vessel) Winslow Anderson designs
continue to dominate the Blenko offerings. Note the illusive
#536, three legged, 11-inch bowl.

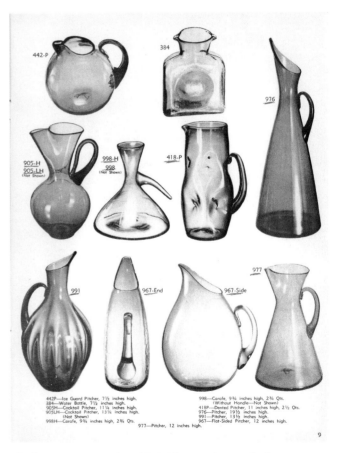

442P—Ice Guard Pitcher, 7½ inches high.
384—Water Bottle, 7½ inches high.
905H—Cocktail Pitcher, 11¼ inches high.
905LH—Cocktail Pitcher, 13¼ inches high.
(Not Shown)
998H—Carafe, 9¾ inches high, 2¾ Qts.

998—Carafe, 9¾ inches high, 2¾ Qts.
418P—Dented Pitcher, 11 inches high, 2½ Qts.
(Without Handle—Not Shown)
976—Pitcher, 19½ inches high.
991—Pitcher, 13½ inches high.
967—Flat-Sided Pitcher, 12 inches high.

977—Pitcher, 12 inches high.

9

Blenko company catalog, 1953. Noteworthy are the long-
produced water bottle #384 (not Mid–Century but earlier yet
modern); shapes like #991 that remain in production for years;
and the diversity of handles being applied in the early 1950s. All
Winslow Anderson designs.

Blenko company catalog 1953. Two popular Winslow Anderson designs appearing in the catalog are the "bent decanter" and #939 pitcher.

550-CT

★-948

550-CT

935-G

939-P

935-G

550CT—Sham Bottom Cocktail, 3 inches high.
948—Bent Decanter, 13 inches high.

935G—Tumbler, 4 inches high.
939P—Pitcher, 14⅛ inches high.

Blenko, bent, Charcoal decanter in crackle with matching colored stopper and colorless applied handle. Pontiled. 13" h.. $60–80.

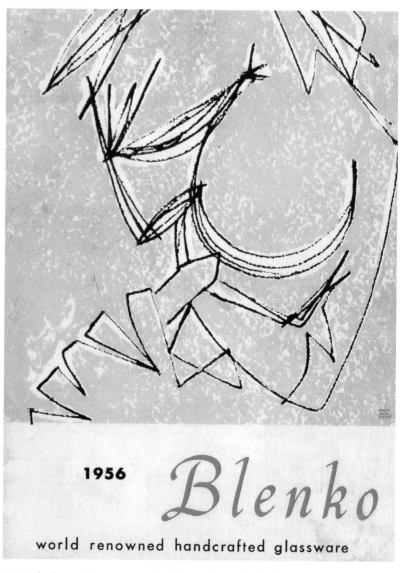

1956 *Blenko*

world renowned handcrafted glassware

1956 Blenko catalog cover. Art by Wayne Husted. Blenko was now self-proclaimed as "world renowned."

Blenko with applied decoration, Husted designs circa 1956–1959. Left to right: #5615, Sea Green, 12½", $400–500; #5935, Mulberry, 9", $150–175; and #551, Gold, 13", $400–450. From the collection of Terry Gartman and Robert Porath.

561

562-L

562

5613

5615

Blenko 1956 company catalog. All designs this page Wayne Husted. The "cut edge" decanters, #562, are very desirable as are a series of vessels with applied surface decoration (#5615, shown here, bottom left).

Blenko with applied decoration, Husted designs. Left to right: #557 in Amber, 12½", $400–500; #551 in Lime, 13", $400–450; #556 in Teal, 16", $500–600. From the collection of Terry Gartman and Robert Porath.

Brief Histories of AMCM Hot Glass Manufacturers

Blenko "flat" decanters. All are more wide than deep. Foreground: #6316 in Gold, 21"
wide, $500–700; center row, three colors of #6315, all 16" wide, Sea Green, $350–400,
Turquoise, $400–450, and Gold, $350–400; rear: #6314 Tangerine (Amberina), 21" h.,
$400–600. From the collection of Terry Gartman and Robert Porath

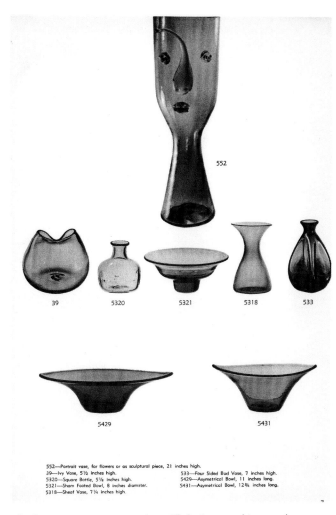

552

39   5320   5321   5318   533

5429   5431

552—Portrait vase, for flowers or as sculptural piece, 21 inches high.
39—Ivy Vase, 5½ inches high.   533—Four Sided Bud Vase, 7 inches high.
5320—Square Bottle, 5⅛ inches high.   5429—Asymetrical Bowl, 11 inches long.
5321—Sham Footed Bowl, 8 inches diameter.   5431—Asymetrical Bowl, 12¾ inches long.
5318—Sheaf Vase, 7¼ inches high.

Blenko 1956 company catalog. All designs on this page by Wayne Husted. The oversized "portrait vase," at 21 inches, is an introduction to sculptural-faced objects that will re-appear in the Blenko line for decades.

★ The Manufacturer guarantees that this article corresponds in every particular to the one chosen by The Museum of Modern Art, New York, for the Good Design Exhibition at The Merchandise Mart, Chicago. A registered description of this article is available for inspection at The Museum, at The Mart and in the Manufacturer's files.

5614

★-901-L

384   45

5414   558

5614—Footed Bowl, 11¾ inches high.
901-L—Giant Salad Bowl, 13½ inch diameter.   45—Plain Muddler, 5½ inches long.
5414—Fruit Bowl, 12¾ inches long, 8½ inches wide.
558—Asymetrical sculptured form; fruit and flowers, 5½ inches high.
384—Water Bottle, 7½ inches high.

Blenko 1956 company catalog page. Note the #558 odd shaped bowl in the lower right corner.

Brief Histories of AMCM Hot Glass Manufacturers

5510

559

559—Cat vase, 13 inches high.
5510—Kitty decanter (one-fifth capacity),
12 inches high.

964-S

964-L—Large Horn Vase, 22 inches long.
964-S—Small Horn Vase, 18½ inches long.

964-L

Blenko 1956 company catalog illustrating the two cat designs and the horn vase.

Blenko kitty decanter #5510 that appeared in the 1956 Blenko Catalog, where it's capacity of "one–fifth" is noted. 13" h. with lid. $320–380. Collection of the Museum of American Glass in West Virginia.

Blenko horn vase, Anderson design. From top: cased, #964–S, 18½", Charcoal, $80–100; Blue, $65–80; and #964–L, 22", Emerald Green, $90–120.

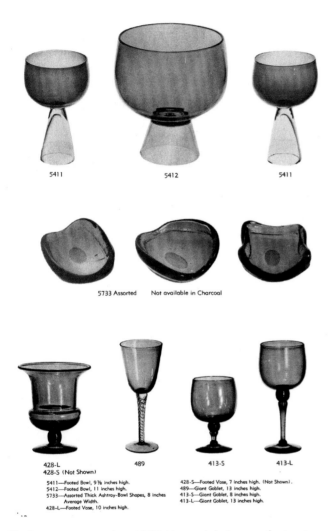

5411

5412

5411

5733 Assorted   Not available in Charcoal

563

564

566

563—Mushroom Decanter, 14 inches high.
564—Decanter, 18 ¼ inches high.
566—Rectangular Decanter, 11 inches high.

5610

428-L
428-S (Not Shown)   489   413-S   413-L

5411—Footed Bowl, 9 ⅛ inches high.
5412—Footed Bowl, 11 inches high.
5733—Assorted Thick Ashtray-Bowl Shapes, 8 inches
       Average Width.
428-L—Footed Vase, 10 inches high.

428-S—Footed Vase, 7 inches high. (Not Shown).
489—Giant Goblet, 13 inches high.
413-S—Giant Goblet, 8 inches high.
413-L—Giant Goblet, 13 inches high.

5610—Water Bottle, 8 inches high.
5616a—Vase, 9 ⅛ inches high.
5616b—Vase, 15 ½ inches high.

5616a   5616b   5616c

Blenko company catalog, 1957. Hustead designs on the top two
rows, and traditional pre–designer shapes on the bottom row.

Blenko catalog page, 1956. All items on this page bear the ware
numbers beginning with "56," indicating new designs that year
and the work of Wayne Husted.

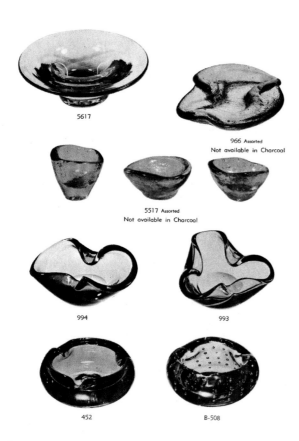

5617

966 Assorted
Not available in Charcoal

5517 Assorted
Not available in Charcoal

994   993

452   B-508

Blenko company catalog, 1957. Husted designs; smoking items were a significant part of most glass houses' production.

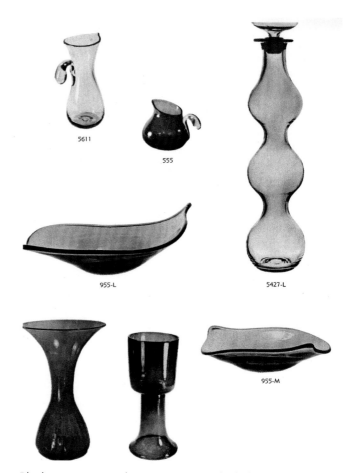

5611   555

955-L   5427-L

955-M

Blenko company catalog, 1957. Note tadpole-like handles on items #555 and #561 and bowl #955–L, the "asymmetrical bowl, 17½ inches in length." There is a striking similarity between this and a pressed form made by Viking Glass. The popular 25" gurgle bottle illustrated is a classic Blenko form.

544   543   939

5612   914

967-Side   967-End   976

Blenko company catalog.

5717   5728   572

5429   5431

Blenko company catalog 1957. #5728 tall jar–vase with lid is an extremely difficult shape to find and the #572 tall spouted decanter at 21" with stopper is equally uncommon.

Blenko company catalog 1957 including classics. The #948 bent neck decanter, #49 pinch bottle and the #920 form as a cruet 10½", decanter at 16½" and 920–L at 21¾". The 18½" Husted #5410 "bird bottle vase" is seldom found today.

948—Bent Decanter, 13 inches high.
920-S—Cruet, 10½ inches high.
37—Decanter, 13 inches high.
49—Pinch Decanter, 10½ inches high.

5410—Bird Bottle Vase, 18½ inches high.
920-L—Decanter, 21¾ inches high.
920—Decanter, 16½ inches high. (Not Shown).

✳948   ✳920-S   ✳37   49
5410   ✳920-L   ✳920 (Not shown)

Blenko #920 decanter, shown on the catalog page at right, in crackle Blue, $80–95, and Ruby, $95–120, both pontiled with the tear drop stopper.

Blenko, 16½″, #920, Emerald Green crackle decanter with stopper, $70–95, showing how the same form is used as the stopper for the #6138 w/s (with stopper) floor vase. See following image.

Blenko floor vase, #6138 w/s in Blue, $350–450, and Emerald Green, $300–380, both with stopper. Towering 35¾", they dwarf the Blenko pinched tumbler at their base. The stopper is formed by an inverted #920, regular-sized decanter.

563—Mushroom Decanter, 14 inches high.
564—Decanter, 18¼ inches high.
566—Rectangular Decanter, 11 inches high.
5723—Bud Vase-Candleholder, 7 inches high.

5724—Bud Vase-Candleholder, 5 inches high.
5732—Mermaidecanter, 15 inches high (head
stopper is removable).

Blenko company catalog, 1957, showing wonderful Husted designs, including the wildly whimsical "Mermaidecanter," 15" in height; the lid is the stopper.

Blenko described this object in the 1957 catalog as "Mermaidecanter," 15" high (head stopper is removable). This example in Gold measures 13", $450–600. From the collection of Terry Gartman and Robert Porath

5427-S—Gurgle Bottle, 13½ inches high.
5712—Vase-Bottle, 10½ inches high.
418-L—Indented Glass, 6 inches high.
418-S—Indented Glass, 4½ inches high.
5516—Architectural decorative bottle, (stopper optional), 32 inches high.

Blenko company catalog, 1957, including the small, #5427, gurgle vase with stopper and the massive, #5516 "architectural decorative bottle," at 32" in height.

Blenko pinched tumbler, shown for scale only, beside the large #5427L, gurgle floor vase with stopper, $350–500, and the gurgle vase, #5427M, Gold, missing stopper; $100–140 as shown.

Blenko #5720, Husted-designed Napoleon Decanter. The name is apparently a reference to the similarity between the stopper and Napoleon Bonaparte's hat.

5729

5727

5720

5729—Rooster Decanter, 12 inches high. Stopper is natural birch and cork.
5727—Very Tall Goblet Vase, 23 inches high.
5720—Napoleon Decanter; 15 inches high.

573

✳5721

573—Cocktail Pitcher with hollow spout ice guard, 11 inches high.
5721—Cocktail Pitcher, 11 inches high.

Blenko company catalog page, 1957, including all designs that were new to that year and all Husted designs. The ware's prefix confirms that they were designs introduced in "57." Included is #5720, captioned as the Napoleon decanter.

Blenko #5823 breast decanter in
Tangerine, 15", $250–300.

Blenko #5921 decanter, Nile Green, 16", $350–400.

View looking into the bowl showing design in base.

Blenko heavy Gold bowl/ash tray with acid signed name on base,
1959–60. $55–70.

Blenko company catalog, 1963.

Blenko tall, Ruby pitcher with straight optic pattern from the Regal line with applied crystal handle and pontil, and with a Blenko acid-stamped signature. Produced in 1960, $120–160.

Blenko #597 vase designed by Wayne Husted. The rose bowl-like form is made entirely new when the randomly applied prunts of glass are attached to the hot surface. The result is a very fun and unexpected object. Tangerine, 5″ h. Sandblasted Blenko signature on the base, triangular crimp at the rim. $160–220. Collection of the Museum of American Glass in West Virginia. Ex-collection of the author.

Blenko Ruby amoeba ash tray with Blenko acid-signed signature, 1959–60. $20–35.

4

6218
22¼" high
$10.00

6217
21½" high
$7.50

*636S
8" high
$4.50

*636L
11" high
$6.50

6223
12½" high
$4.00

635 assorted
7" diameter $2.50 ea.
6" diameter $2.50 ea.
7" x 4" $2.50 ea.

6212L
28" high
$15.00

6212
20½" high
$9.00

*6212S
16" high
$7.00

6210
13⅞" high
$7.50

6215
19" high
$7.50

639
14" high
$6.00

6310
14" high
$7.50

Blenko company catalog, 1963. Noteworthy are long spire stoppers, the #635 organic
shaped bowl, and the briefly produced, rose-colored objects.

Blenko textured line, left to right: 18" h., Charcoal, #6228 bottle with stopper, $120–180; 10½" h., Crystal, #6226L, $20–30; vase in Tangerine (Blenko's name for their Amberina-like color), #6223, 12½" h., $45–55. This textured line first appears in 1962 and was a Husted design.

Blenko pinched bottles with stoppers. #638M in Tangerine, 15", $120–150; #638S in Sea Green, 10", $75–100; and #638L in Tangerine, $180–200. The three appeared together in different colors on a page of the 1963 catalog (see page 52). From the collection of Terry Gartman and Robert Porath.

6

*6030L	*6030M	*6030S	*6027		6222	6222	6226		6227
18½" high	13" high	10½" high	17" high		8¾" high	8¾" high	15" high		15" high
$8.00	$6.50	$5.50	$10.00		$3.50	$3.50	$7.50		$6.00

6225L	6225S	6224S	6224S	6224L	6219S	6219L	6220S	6221
21¼" high	15⅝" high	7½" high	7½" high	10⅜" high	6⅞" high	9" high	10¾" high	12½" high
$9.00	$6.50	$5.00	$5.00	$7.00	$4.00	$5.00	$4.00	$6.00

Blenko company catalog page, 1963, including a number of the #6200 textured line pieces.

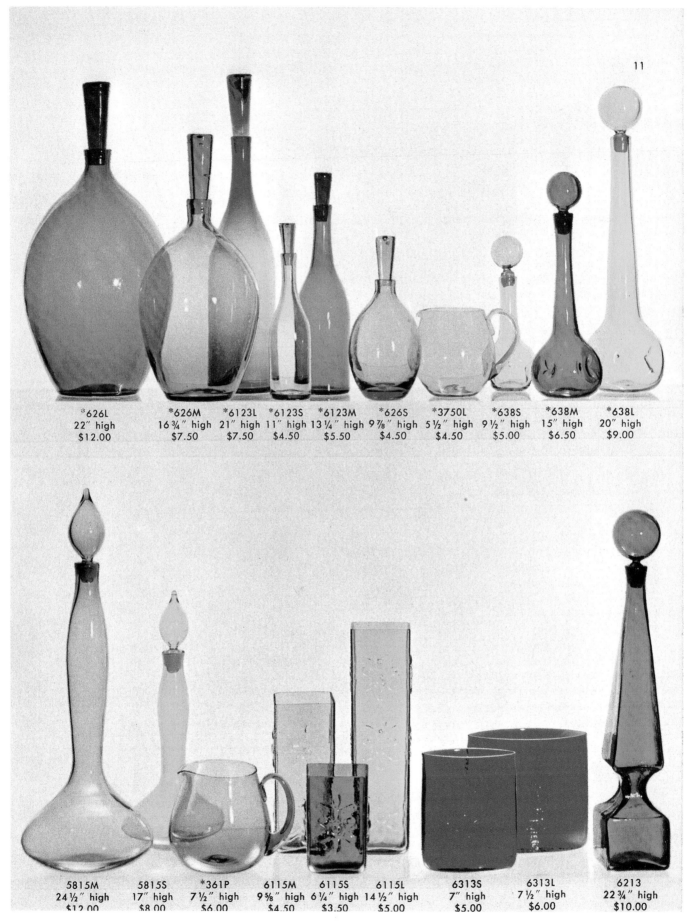

11

*626L
22" high
$12.00

*626M
16¾" high
$7.50

*6123L
21" high
$7.50

*6123S
11" high
$4.50

*6123M
13¼" high
$5.50

*626S
9⅞" high
$4.50

*3750L
5½" high
$4.50

*638S
9½" high
$5.00

*638M
15" high
$6.50

*638L
20" high
$9.00

5815M
24½" high
$12.00

5815S
17" high
$8.00

*361P
7½" high
$6.00

6115M
9⅝" high
$4.50

6115S
6¼" high
$3.50

6115L
14½" high
$5.00

6313S
7" high
$5.00

6313L
7½" high
$6.00

6213
22¾" high
$10.00

Blenko company catalog page, 1963. Stoppers ruled the Blenko offerings in 1963.

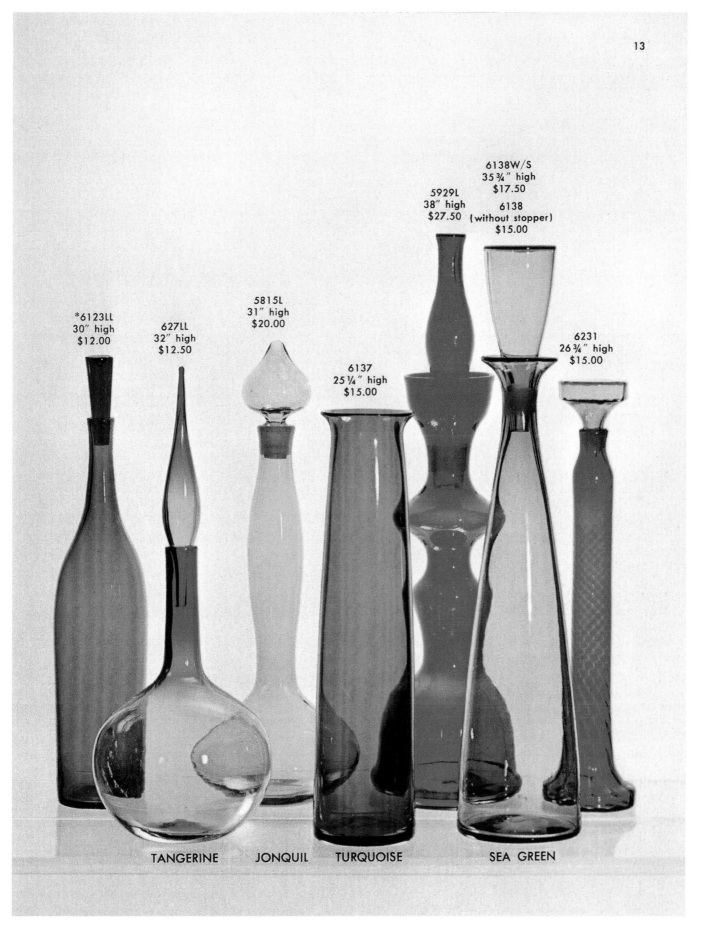

*6123LL
30" high
$12.00

627LL
32" high
$12.50

5815L
31" high
$20.00

6137
25 ¼" high
$15.00

5929L
38" high
$27.50

6138W/S
35 ¾" high
$17.50

6138
(without stopper)
$15.00

6231
26 ¾" high
$15.00

TANGERINE   JONQUIL   TURQUOISE   SEA GREEN

Blenko company catalog, 1963. Here are some of the early forms for the large floor vases, called "architectural vases" in Blenko literature, 16¾" to 38" in height.

Blenko #6030L pitcher, 18½" h., in Rose crackle with applied handle and pontil. Rose was shown in the 1963 and 1964 catalog, but does not appear in 1965, making it a color produced a very short time. $250–300. Short crackle Ruby tumbler shown for scale only.

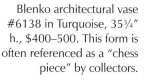

Blenko company catalog cover, 1964. The claim on this cover has been scaled back from the 1956 "world renowned" to be touted as merely "A famous name in American Glassware."

Blenko architectural vase #6138 in Turquoise, 35¾" h., $400–500. This form is often referenced as a "chess piece" by collectors.

6213
22¾″ high
$10.00

*6030M
13″ high
$6.50

*6030L
18½″ high
$8.00

6310
14″ high
$7.50

6410
11½″ high
$6.00

5616C
approx. 22″ high
$6.00

*6425
27″ high
$7.50

*6427
25½″ high
$6.00

6322
6¼″ dia.
$3.50

6426
25¼″ high
$7.50

*6211
15¾″ high
$9.00

5815S
17″ high
$8.00

5815M
24½″ high
$12.00

Blenko company catalog, 1964, including items in the color Rose. New items from that year, all bear a ware number in the 6400s, including the pitcher next to last on the top row and the two tall bottles and vase on the bottom row.

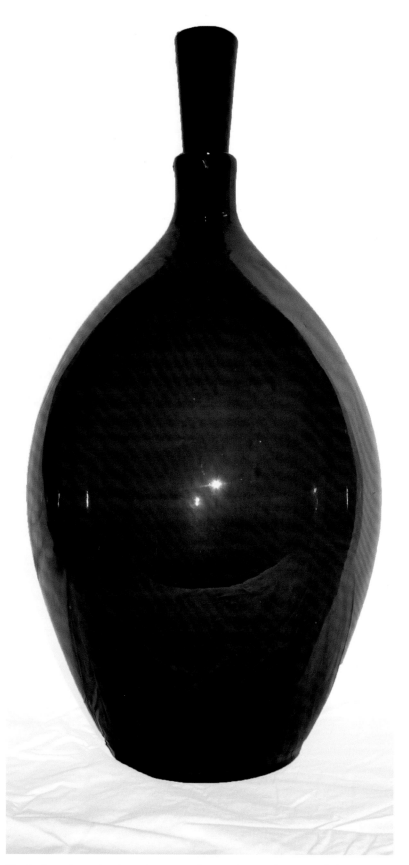

Blenko #6310, Wayne Husted-designed bottle or decanter, blue with large hollow stopper. 14" h., $75–100. (Originally introduced in 1963 this form was re–issued in the 2010s by Blenko.)

Blenko large jug or bottle and stopper, #626L, in Amethyst. Pontiled, 22", $140–180. Also made in a medium size, #626M, at 16¾", and a smaller #626S. Illustrated in the 1964 catalog, opposite.

*626L
22″ high
$12.00

*626M
16¾″ high
$7.50

*3744X
7″ dia.
$3.50

6224L
10⅜″ high
$7.00

6224S
7½″ high
$5.00

5433
10″ high
$12.00

639
14″ high
$7.00

*6323L
12½″ high
$6.00

*6323M
9″ high
$5.00

*6323S
6″ high
$4.00

971M
16″ long
$15.00

971L
25″ long
$30.00

971S
12½″ long
$8.00

6217
21½″ high
$7.50

Blenko company catalog, 1964, including the iconic fish as well as a 1962 fish bottle, #6217 (bottom row, far right).

8

*64A
11¼″ high
$3.00

*64B
13″ high
$3.00

*64C
8″ high
$3.00

*976
19½″ high
$10.00

*623S
8″ high
$5.00

6313S
7″ high
$6.00

6218
22¼″ high
$10.00

6212L
28″ high
$15.00

6212
20½″ high
$9.00

*6212S
16″ high
$7.00

*628S
24⅝″ high
$9.00

*6424
5″ high
$2.50

*6029
27½″ high
$12.50

Blenko company catalog page, 1964.

Blenko company catalog cover, 1965.

Blenko #427M decanter, Tangerine with teardrop stopper, $85–110; #647 indented bottle vase, Olive Green, shown with wrong stopper (which is a cautionary note for Blenko and other pieces that require stoppers), 18" without any stopper; as shown, $60–80.

8

Blenko company
catalog, 1965.

6415	†641L	°37	659L	659S	°649
12½″ high	12″ dia.	13″ high	16″ high	9¾″ high	13¼″ high
$7.50	$5.00	$6.50	$8.00	$6.50	$7.00

6418	°920S	°920	°920L	†633	°6427	°6425
23″ high	10½″ high	16½″ high	23″ high	14″ long	24″ high	27″ high
$10.00	$5.00	$6.50	$9.00	$4.00	$6.50	$8.00

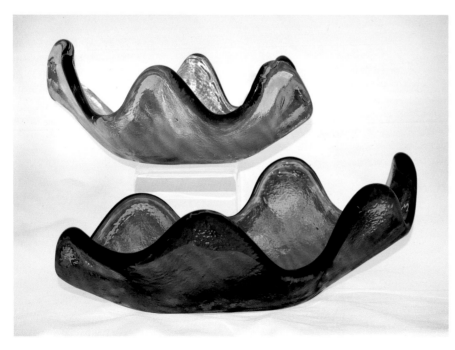

Blenko #633 bowl, 14″
in length, Crystal (end
view), $40–65; Green
(side view), $50–70 .

6417
16" high
$9.50

*3750L
5½" high
$5.00

6525
13¼" high
$9.00

6410
11½" high
$6.00

6420
11¾" high
$7.50

6421
16" high
$7.50

6212
20½" high
$10.00

*6212S
16" high
$8.00

*6512
6" high
$5.00

*6516
14½" high
$6.00

†641S
9¼" dia.
$3.00

†631S
6" dia.
$2.00 ea.

†625L
14" dia.
$5.00

§6326
4" dia.
$1.20 ea.

Blenko Company, 1965, catalog page.

Blenko Company, 1965, catalog page.

Blenko #6027 long necked bottle with stopper, 17" h., Turquoise, $80–100.

Blenko #991 pitcher in Green and Turquoise, 13½" h., $60–85.

656L
14″ high
$8.00

656M
10½″ high
$6.00

656S
8½″ high
$5.00

6517
10″ high
$6.00

418S
4½″ high
$2.00 ea.

418L
6″ high
$2.00 ea.

6526
15¾″ high
$9.00

6211
15¾″ high
$10.00

3744X
7″ dia.
$3.50

657S
12″ high
$5.50

657M
14″ high
$7.50

657L
18½″ high
$9.00

657LL
22¾″ high
$11.50

Blenko Company catalog page, 1965.

Blenko #6512 pitcher with one of the distinctive handles that rises far above the objects rim and is attached, lightly, at the rim. Pontiled; Tangerine, $35–50; Green, $25–40.

Blenko architectural or floor vase with straight optic, pontiled, and hollow-blown stopper. Blenko hand grinds each stopper to specifically match the bottle/decanter. Note the difference in the overall height of these two large vases with stoppers. $500–600 each.

Blenko pinched tumbler, shown for scale only, beside the #6955 bottle in Ruby with straight optic design. Hollow stopper and pontiled, 22¾" h., $600–680.

Blenko paperweight stoppered bottle #6716 in Cobalt Blue, $200–250; shown with a paperweight (smooth ground base) with the same air twist treatment. Paperweight stoppers first appear in the 1967 catalog, with only one design offered #6716, 6724, 6736, 6741, and 6745. The designer in 1967 was Joel Myers. 14½" h., pontiled. The paperweight with air-trap twist is #68B; see photo at right.

Blenko's 1968 catalog featured the tall, air-trap twist candlesticks on the cover. #6825 6 ¼" h. Amber core $30–40 each; same in green $30–45 each and paperweight #68B $30–40.

Blenko face vase #6625, 7¾" h., pontiled. Turquoise, $180–220; Green, $180–220. This Joel Myers design appeared in the 1966 catalog. It did not appear in the 1967 catalog, suggesting production for one year only.

Blenko #6424 bottle vase, 5" h., pontiled. Tangerine, $16–24; Green, $12–18; Crystal crackle, $14–20; Turquoise, $14–18.

Blenko blown-out vase. Purchased from the factory warehouse by the author, circa 1986. Cased glass Amber, Green and Turquoise. Possibly unique, No value determined.

Blenko experimental, Amber and Turquoise bottle. Purchased by the author from the Blenko warehouse in 1988. Ground top, pontiled base. Possibly unique, $300–450.

Blenko blown out vase #5422, Charcoal. 14", $350–400. From the collection of Terry Gartman and Robert Porath

Blenko vase, #6833, 10⅝" h.. Lemon body and Ruby color threading near the crimped top, pontiled; $60–80.

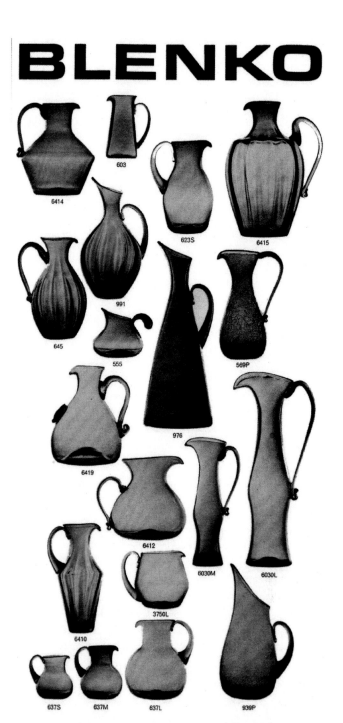

BLENKO

An almost endless variety of miraculous pitchers to add a special note of charm and warmth to your home — at Christmas! Each of these lovely pitchers has its own unique and very personal beauty — a beauty that says so unmistakably that this is glassware — by BLENKO. Every piece of Blenko ware is made completely by hand and because each step in the glass blowing process is dependent upon the eye and hand of the master craftsman, each is an original. And Blenko ware is as practical as it is decorative; it is made to be used and enjoyed — yet its incomparable quality will make it a possession to be cherished through the years. There are six beautiful colors and crystal to choose from. Blenko glassware can be seen in leading department stores and gift shops throughout the world. It is an ideal gift for Christmastime.

BLENKO GLASS COMPANY
Department A, Milton, West Virginia

Blenko trade advertisement featuring the diversity of pitchers in their line, which the text described as "An almost endless variety of miraculous pitchers to add a special note of charm and warmth to your home—at Christmas". 1964.

Blenko #6744 air-trap Tangerine (Amberina), pontiled vase, 14½" h., $75–85; Tangerine/Amberina pitcher with applied handle pitcher attributed to Greenwich Flint or other manufacturer producing in the style similar to Blenko; shown for contrast.

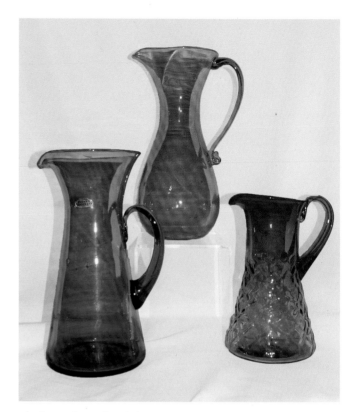

Blenko pitchers all with hand applied handles and pontiled (left to right): Turquoise, #7111, 12" h., $45–60; Lemon, #569–P 13", $30–45; Tangerine with diamond optic and etched block letter Blenko signature on base (1959–60), $50–70.

Blenko's enduring forms include the Winslow Anderson bent neck decanter, here in Green, $50–60; and 939–P ,14½" h. pitcher in Peacock, $50–70.

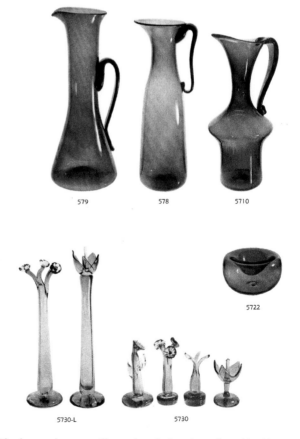

Blenko catalog page illustrating designs introduced in 1957. Intriguing is the #5730 line at the page bottom in both large and regular sizes. Described as "Blenko accents serve as paperweights or as decorative accents."

Blenko's Rialto line was produced in 1960 only. The line features milky white glass with applied, bold, Ruby Red highlights. Being a product of the year 1960 (one of two years Blenko marked their glass during the timeframe of this book's interest), Rialto bears the acid mark of Blenko on the base. Left to right: pitcher #7–T0, 9½– 10", $200–225; vase, band at middle, #12–TO, 8½ –9", $300–350; tall decanter/bottle with stopper #1–TO, 20–21", $700–900: and vase, band at top, #15–TO, 9–10", $225–275.

Blenko ran advertisements in national magazines including this colorful and fanciful "Blenko Loves Blenko" campaign in 1961.

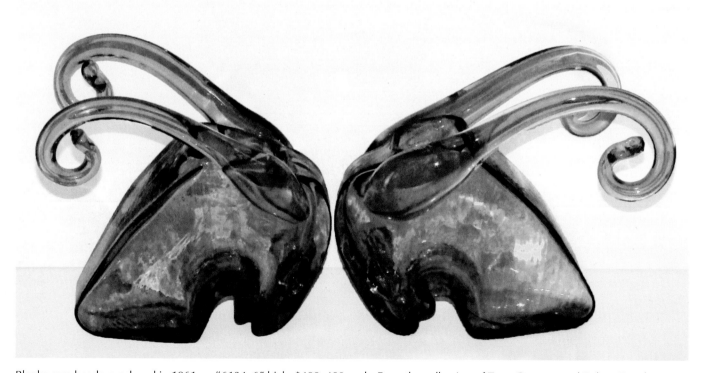

Blenko ram heads, produced in 1961 as #6134. 6" high, $400–480 each. From the collection of Terry Gartman and Robert Porath

Blenko lamp. From the collection of the Museum of American Glass in West Virginia.

Blenko lamps as featured in the company catalog of 1953.

Blenko lamps as featured in the company catalog of 1953.

Brockway Glass

Clarksburg, West Virginia
1972–1983

Good

A large glass factory was built in Clarksburg, West Virginia, in 1901. Over the decades between 1901 and 1956, Hazel-Atlas Glass expanded and enlarged the factory to mammoth proportions. Hazel-Atlas was a giant glass producer with multiple plants across the country. Their Clarksburg plant produced tumblers and tableware pieces by the literal millions. From 1956 until 1972, it operated as the consumer products division of Continental Can Company, Inc., producing a line marketed as Hazelware, a name crafted to retain the popularity and reputation of Hazel-Atlas.

When Hazel-Atlas was acquired by Continental Can, the design department relocated from Wheeling, West Virginia (the old corporate headquarters for Hazel-Atlas), to Clarksburg. One of those relocating was designer Kay Herpel. Herpel was a prolific designer of the almost endless products at the Clarksburg plant under a series of owners. Her designs include products for Hazel-Atlas, Continental Can, Brockway Glass and a multitude of others for whom the factory made wares which were marketed under wholesale names. Herpel was little known until a significant collection of her designs came to the Museum of American Glass in West Virginia in 2013. Time and scholarship will help define her contribution to popular mid-century and modern designs as an unsung industrial designer.

In 1972, the factory was acquired by Brockway Glass. Brockway had other glass manufacturing facilities across the nation and operated this West Virginia location until approximately 1983 when it was acquired by Anchor-Hocking, which closed the factory for good in 1987.

Brockway Glass, from the Clarksburg, West Virginia, factory, introduced a line called Icelandic and featured it on the cover of their 1973 catalog. While it is modest in its AMCM influence and late to the market, in name and design, Icelandic seeks to identify with the Scandinavian influences of modernity that remained prevalent well into the 1970s in American glass. If there is a glass line that aspires to place the design influences of Scandinavian glass within the financial reach of every household this machine-made, commercially priced line indeed achieved that goal.

Brockway Glass company catalog, 1973, featuring the Icelandic pattern in colorless crystal.

Brief Histories of AMCM Hot Glass Manufacturers

GOLD

icelandic
BULK
1 DOZEN CUT CASE

A7040

A7041

A7043

A7042

AVOCADO

icelandic
BULK

G7002

G7003

G7006

G7001

G7000

PAGE 7

Brockway Glass company catalog, 1973. Icelandic in Gold and the ever-present Avocado color.

CONSUMER PRODUCTS

DIVISION OF

CONTINENTAL CAN COMPANY, INC.
CLARKSBURG, WEST VIRGINIA

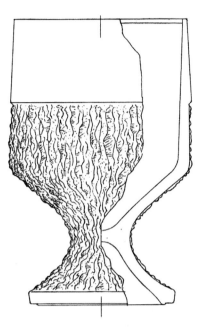

refer to sh. 70-1059

DESIGNED FOR: _general trade_   DESIGN NO.: _70-1071_
DESCRIPTION: _footed rocks (stackable)_ AV. CAPACITY: _9 oz._
DRAWN BY: _kay herpel_   DATE: _12-30-70_

Before Brockway Glass, the factory was operated by Continental Can Company. The long term and unsung designer was Kay Herpel. This December 1970 design for a stackable, footed rocks glass may have been original idea that became Icelandic. Herpel archive, West Virginia Museum of American Glass collection.

Icelandic pattern by Brockway Glass. Covered candy with lid, 6¼" h., $5–9; footed cake plate, 5" h. x 6½"-diameter, $8–12.

Bryce Brothers Company

Mt. Pleasant, Pennsylvania
1895–1965

Good

Better

Best

Bryce Brothers operated in Mt. Pleasant, Pennsylvania, from 1895 until 1965. The Bryce family had ties to glass production in and around Pittsburgh, Pennsylvania, for decades prior to the opening of the Mt. Pleasant factory.

Bryce ware of the mid-twentieth century was largely hand-formed, mouth-blown stemware, tableware, and giftware. The utilization of acclaimed designers was not ignored at Bryce. The Silhouette line was the creation of Eva Zeisel.

Lenox obtained a controlling interest in Bryce circa 1965 and utilized the name Bryce Crystal for a short time before it became Lenox Crystal in 1966. The factory ceased all hot glass production in 2003.

Bryce was predominately a handmade tableware factory. Within the tableware lines, accessories were sometimes included. In the El Rancho line, containers with lids were produced and called turnabouts, as the lid served as a base or supplemental small serving dish. Examples of Bryce giftware during the AMCM period would be limited to occasional utility objects like the turnabout and vases.

The Bryce El Rancho pattern first appeared in Bryce Brothers literature in 1955. It last appeared in 1966. Over that decade plus, it was produced in a variety of colors. In the circa 1957–58 Bryce catalog, it is offered in "Milk Crystal" and that color alone is priced about 10% higher than the other seven colors then offered. The other El Rancho color offerings in that catalog were Crystal, Amethyst, Cerulean (a light, bright blue), Dusk (a smoky color), Gold (a light, honey Amber), Greenbrier (a dark, forest-like green), Morocco (a less dark, less purple Amethyst) and Caribbean.

In 1964-65, the catalog illustrates El Rancho in Greenbrier, Morocco, Pink, Amber, Blue, Gold, Green, Cerulean, Flamer, Dusk, and Flame. Eleven colors were then available.

The El Rancho colors are Blue (a dark, cobalt-like color), Citron (a mossy or tending-toward-avocado green), Flame (a true Amberina, fading from light Amber to Ruby red), Green (a light, transparent green resembling depression-era greens), Pink, and Ruby. El Rancho can be found in fifteen different colors.

Tempo has a rounded design over a square foot that has the appearance of handmade shaped glass. Sharon Hybril, writing in the Mount Pleasant Glassblower, Volume 1, No. 2, Summer 2013, recalled that "Alvin Pfrogner, cut & down man (at the Bryce factory) invented this pattern for Bryce in the 1960s."

Show in a circa 1957 Bryce Brothers catalog is the line titled Silhouette. Including an ice tea, goblet, sherbet or old fashion, juice and sherry the line, designated #1138, was designed for Bryce by Eva Zeisel.

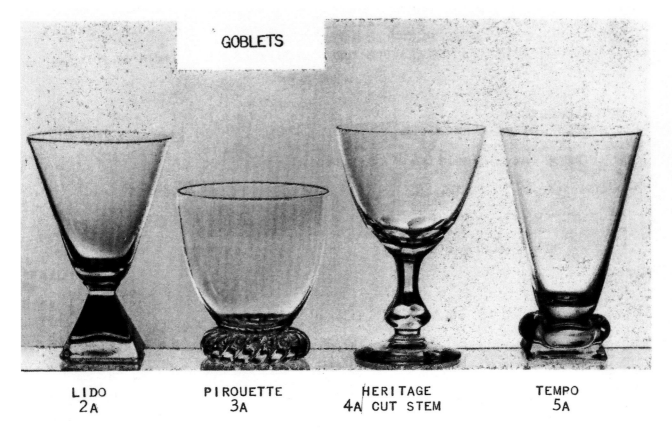

GOBLETS

LIDO
2A

PIROUETTE
3A

HERITAGE
4A CUT STEM

TEMPO
5A

Bryce catalog page illustrating the Lido pattern (relatively modern), Pirouette, Heritage (very traditional in name and form), and Tempo (AMCM). Pirouette was available in Crystal, Morocco or Amethyst bowls. The pieces types offered were goblet, sherbet, claret, cocktail, cordial, juice, footed ice tea, and 8" salad plate. Bryce catalog date circa 1957.

Bryce Pirouette pattern. Morocco (amber) bowl with crystal foot. 4¹/₈" h. x 4¾" w.. $12–18.

Bryce cobalt bowl with modern finial on the sterling silver lid. The crystal was sold to Gorham, a silver manufacturer, who added a lid which bears their mark. Often objects with additional components were merchandized under the silver companies name with no mention of the glass manufacturer. Also known with an Amethyst bowl. $35–45. Jaime Robinson collection.

Bryce catalog illustration for the #1138 pattern Silhouette. Shown are the iced tea, goblet, sherbet or old fashion, and juice glass. The undated catalog is circa 1957.

Bryce Silhouette pattern, juice 4 ¼" h. $6–8.

Bryce catalog page illustrating EL Rancho, Plymouth, Monterey, Silhouette, and Tempo period patterns. Bryce catalog circa 1957.

Bryce Tempo pattern. Left to right: 3 oz. footed tumbler, 3½" h. x 2¾" d., Green and colorless $20–24; juice, 4¼" h., Morocco (brown) and colorless, $22–26; goblet, 4½" h., Morocco and colorless, $24–30. Also known in Tempo are liquor cocktails (2¾" h. x 3¼" d.) and champagne–sherbets (3" h.).

A trade journal advertisement for Bryce Brothers Company. "Follow The Casual Trend With These Fast–Selling Bryce Designs." From left to right: Silhouette, El Rancho (footed), Plymouth, Monterey, El Rancho, and Holiday. All of the patterns shown are more modern than traditional, despite pattern names like Plymouth. *Crockery and Glass Journal*, July 1956.

Tempo pattern, left to right: tumbler, goblet, tumbler, juice, tumbler, all with the colorless stylized Italian base.

Announcing four new Bryce gift items in milk crystal

Spurred by popular demand, Bryce has now added four more pieces to its new milk crystal line— the fastest selling offering it has made in recent years. Much of this rapid acceptance is unquestionably due to the fact that even though each piece is carefully hand-blown in fine lead crystal in the traditional Bryce manner, prices are surprisingly reasonable. Suggested retail prices of the items shown above, from left to right, are: Toddy Vase, $3.50; Flared Vase, $5.00; Footed Vase, $1.50; Ivy Vase, $2.75. Write to Bryce now for details and shipping date.

Bryce Brothers Company

MT. PLEASANT, PENNSYLVANIA

Bryce Brothers Company advertisement for El Rancho in milk crystal. The text reads "Announcing four new Bryce gift items in milk crystal…spurred by popular demand, Bryce has now added four more pieces to its new milk crystal line– the fastest selling line it has made in recent years. Left to right: toddy vase, flared vase, footed vase, and ivy vase. *Crockery and Glass Journal*, December 1955.

Bryce El Rancho grouping showing the wonderful color and diversity of form.

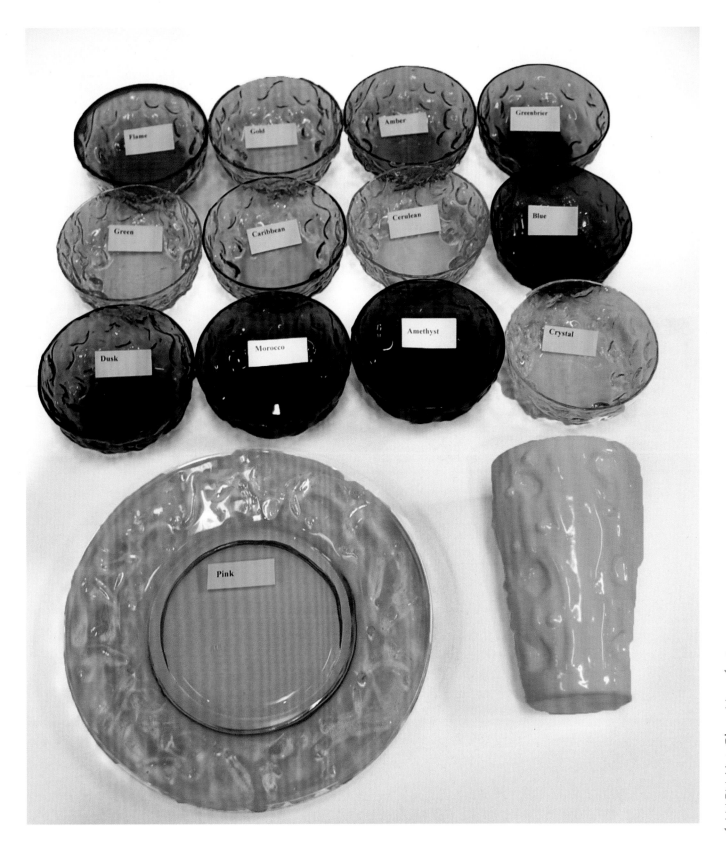

Bryce EL Rancho colors offered. Flame, Gold, Amber, Greenbrier, Green, Caribbean,
Cerulean, Blue, Dusk (smoke gray), Morocco (brown), Amethyst, Crystal, Pink, Milk.
Harley Trice collection.

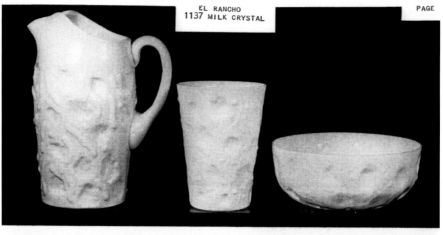

EL RANCHO
1137 MILK CRYSTAL   PAGE

1137-5 PINT JUG   1137 TODDY VASE   1137 BERRY BOWL

1137 FOOTED IVY   1137-15   1137-12   1137-6   1137 DESSERT
                   CRIMPED VASE   CRIMPED VASE   CRIMPED VASE

Bryce Brothers Company, 1958 catalog page, for El Rancho in Milk Crystal.

PAGE 12   EL RANCHO
                                   MILK CRYSTAL

1137-1   1137-2   1137-3
TURNABOUT   TURNABOUT   TURNABOUT

1137 COUPETTE   1137 JAM JAR   1137 LARGE CRIMPED VASE
OR LARGE TURNABOUT   AND COVER
COVER

Bryce Brothers Company, 1958 catalog page, for El Rancho in Milk Crystal.

EL RANCHO
MILK CRYSTAL

15 OZ FOOTED ICE TEA   12 OZ FOOTED WATER   7 OZ FOOTED SHERBET   6 OZ FOOTED JUICE   DESSERT LARGE

16 OZ ICE TEA   12 OZ WATER   8 OZ OLD FASHION   5½ OZ JUICE   1138-1 VASE

Bryce Brothers Company, 1958 catalog page, for El Rancho in Milk Crystal.

Bryce El Rancho salt and pepper shakers, Gold with lids. Pair $24–30.

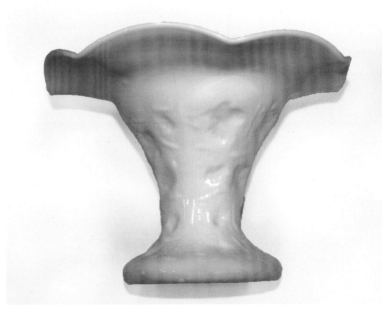

Bryce EL Rancho large flared vase in Milk Crystal, $24–36.

Bryce El Rancho in the color Flame. 5-pint pitcher #1137–5 with applied handle, 9½", $80–110; top row: flat tumbler 4⅝", $14–20; flat iced tea 5½", $16–24; bottom row footed sherbet, 2¾" x 3 ⅞ diameter, $10–14; footed juice 3¾", $16–24; footed water goblet, 5¼", $18–26; footed iced tea, 5½", $18–26. Collection of Jaime Robinson

Bryce El Rancho, Milk Crystal, #1137–6 crimped vase, footed. $10–14

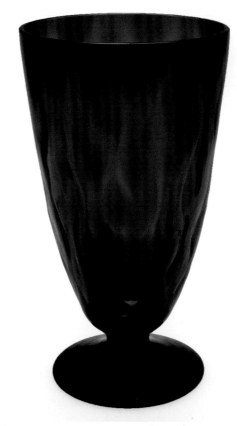

Bryce Monterey pattern in Morocco (brown) Optic pattern, footed iced tea. The form is not modern but the color, a sultry brown, was popular only in MCM. 6¼" h., $10–16.

Bryce El Rancho
Turnabout, Cerulean
(blue), with lid. Left,
#1137–2, 6$\frac{1}{8}$" h.,
$20–28; center,
#1137–1, 7$\frac{3}{8}$" h.,
$24–34: right, #1137–
3, 4$\frac{3}{4}$" h., $16–24.
(Paper label adds 10%.)

Bryce El Rancho turnabout with lid. Dusk, #1137–2 (middle size), 6$\frac{1}{4}$" h., $18–24

Bryce El Rancho turnabout with lid, Milk Crystal, #1137–3 (small size), 4$\frac{3}{4}$" h., $12–16.

Cambridge Glass Company

Cambridge, Ohio
1902–1958

Good

The factory that housed Cambridge Glass was financed and built by the large glass monopoly National Glass. However, National never operated it. In 1902, production began there as Cambridge Glass. Cambridge products were predominately hand blown or hand-pressed tableware. Cambridge Glass produced quality tableware that was largely sold in department stores, jewelry stores, and other mid to high-end outlets.

Cambridge made elegant tableware and, to a lesser extent, accessories and giftware. Mid-century designs were modest in their homage to Modern at Cambridge. One AMCM example was the Cambridge Square line. Consisting of a boldly simple circle and square, the minimalist design is strongest when undecorated and uncompromised by cutting, etching, or other decoration. Originally offered only in clear crystal, other colors were added later including Ruby-red and black.

The Cambridge factory closed in 1958 and assets were sold to Imperial Glass of Bellaire, Ohio. Cambridge production spanned 56 years.

Cambridge square pattern items constitute the bulk of giftware or accessories of AMCM influence. Cambridge Glass introduced the simple and modern line in 1951 called Cambridge Square. It related to Heisey Cabochon in the use of a rounded body and a squared foot or stem. The overall Cambridge Square pattern included items in the #3797 line, which had square bases, and #3798 line that had round based stemware with cubes in the stem. Items were produced from 1951 until the factory closed in 1958.

Cambridge Square moulds passed to Imperial Glass after Cambridge ceased production.

To Learn More:
National Cambridge Collectors, Inc. *Colors in Cambridge Glass II: Identification and Value Guide.* Paducah, Kentucky: Collector Books. 2007.

Cambridge Square cup and saucer. The "modern" use of opposing geometrics (circle and square), as well as the unattached handle, was touted as the modern design from Cambridge glass. Set $7–10.

Cambridge square Ebon (black satin) ash tray #151, 3½", with Gold decoration "Birds," $12–16 each; #48 oval bowl, 9", $60–75; colorless candlestick #67, $8–12 each. The birds decoration on Ebon was noted in the October 1953 catalog supplement, a very short time before Cambridge Glass closed.

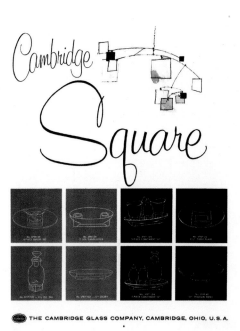

From the Cambridge glass catalog circa 1956, this page makes certain a prospective buyer understands that Cambridge Square is modern by the company it keeps. Visually the message is that the Cambridge Square is in the same cool style as a mobile, a relatively new and hip art idea for home decorating in the 1950s.

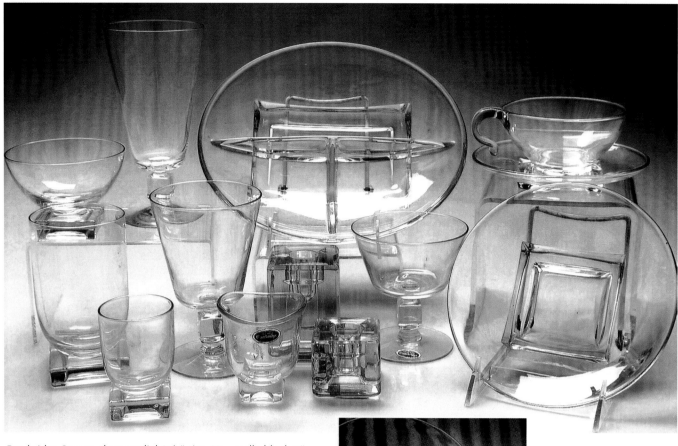

Cambridge Square clear cordial 2⅛″, $7–10; candle block 3″
h., $10–14; Relish, 8¼″, $10–14; salt and pepper shakers, 2¾″,
$12–16 pair; tall water goblet, 5⅜″, $14–18; flat water goblet,
5″, $15–20; cup, 2½″ h., and saucer, 5⅞″diameter, $7–10 set.

CAMBRIDGE SQUARE

It dares to be different — this
sparkling new Cambridge crystal
with its forthright, modern square
base! It's "special occasion" for
the ah-inspiring table or buffet.
It's the swank touch to pleasant
entertaining. Choose from a
variety of beautiful, functional
and decorative pieces: Cambridge
Square goblets, cocktails and
sherbets — relishes, canape plates,
sugar & cream, bowls, candy box,
vases and others. Yours for smart-
ness, yours at the most modest
prices! Now featured in good
stores everywhere.
The Cambridge Glass Company,
Cambridge, Ohio.

Pictured at top: Lovely Cambridge
Square canape plate and low bowl.
At left: Stemmed goblet and sherbet;
footed goblet and sherbet. These styles
also available in cocktail, wine,
cordial, iced tea and juice glass.

Cambridge Square
pattern.
Advertisement
appearing in *House
Beautiful*, Sept. 1952

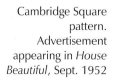

Cambridge

fine American hand-made crystal

Canton
Glass Company

Marion, Indiana
1893–1958

Best

Canton Glass Company operated in Canton, Ohio, from 1883 until 1892, when it was destroyed by fire. It relocated to in Marion, Indiana, in 1903. In March of 1958, it relocated to Hartford, Indiana, and occupied the then-vacant Sneath Glass site.

Canton produced pressed and blown ware ranging from private mould work to tableware and giftware. When Paden City Glass closed in 1951, Canton acquired most, if not all, of Paden City's moulds. Thus, post-1951 Canton includes a number of patterns and forms from Paden City.

One unique Canton line, unrelated to Paden City, that clearly embraces the aesthetic of American Mid-century Modern was Canton Casual. Canton Casual was a thick, heavy line of two heavily cased or layered glasses. Canton Glass ceased operations in 1958.

Canton Casual is the only Mid-century Modern design made by Canton Glass currently identified. Amidst a number of very conservative and traditional forms, it is a bold departure from the firm's usual offerings. The forms are a gather of one color, with a second gather of a contrasting color heavily applied to the exterior and partly encasing the original color. The result is very Modern in appearance. Mention in *Chain Store Age*, August, 1951, noted vases, divided dishes, bowls (7-, 10-, and 12- inch), candleholders, nut dish, candy dish with lid, handled bonbon, and cigarette server and ashtray.

Casual line pieces incorporate colorless crystal and a color, but also are found in two-colored glasses. The color combinations known are Crystal/Green, Crystal/Blue, Crystal/Amber, and Black/Amber. The era of production for Canton Casual is circa 1951 and probably ending prior to 1958.

Canton Casual Green and Crystal. Front row, left to right: small bud vase, 8" h., $18–24; cigarette server, 2½" h. x 2½" w., $16–22; mint dish, 2½" h. x 3½" w. $18–22; candleholder, 2⅛" h. x 4" w., $12–20 each; mint bowl, 3½" h. x 6¾" w.; back row: divided bowl, small, $20–24; divided bowl, large, $32–40.

Canton Casual Amber and Crystal mint dish, $18–24; divided bowl, $22–28; nut dish (top view), $14–18.

Canton Casual Blue and Crystal: top, cocktail pitcher with pouring spout, 8" h., $28–38; cigarette server, 2½" h. x 2½" w., $16–22; divided bowl, small, 6½" w. x 2¼-tall, $20–24.

Canton Casual Amber and Black. Left to right: nut dish 3⅛″ d., $12–18; center-handled "bon bon" 6½″ d., $30–38; cigarette server, 2½″ h. x 2½″ d., $28–34; large bowl, 2½″ h. x 8″ d., $30–38; and nut dish again.

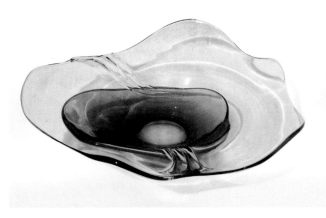

Canton Casual large Crystal and Amber ash tray, with three band patterns/cigarette rests on two sides. 2½″ h. x 11″ w., $38–45.

CANTON CASUAL glassware line includes cigarette server and ash tray, bud and flower vases, divided relish dish and large divided dish, flared bowls in rim dimensions of seven, ten and twelve inches, candle-holders, nut dish, candy dish with cover, and handled bon bon. Colors include: crystal with green, blue or gold base, and amber with black base. Canton Glass Co., Marion, Ohio.

Canton Casual advertisement appearing in *Chain Store Age*, August, 1951.

Canton Casual large vase, Green and Crystal, 8″ h. x 8″ w. at rim, $55–65

Chalet
Artistic Glass

Cornwall, Ontario, Canada

1962–1975

Chalet Artistic Glass was founded by glass workers from Murano, Italy, who originally established a factory in Montreal, Canada, circa 1960, before relocating to Cornwall, Ontario, in 1962.

Some, but not all, Chalet production bears a "Chalet" acid stamp on the base. Chalet was one of a small group of mid-century hot glass producers in Canada that included Altaglass of Medicine Hat, Alberta, and Lorraine Glass Industries Ltd. of Montreal, Quebec. Chalet declared bankruptcy and ceased production of hot glass in 1975.

To Learn More:
Patterson, Deborah. "Enduring Magic of Shape and Colour-Chalet Art Glass." *All About Glass.* Vol. XI No. 3. October 2013.

Chalet label close up.

Chalet Green, Blue, and Crystal heavy ash tray, $25–30.

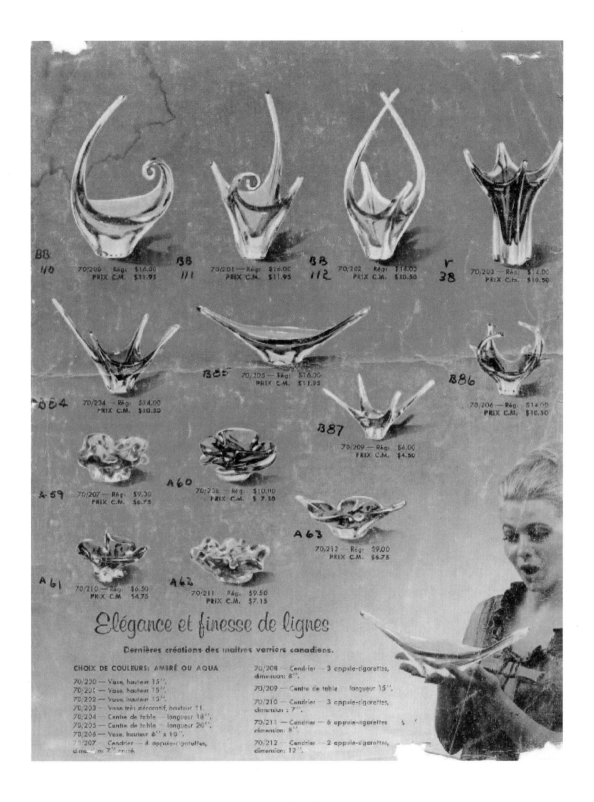

Chalet catalog page, circa 1960s. The text is in French, of course!

Dunbar Glass Corporation

Dunbar, West Virginia
1930–1955

Best

In the earliest years, Dunbar was called Dunbar Flint Glass Company (circa 1912–1923) and produced only lamp chimneys. By the 1920s, Dunbar Glass had expanded and was manufacturing novelties, giftware, barware, and tableware. In 1923, Dunbar Flint Glass Company became Dunbar Flint Glass Corporation and later Dunbar Glass Corporation. Located in the town of Dunbar, West Virginia, the firm employed a line of designers producing some award winning designs for the firm in handmade tableware and barware. Late production at Dunbar turned to lighting goods exclusively, and, in 1953, Dunbar withdrew from pressed and blown glass to concentrate only on the production of glass tubing. The firm ceased production in 1955.

Dunbar Giftware and Accessories
Most striking as examples of Dunbar American Mid-century Modern was a line of handmade crystal in black metal frames. Called Contrast, the ware was produced in 1952 and 1953 only. Contrast included seventeen different forms created by designer Michael Lax. The line contains decorative and food-serving pieces, but not table-set pieces. Contrast won a good design award. This use of undecorated industrial like holders and colorless glass was stark and futuristic for the post-World War II brides. Dunbar ceased production of all glass in 1953, except glass tubing, and thus ended production of the Contrast line.

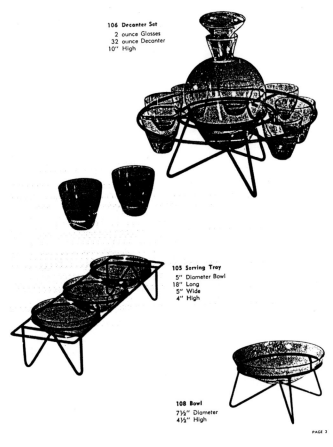

Dunbar Contrast, colorless glass in black wire, catalog page, 1953. Decanter set 10" h., $50–80; serving tray, 18" long, $30–50; and bowl, 7½" d., $20–30.

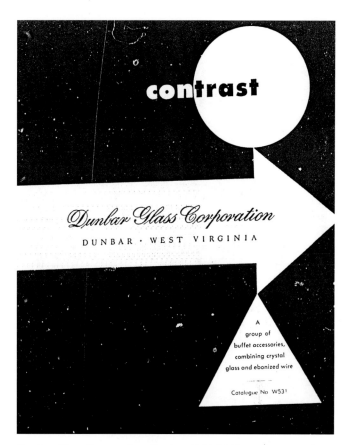

Dunbar Glass Corporation, Dunbar, WV, 1953 catalog cover for their colorless glass in black wire stands. The line was designed by noted industrial designer Michael Lax.

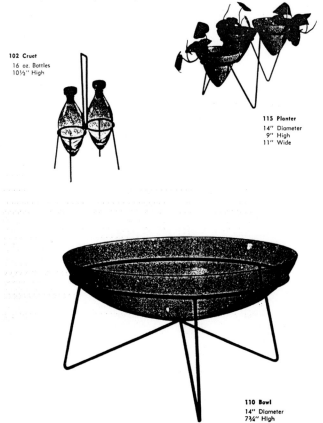

Dunbar Contrast, colorless glass in black wire, catalog page, 1953. Cruet set, 10½" h., $25–35; planter, 9" h., $20–30; bowl, 14" d., $35–50.

Dunbar Contrast, colorless glass in black wire, catalog page, 1953. Punch set, 12 glasses, bowl, stand, and ladle 11½" h., $100–120; cocktail tray, 18" long, $25–35.

117 Susan Server
21" Diameter
6½" High

Center bowl 9¾" Diameter
8 bowls 5" Diameter

118 Sandwich Server
Glass Tray 13" Diameter
Stand 3½" High

Dunbar Contrast, colorless glass in black wire, catalog page, 1953. Susan Server, eight 5" bowls, and one 9¾" bowl; overall diameter 21", $60–80; sandwich server, 13" d., $25–35.

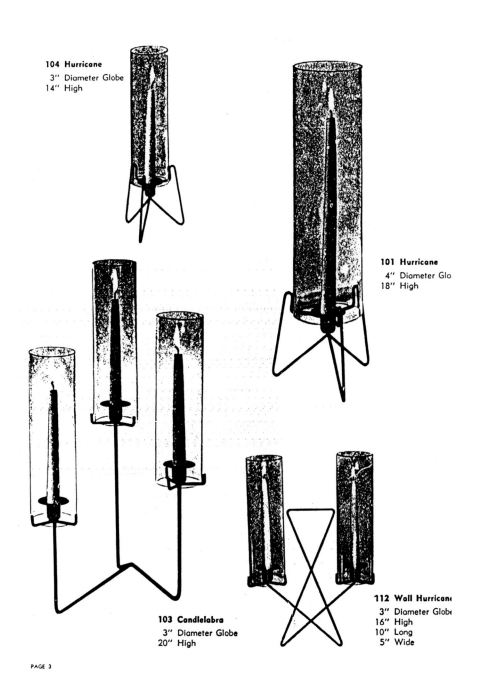

104 Hurricane
3" Diameter Globe
14" High

101 Hurricane
4" Diameter Glo
18" High

103 Candlelabra
3" Diameter Globe
20" High

112 Wall Hurricane
3" Diameter Globe
16" High
10" Long
5" Wide

PAGE 3

Dunbar Contrast, colorless glass in black wire, catalog page, 1953. Hurricane, 14" h., $15–23; hurricane, 18" h., $20–28; candelabra, 20" h., $35–50; wall hurricane, 16" h., $35–45.

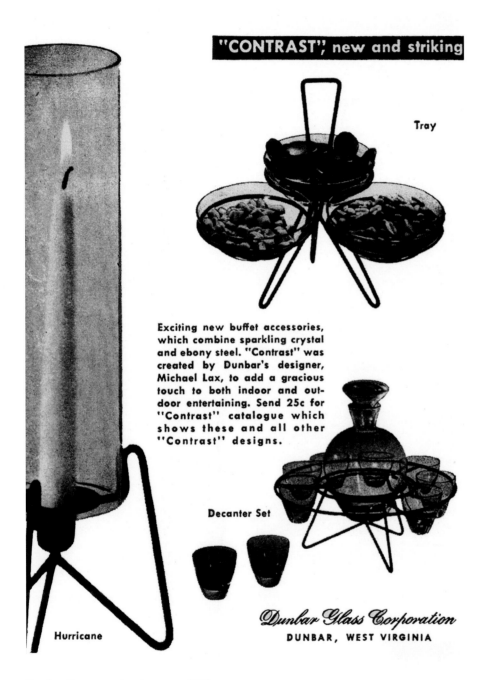

"CONTRAST", new and striking

Tray

Exciting new buffet accessories, which combine sparkling crystal and ebony steel. "Contrast" was created by Dunbar's designer, Michael Lax, to add a gracious touch to both indoor and outdoor entertaining. Send 25c for "Contrast" catalogue which shows these and all other "Contrast" designs.

Decanter Set

Dunbar Glass Corporation
DUNBAR, WEST VIRGINIA

Hurricane

Dunbar Contrast advertisement. 1953

For Gracious Entertaining

The Dunbar "Contrast" decanter set . . . decanter and ten glasses in sparkling hand-made crystal, set off by the stand of ebonized steel wire . . . for the modern touch in entertaining . . . for an ideal gift.

One of seventeen "Contrast" contemporary designs of dining and buffet accessories by Dunbar. See the "Contrast" decanter set, bowls, hurricanes, punch set, and other striking "Contrast" crystal and ebonized wire accessories at leading department stores and gift shops.

Dunbar Glass Corporation
DUNBAR   WEST VIRGINIA

Dunbar Contrast advertisement "for the modern touch in entertaining" and noting that there were seventeen designs in dining and buffet accessories.

Duncan & Miller Glass Company

Washington, Pennsylvania
1893–1955

Good

Better

Best

The origins of Duncan and Miller lie in the 1893 organization of Geo. Duncan's Sons & Co. The firm relocated to Washington, Pennsylvania, in 1893. The Duncan family had a long history of involvement with hot glass production in Pittsburgh, Pennsylvania. When John Mill, a financial partner, joined the firm the name was changed to Duncan & Miller Glass Company in 1890.

Duncan and Miller's major ventures into American Mid-century Modern were the lines Raymor Connoisseur (designed by Ben Seibel for exclusive distribution by Raymor), Laguna (designed for Duncan by James Rosati), and Festive (designed for Duncan by Michael Lax).

Duncan's Laguna was produced in what has been described as "dull earth tones." Smoky Avocado, Teakwood Brown, and Biscayne Green were the color names Duncan used to describe Laguna. The line, numbered pattern 154, was a tableware line that included salt and pepper, cream and sugar, cruet, iced tea glass, individual celery, salad bowl, and even a "one-handled celery," as well as other shapes. In addition to tableware, Laguna included accessories for smoking, nut bowls, candy bowls, and other casual entertaining pieces. Laguna was an extensive line with approximately fifty shapes being produced. It was designed by James

Rosati and won a good design award from the Museum of Modern Art in 1953.

Raymor Connoisseur was produced by Duncan & Miller for exclusive distribution by Richards Morgenthau & Co. Raymor and Richards Morgenthau were interconnected New York-based firms that created and marketed modern designed domestic products. The line was designed by noted industrial designer Ben Seibel. Introduced in 1953, the line came in Mocha Brown, Contemporary Crystal (colorless) and Avocado Green. All pieces were produced with a crackle finish. A list of twenty-seven shapes is enumerated in original sales literature. They range from a large punch bowl to small, 6 oz. juice glasses. Raymor Connoisseur covered a range of objects from food serving to smoking accessories and and candleholders. The candleholders and several other pieces are described as having "cadmium stands." Today all of these pieces are difficult to find, with some being known only in literature.

Festive was the third and final American Mid-century Modern pattern undertaken by Duncan & Miller. Introduced in July 1954, it came on the eve of Duncan's closing in mid-year 1955. The production of Festive was thus confined to less than one year. When first noted in *China, Glass and Tableware* in August 1954, the line included twelve items incorporating what had been described as "Duncan's exquisite glass with hand rubbed Hondorus Mahogany and solid brass." It must have met with some sales success. When mention of Festive was made in *Crockery & Glass Journal* of 5 May 1955, it was noted that five additional and new pieces were being offered.

The Duncan & Miller company was sold to the U.S. Glass Company of Tiffin, Ohio, in 1955. The assets of the firm were relocated to either the U.S. Glass factory in Glassport, Pennsylvania, or to Tiffin, Ohio.

To Learn More:

"Festive: A Charming Pattern in Contemporary Design." *The National Duncan Glass Journal.* Volume 32 No. 4, October–December 2006.

"Duncan & Miller's Raymor Connoisseur." *The National Duncan Glass Journal.* Volume No. 1, January–March 2007.

"Duncan & Miller No. 154: Laguna." *The National Duncan Glass Journal.* Volume 34 No. 4, October–December 2008. Styled and designed by James Rosati.

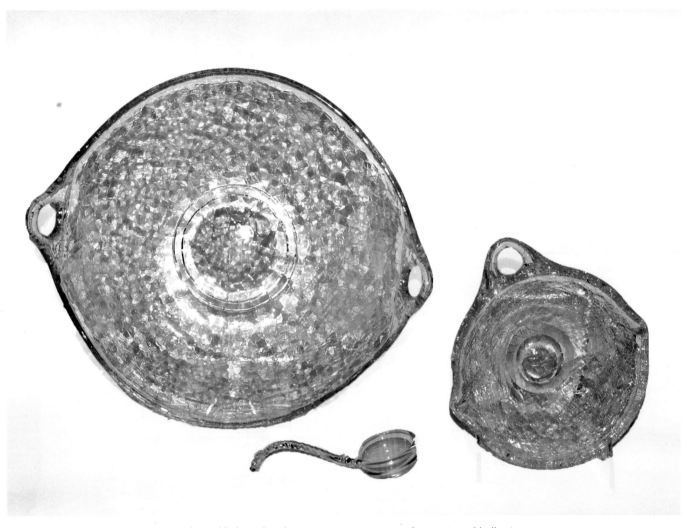

Duncan-made Raymor pattern Crystal Crackle large bowl, 10–12", $75–80; sauce boat, 6"; and ladle, $50–60.

Duncan-made Raymor pattern Smoky Avocado juice tumbler, 3", $30–45; and cup, 2", $30–50.

Duncan-made Raymor pattern, Teakwood Brown celery tray, $75–80.

Duncan Laguna pattern, Smoky Avocado one-handle bowl, 8", $50–60; Teakwood Brown salad bowl with dressing compartment, 14", $80–95; and Teakwood Brown individual salad, 6", $35–45.

Duncan Laguna #154/5 Biscayne Green 8" ash tray, $40–50; #154/3 Teakwood Brown 9" plate, $60–70.

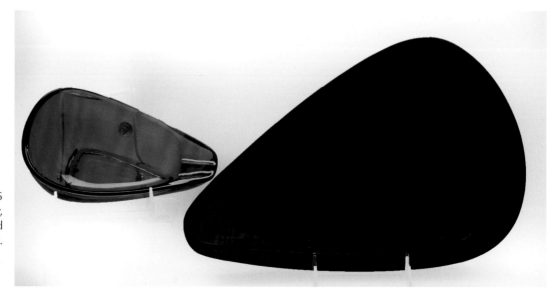

154/24
14" Floating Garden

154/26
12" Salad Bowl

154/27
6" Individual Salad

154/25
14" One Handled Celery

154/29
17" Oblong Plate

154/31 12" Salad Bowl
w/Dressing Compartment and Ladle

Sell *Laguna* Salad Service in seven piece sets. The large bowl is 12" x 9½" x 4⅝". The individuals are 6¼" x 5¼" x 3½". The salad bowl doubles as a centerpiece, and the individuals also serve as bon-bon or nut dishes, or desserts.

154/30 14" One Handled,
Two Compartment Relish

154/32
15" One Handled Plate

154/28
14" Three Compartment Relish

Laguna

Styled and Designed by James Rosati

The ware shows Rosati's nice feeling for modern informal design, and his fine perception of the niceties of line and form. Notice too, the precise clean definition of detailing — the flawless undistorted clarity of the glass — both characteristic of well practiced hand craft by the old traditional methods.

THE DUNCAN & MILLER GLASS CO.

"The loveliest glassware in America"

Washington, Pennsylvania

Page 34

Duncan catalog page for Laguna pattern. Illustrated are floating garden, 14"; salad bowl, 12"; individual salad, 6"; open-handled celery, 14"; oblong plate, 17"; salad bowl with dressing compartment and ladle ,14"; one-handled, two-compartment relish, 14"; one-handled plate, 15"; three-compartment relish, 14".

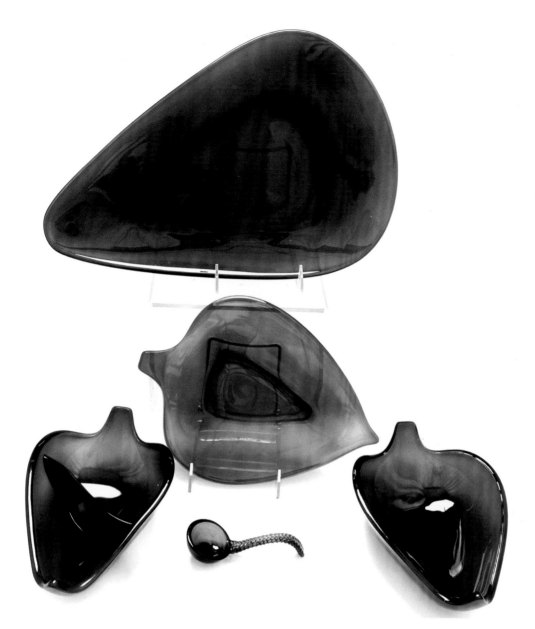

Duncan Laguna, all Teakwood Brown. Top: #154/3, 9" plate, $60–70. Front: #154/13 one-handled two-compartment relish with ladle, 8", $50–60; #154/10 one-handled plate, 10½", $40–50; #154/9 one-handled bon-bon, 9½", $40–50.

Duncan Laguna cigarette box with handled cover, Smoky Avocado, 6", $40–50; bowl with lid, Teakwood Brown, $50–60.

154/16
10" Two Handled Plate

154/5
8" Ash Tray

154/15
9" Two Handled Bon Bon

154/12
8" Four Piece Twin Dressing Set

154/17
10" Two Handled Celery

154/8
8" One Handled Bowl

Laguna { THE <u>GOOD</u> MODERN AT MODERATE COST

154/44
Salt
154/45
Pepper

154/46
Oil or Vinegar Cruet

154/43
7 oz. Cream

154/48
6½" Candy Box & Cover

154/42
7 oz. Sugar

The Nicest Table Accessories are--

HAND-MADE
Duncan

Duncan catalog page for Laguna pattern. Illustrated are #154/5, 8" ash tray; #154/16, 10" two-handled plate; #154/15, 9" two-handled bon-bon; #154/12, 8" four-piece twin dressing set (bowl, two ladles, and under plate); #154/17, 10" two-handled celery; #154/8, 8" one-handled bowl; #154/44 and 154/45, salt and pepper shakers; #154/46, oil or vinegar cruet with stopper; #154/43, 7 oz. cream; #154/48, 6½" candy box with cover; #154/42, sugar, 7 oz.

Duncan Laguna, all Smoky Avocado. Cocktail mixer with stirrer #154/22, 18 oz., $100–110; #154–B, 10 oz. water, $15–20; #154–D, 7 oz. sherbet or old fashion, $8–10; #154–E, 3½ oz. cocktail, $20–30.

Two Duncan Laguna pieces in the uncataloged aqua color. While uncommon, several examples of Laguna aqua are known. Decanter #154/49 with stopper, 32oz., $150–180; #154/46 oil or vinegar cruet with stopper, $100–125.

Duncan Laguna, all Teakwood Brown. #154/44 salt and 154/45 pepper set, $60–70; #154/21 vase, 10", $80–90; #154/A, 14 oz. beverage, $15–20; #154–C, 6 oz. juice, $8–10.

The Duncan & Miller Glass Co.
WASHINGTON, PA.

Laguna
PATTERN
NO. 154

Catalog 89
Page 29

The Duncan hand made crystal tumblers shown here were all selected by The Museum of Modern Art for GOOD DE-SIGN. They are hand blown and flame polished.

Duncan Laguna tumblers from catalog 89.

Two Duncan Laguna glasses in Smoky Avocado: #154–B, 10 oz. water, $15–20; #154–D, 7 oz. sherbet or old fashion, $8–10.

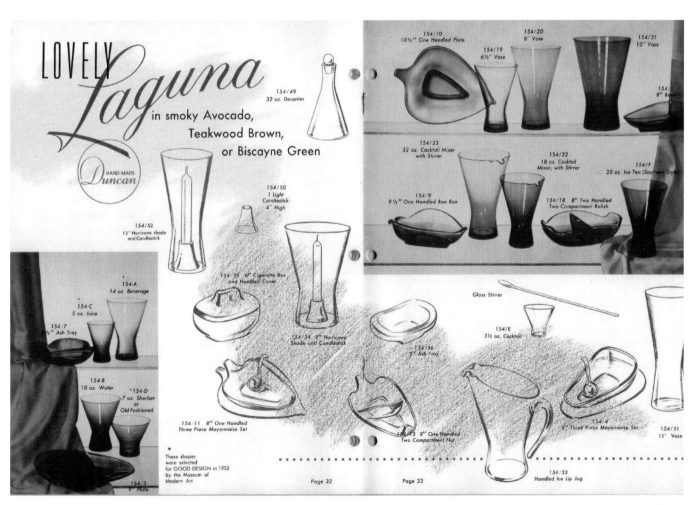

Duncan catalog page for Laguna pattern. Illustrated are #154/7, 6½" ashtray; #154–C, 5 oz. juice; #154–A, 14 oz. beverage; #154/3, 9" plate; #154–B, 10 oz. water; #154–D, 7 oz. sherbet or old fashion; #154/49, 32 oz. decanter; #154/52, 12" hurricane shade and candlestick; #154/50, one light candlestick, 4"; #154/35, cigarette box and handled cover; #154/34, 9" hurricane shade and candle stick; #154–36, 5" ash tray; #154/E, 3½ oz. cocktail; glass stirrer; #154/11, 8" one-handled three-piece mayonnaise set; #154/13, 8" one-handled, two-compartment nut; #154/33, handled ice lip jug; #154–4, 8" three-piece mayo set (no handle); #154/51, 12" vase; #154/10, 10½" one-handled plate; #154/19, 6½" vase; #154/20, 8" vase; #154/21, 10" vase; #154/?, 8" bowl; #154/9, 9½" one-handled bon-bon; #154/23, 32oz. cocktail mixer with stirrer; #154/22, 18 oz. cocktail mixer with stirrer; #154/18, 8" two-handled, two-compartment relish; #154/F, 20 oz. ice tea (southern style).

Brief Histories of AMCM Hot Glass Manufacturers

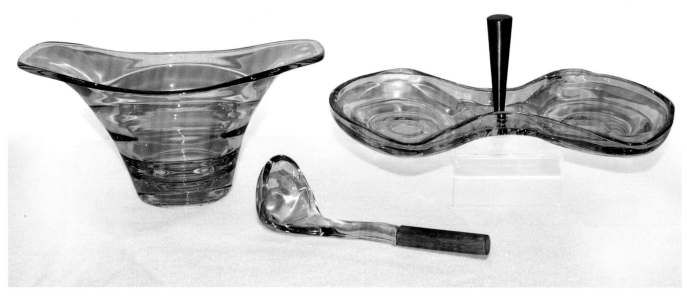

Duncan Festive, Golden Honey color, oval sauce bowl, $40–60; glass ladle with threaded wooden handle, $30–40; and two-part relish/tray with solid brass handle, $50–60. Note: all wood parts are mahogany

Duncan Festive, Aqua, round sauce bowl, 2½" h., $30–40; serving tray/chip–n–dip tray, $70–80; bowl on wood stand/base, $100–120.

Duncan Festive (left to right): cream and sugar sets, mahogany base tray and lids with brass handles: Aqua cream, sugar with lid, and tray (four pieces), $100–120; clear four-piece set, $85–100. Honey Amber cream, $30–35, and sugar with no lid, $30–35 (shown with lid missing brass handle). Oil bottle, aqua (back right), $80–100 as shown (add $20–25 for wood stopper with brass handle); tumbler (front center), aqua, $30–35; salt and pepper with wood lids, aqua, $30–45 pair with lids a shown.

Duncan Festive pattern, sugar bowl (no lid), Aqua, $15–20 as shown; platter, Golden Honey, $80–100; creamer, Aqua, $15–20.

Duncan Festive,
reversible candlestick
#155/60, Golden
Honey color, 5½" h.
(made only 1954–55).
Two glass parts with
wood wafer. Inverted it
was a violet vase. Each
$45–50.

Duncan Festive, Golden
Honey and mahogany.
Candlesticks, $45–50
each; compote, 10",
$80–100.

Erickson Glass Works

New Bremen, Ohio
1943–1960

Good   *Better*

Carl Erickson (b. 1899), like many glass workers, worked at many places. Erickson hailed from Reijmre, Sweden, and was from a family of famed glass workers. He worked at Pairpoint Manufacturing Company in New Bedford, Massachusetts, for twenty years. He then worked in Toledo, Ohio, at Libbey glass for four years. In 1937, he joined Blenko Glass as shop foreman. Upon leaving Blenko, he and his brother Steven acquired a closed glass plant in Bremen, Ohio, which they re-opened in 1943.

In Erwin Kalla's obituary in the *Pittsburgh Post-Gazette* (July 28, 2005), it is noted that Kalla had designed the Raymor Holiday Glass line that was produced by Erickson Glass in the 1950s.

In time, Carl Erickson became the sole owner, and he continued to produce hot glass until shortly before the works were dismantled in the summer of 1960. The company officially ceased to exist in 1961.

The Museum of Modern Art in New York awarded Erickson its accolade for good design. His creations included the use of heavy crystal, controlled bubble inclusions, and often two-color creations. Carl Erickson died in 1966.

Erickson raindrop ball ashtray, Grape and Crystal, 14" d., $65–85; Emerald and Crystal, 8" d., $40–60.

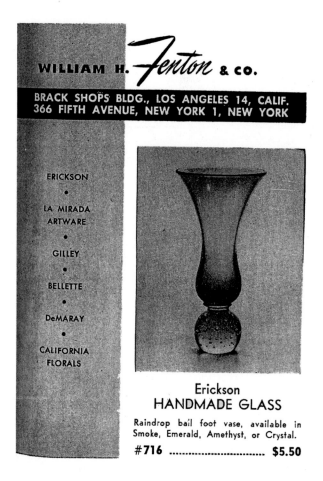

WILLIAM H. *Fenton* & CO.

BRACK SHOPS BLDG., LOS ANGELES 14, CALIF.
366 FIFTH AVENUE, NEW YORK 1, NEW YORK

ERICKSON
•
LA MIRADA
ARTWARE
•
GILLEY
•
BELLETTE
•
DeMARAY
•
CALIFORNIA
FLORALS

Erickson
HANDMADE GLASS

Raindrop ball foot vase, available in
Smoke, Emerald, Amethyst, or Crystal.
#716 .... $5.50

Erickson "raindrop ball foot" period advertisement.

Erickson raindrop ball foot Emerald and Crystal ice tea, 8",
$45–55; Grape and Crystal crimped vase, 6", $60–80.

ONE OF THE WORLD'S FINE GLASSWARES

#642 – $3.00

#527 – $6.00

#902 – $5.50

HANDMADE
by
Erickson

#541 – $3.00

#701 – $7.50

Ashtrays
Perfect Gift for Men

USEFUL
Men like these man size ashtrays

HANDSOME
To a man's taste – In emerald, crystal or smoke

SALEABLE
The answer to your customers' gift problem for that hard-to-please man. Priced from $3.00 to $7.50

IMMEDIATE DELIVERY

WILLIAM H. *Fenton* & CO.

366 Fifth Ave., New York, N.Y. • 2555 W. Fifth St., Los Angeles, Calif.

Bolender and Company   Grace Hunter
Merchandise Mart, Chicago, Ill. Parker House, Boston, Mass.

Advertisement for Erickson ashtrays.

Erickson Crystal square foot and raindrop Emerald bowl, 4¼" h. x 8¼" d., $120–145.

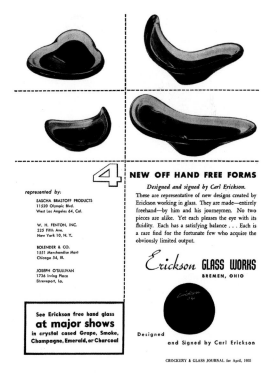

represented by:

SASCHA BRASTOFF PRODUCTS
11520 Olympic Blvd.
West Los Angeles 64, Cal.

W. H. FENTON, INC.
225 Fifth Ave.
New York 10, N. Y.

BOLENDER & CO.
1551 Merchandise Mart
Chicago 54, Ill.

JOSEPH O'SULLIVAN
1736 Irving Place
Shreveport, La.

See Erickson free hand glass
at major shows
in crystal cased Grape, Smoke,
Champagne, Emerald, or Charcoal

4 NEW OFF HAND FREE FORMS

Designed and signed by Carl Erickson.

These are representative of new designs created by Erickson working in glass. They are made—entirely freehand—by him and his journeymen. No two pieces are alike. Yet each pleases the eye with its fluidity. Each has a satisfying balance . . . Each is a rare find for the fortunate few who acquire the obviously limited output.

Erickson GLASS WORKS
BREMEN, OHIO

Designed   and Signed by Carl Erickson

CROCKERY & GLASS JOURNAL for April, 1955

Erickson advertisement for "new off hand free forms" noted that they are signed by Carl Erickson and the colors were Crystal, cased Grape, Smoke, Champagne, Emerald and Charcoal. *Crockery & Glass Journal,* April, 1958.

Erickson advertisement for new pieces introduced in 1957 and to be offered at the Pittsburgh glass show.

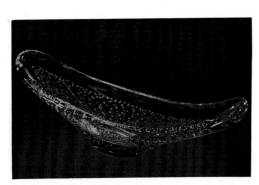

Erickson Crystal and Emerald bowl/ashtray in flame pattern, 3⅛" h. x 8¼" d.. $45–55.

Erickson free form bowl with "its unique treatment of symmetrically spaced bubbles caught in a clear crystal body." Noted to "retail for as little as $15.00." *Crockery & Glass Journal,* January 1958.

Erickson advertisement for "sophisticated miracles in glass by Erickson." The top three objects are tulip shape glasses on tear drop base," man-size beer mugs with thumb rests, and double capacity glassware in the unique Erickson Flame.

Erickson Flame decanter with raindrop stopper, Champagne color, 10½" h., $100–125; tumbler, Emerald, 6½" h., $18–26; tumbler, Charcoal, 4" h., $14–20.

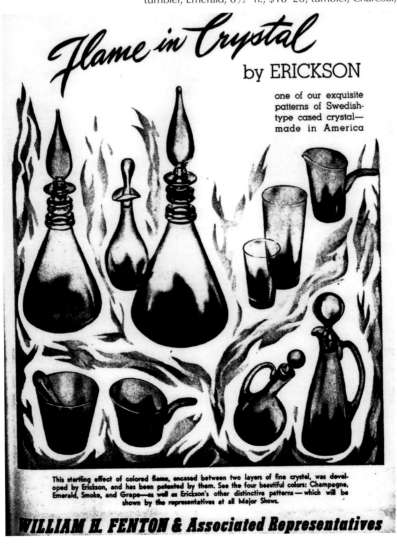

Advertisement for Flame in Crystal. Noted as "one of our exquisite patterns of Swedish—type cased crystal—made in America." The copy reads "the startling effect of colored flame, encases between two layers of fine crystal, was developed by Erickson, and has been patented by them. See the four different beautiful colors: Champagne, Emerald, Smoke, and Grape…"

WILLIAM H. Fenton & CO.

BRACK SHOPS BLDG., LOS ANGELES 14, CALIF.
366 FIFTH AVENUE, NEW YORK 1, NEW YORK

ERICKSON
•
LA MIRADA
ARTWARE
•
GILLEY
•
BELLETTE
•
DeMARAY
•
CALIFORNIA
FLORALS

Erickson Glassware
Decanter and Glasses
#506-600 ....Set, $10.75

William H. Fenton & Co. advertisement for Erickson. Note that the decanter with teardrop stopper, ringed neck, and four glasses was priced at $10.75.

Erickson raindrop-based, Emerald bowl compote, 7"-tal x 13" wide, $75–95.

Erickson raindrop-based, Champagne color bowls. Left: 5"-tal x 6⅛" d.; right: 6" h. x 12⅛" d..

Erickson #3725CH candlesticks, crystal-cased Emerald with raindrop, 3¼" h., $30–40 each.

Erickson vase bookends with raindrop in Smoke and Emerald, 6" h., $85–110 per pair.

Fenton Art Glass Company

Williamstown, West Virginia
1905–2011

Good

Better

Best

Fenton Art Glass Company began in 1905 as a decorator of glass made by others. Fenton built a new factory in Williamstown, West Virginia, and moved there from their site in Ohio, with the first hot glass production being in 1907. Fenton's success often rested on selling to traditional markets and their designs were largely those adapted from historical precedents. There were, over time, several efforts to expand into designer-influenced glass, art glass, and less traditional lines. With few exceptions these efforts were all unsuccessful. The Fenton lines that qualify as Mid-century Modern are few and all were very short lived.

Fenton ceased production of hot glass in the summer of 2011, after 106 years.

Fenton ventured into Mid-century Modern in 1953, with their introduction of the New World line. The Fenton catalog supplement of that time said of the line, "designed by Stan Fistick to adapt to our particular skills and distinctive processes to contemporary living. The beautiful color effects and new feeling in Modern of the wine bottle (No. 1667) and wine glass (No. 1647) cruet, salt and pepper, sugar and cream, and others will stimulate your sales of Fenton. They are made in Cranberry and Lime. The cruet (No. 7369) is made in solid gray with black handle and black stopper. The wine bottle (No. 7367) is gray with a black stopper, while the wine glass is black on the outside and gray on the inner surfaces. Plates and

bowls are all gray on the upper surface and black on the underside except the 8" plate (No. 7318) which is solid black."

By the end of 1953, a short few months later, sales of the gray and black items were so slow that they were discontinued. Few of the items remained in production beyond a few years. Cranberry was the most popular color. The most popular item was the tall wine bottle in Cranberry. Authors Ken and Margaret Whitmeyer report the Cranberry and opalescent decanter remained in production for ten years.

The leadership at Fenton was not willing to accept being locked into only the historical and traditional glass market. In 1957, roughly three years after the New World line had failed to sell, they again engaged a designer to lead Fenton in the Modern design market. An agreement with Michael Lax was entered into in 1957, and the designs were ready for production by 1958. At the time, sales of traditional glass design in the Fenton line were strong, and the company delayed introduction of the Lax designed Horizon line until it was nicluded in the announcement of mid-year (July) offerings by Fenton in 1959.

The bold colors of the earlier New World line were replaced in Horizon with Amber, Jamestown Blue, and French Opalescent (milk white and crystal). Into a late 1950s world of wood-finished Swedish Modern furniture came the Fenton Horizon line, which coupled rawhide strips, walnut wood, and white porcelain

elements with glass. Horizon had a very modern vocabulary.

Fenton literature had this to say about Horizon: "For well over half a century Fenton has specialized in Early American designs–and very successfully too! However, knowing that you have a number of contemporary minded customers we have had Michael Lax, a young inspirational designer, develop the 'Horizon' line… Horizon is a marriage of beautiful Fenton colors, rubber walnut wood tops, porcelain candle cups and bases, and rawhide thongs—as new as tomorrow…"

Sales of modern glass, this time the Horizon line, were again notably slow, and did not live up to the hype and expectations of Fenton. The 1960 catalog (introduced in January 1960) did not include Horizon, making the window of availability for the line an amazingly brief one half of a year.

Fenton Giftware and Accessories
Most noted as AMCM Fenton would be the small wooden table that held three vases and was an updated version of the traditional all glass epergne. Additional pieces with striking modernity are the hanging vases, suspended on leather cords.

To Learn More:
Whitmyer, Margaret and Kenn. *Fenton Art Glass Patterns: 1939–1980.* Paducah, Kentucky: Collector Books. 2001

Fenton New World wine bottle, #1667–CR, with Crystal stopper (1953–1963), 12", $100–135.

Fenton New World pepper shaker, #7305, in Lime opalescent, $30–40 per shaker.

Fenton Glass catalog supplement, January 1, 1953.

Fenton New World #1605 pepper and salt shakers with metal caps. 5" and 4 1/8" tall, respectively, Cranberry rib optic, $30–38 each.

FENTON'S NEW LINES
FOR 1953

NEW WORLD:

Designed by Stan Fistick to adapt our particular skills and distinctive processes to contemporary living. The beautiful color effects and new feeling in modern of the wine bottle (No. 1667) and wine glass (No. 1647), Cruet, Salt and pepper, sugar and cream and others will stimulate your sales of Fenton. These are made in Cranberry and Lime.

The spell of Dusk is captured by the same shapes made in the very smart color combination of black and gray. The cruet (No. 7369) is made in solid gray with black handle and black stopper. The wine bottle (No. 7367) is gray with black stopper, while the wine glass is black on the outside and gray on the inner surfaces. Plates and bowls are all gray on the upper surface and black on the under side except the 8" plate (No. 7318) which is solid black.

No. 1614
14" Torte Plate
(CR & LO)

No. 1624
14" Floater Bowl
(CR & LO)

No. 1623
12" Salad Bowl
(CR & LO)

No. 5156
7" Fish Vase
(KM, MK)

No. 1647
Wine
(CR & LO)

No. 1604
Sugar & Cream Set
(CR & LO)

Fenton New World January glassware for the 1953 catalog supplement promoting "Fenton's New Lines for 1953" and noting Stan Fistick as the designer. Image compliments of Fenton Art Glass Co.

Fenton Horizon glassware in the color Jamestown Blue, #8122 bowl, 7¾"-diameter x 5" h. $30–45; and #8123 bowl, 10½"-diameter x 6⅜" h., $55–65. They bear alternating panels of smooth glass and raised, textured pattern. Both were purchased from the Fenton factory during the final months of their gift shop being open. They were from the factory collection and bear the label "Frank's Closet" indicating they were retained by Frank Fenton. Courtesy of the Museum of American Glass in West Virginia collection.

HORIZON

signed by Michael Lax for

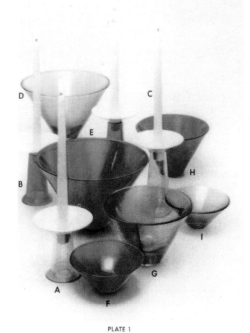

PLATE 1:

A 8175 AR 5" Candleholder with Insert
B 8176 JT 6½" Candleholder with Insert
C 8177 AR 8" Candleholder with Insert
D 8123 AR Bowl
E 8123 JT Bowl
F 8121 JT Nut Dish
G 8122 AR Bowl
H 8122 JT Bowl
I 8121 AR Nut Dish

PLATE 2:

A 8176 FO Candleholder with Insert
B 8126 FO 10½" Bowl with Base
C 8157 FO 8½" Vase
D 8101 FO Sugar & Cream Set
E 8162 FO Oil
F 8106 FO Salt & Pepper

FRONT COVER

A 8105 JT Hanging Bowl with Thong
B 8105 AR Hanging Bowl with Thong
C 8104 AR Hanging Vase with Thong
D 8104 JT Hanging Vase with Thong
E 8102 JT Epergne

PLATE 2

For well over a half a century Fenton has specialized in Early American designs — and very successfully too!

However, knowing that you have a number of contemporary minded customers we have had Michael Lax, a young inspirational contemporary designer, develop the "Horizon" line as shown on the front and back covers. "Horizon" is a marriage of beautiful Fenton colors, rubbed walnut wood tops, porcelain candle cups and bases, and rawhide thongs — as new as tomorrow; functional and beautiful, truly a pace setting achievement that has long been our forte — and always with you our customers in mind.

8103 Hangers needed with 8104 & 8105

PLATE 1

Fenton Horizon, summer catalog supplement 1959. Image compliments of the National Fenton Glass Society.

Fenton Horizon, Jamestown Blue
Cream, #8101, $24–30; oil, #8162
(missing wooden stopper–lid), $35–42;
nut dish, #8121, $24–28

Fenton Horizon, Amber Cream, #8101,
$14–18.

Fenton Horizon French
Opalescent Cream,
#8101 $20–30; and
salt shaker with wood
lid, #8106, $20–25
per shaker.

...because you ask for them-

NEW STYLES
in
Proven Patterns
..... and Colors

SUMMER CATALOG SUPPLEMENT 1959

Fenton Horizon catalog summer supplement, 1959. Image compliments of the National Fenton Glass Society.

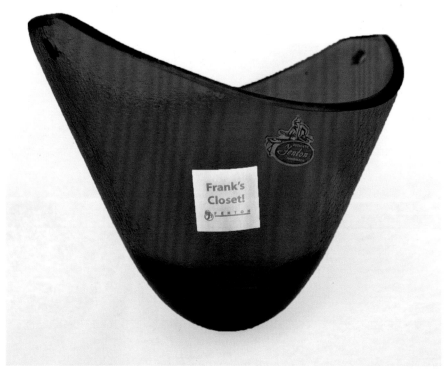

Fenton Horizon hanging vase, Amber glass with two holes for rawhide hanging thong, 6¾" w. x 5" h., $40–55. Purchased at the Fenton Factory September 2013. Courtesy of the Museum of American Glass in West Virginia Collection.

Fenton Horizon, Jamestown blue hanging vase, with leather thong, #8104, 12" h., $100–140. Courtesy of the Museum of American Glass in West Virginia Collection.

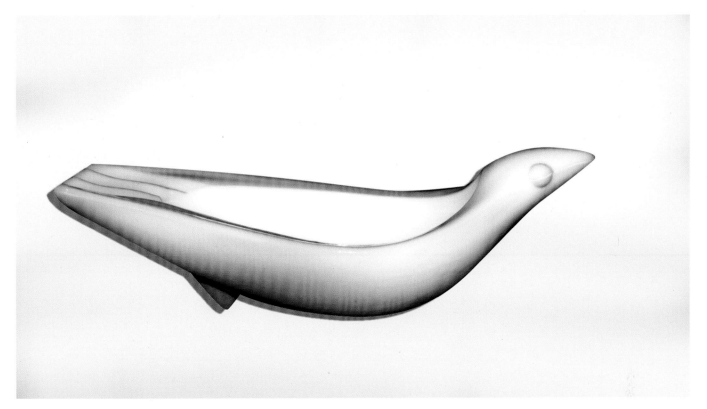

Fenton bird ash tray in milk glass, illustrated as one of three bird–like forms in the January 1954 catalog supplement. 8⅝"-long x 2½" h., $24–30. Courtesy of the Museum of American Glass in West Virginia collection.

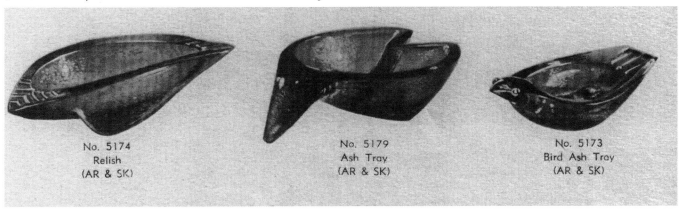

No. 5174
Relish
(AR & SK)

No. 5179
Ash Tray
(AR & SK)

No. 5173
Bird Ash Tray
(AR & SK)

Fenton mid century modern designs #5174 relish, #5179 ash tray, and #5173 bird ash. All three pieces are captioned as being offered in Amber and Smoke, an uncommon Fenton color. January 1954 Fenton catalog supplement.

Fenton glass made for Rubel: Amber with straight optic vase, $45–60; and pitcher, $40–50. Purchased by the Museum of American Glass in West Virginia from the Fenton Art Glass factory at public auction of the factory glass collection.

Fenton offered this line as early as their 1961 catalog, where two sizes (5" and 9") of ash trays appear in blue, green, crystal and Amber. As late as 1977–1978, two ash trays described as "Swirl" were offered in the catalog with sizes cited as 7½" and 5½". Colors in 1977 were Colonial Blue, Springtime Green, Wisteria, and Amber. The same shape was produced at one time for Rubel and may have originated as Rubel designs? Shown here, left to right: ash tray, blue (not colonial blue), 5", $5–8; coaster and cigarette rest combination (top view and side view) in colonial green (no catalog information found, but purchased from the estate of Frank Fenton), $10–14; red toothpick or cigarette urn, $14–20.

Fenton produced these AMCM glass tiles in the 1960s for an unknown private contract. These examples were purchased in 2012 at one of the factory's closing special sales, held in the Blue Ridge Room adjacent to the Fenton Museum. $20–28 each. Collection of the Museum of American Glass in West Virginia.

Fostoria Glass Company

Moundsville, West Virginia 1887–1984

Good   *Better*   *Best*

Fostoria Glass began in 1887 in Fostoria, Ohio, from which the company took its name, and relocated to Moundsville, West Virginia, in 1891. The relocation was spurred by a shortage of natural gas in Ohio. Fostoria was largely a producer of higher-end tableware and giftware.

Fostoria utilized designers, like George Sakia, and they created a number of designs that drifted into Mid-century Modern designs. As early as 1949, their introduction of Contour line pieces entered the modern design movement. Fostoria closed their factory in 1984, after 97 years of glass production. The assets were purchased by Lancaster Colony of Ohio.

In the Fostoria catalog dated July 15, 1961, a short line of objects titled "Glass Combinations With Brass" is shown and designated as lines 2702 and 2708. The 2702 objects have a pattern or design inside the glass elements; the line 2708 objects are unpatterned glass. The lines consist of candleholders and one comport.

The same 1961 catalog features the Hawaiian Pattern, No. 2737. While there are some food service pieces, the casual table items, like appetizer sets, a few bowls, shrimp and dip set, torte plate, and cheese and cracker plate. There were no true tableware or place setting pieces in Hawaiian. The line was offered in Amber with brown accents color and Amber with Peacock Blue accent colors.

A line in 1961 that was very much in the manner of Mid-century Modern was Fostoria's Sculpture Pattern, noted in the catalog as being made of lead crystal. Few of the forms are tableware; one might suggest that few are even functional, but instead are, indeed, glass sculpture, as the line name suggests. Piece type names are "shell, oblong, spire bowl, lineal, bowl, and Tricorne." By the 1965 catalog, three additional pieces had been added to the line, then totaling an offering of 19 shapes.

Also in the 1961 catalog are a number of items grouped together as garden club items. The line has two footed bowls of 5 and 9 inches in diameter that incorporate a textured surface and conical, modernistic base. A free-form oblong bowl and other random items are included in the selection.

Fostoria Glass reigned for decades as one of the premier makers of elegant handmade crystal for American tables. To the mothers of the baby-boomers, it was a known staple for holiday and Sunday table settings. But, as casual dining grew, Fostoria could not ignore the shifting market. Their efforts to redefine themselves from elegant to casual was rarely successful. They had many lines that addressed the heavier, textured, casual glass for American's tables. While the heavy casual lines were mid-century, not all engaged a design concern for Modern.

Pebble Beach was one of the heavy, textured, pressed glass lines produced by Fostoria. It appeared in the January 1, 1970, catalog, and was offered in Crystal Ice, Black Pearl, Lemon Twist, Pink Lady, Mocha, and Flamingo Orange, in sixteen shapes. By January 1972, the offering had fallen to include only the colors Black Pearl, Lemon Twist, and Flaming Orange, and a modest seven shapes were all that remained in production. 1973 saw the same colors but only five shapes, all drinking vessels. Any serving pieces in Pebble Beach are difficult to find.

Sorrento was new in January 1972, barely sneaking under the timeline accepted here to qualify as Mid-century. The design is very typical of the heavy, textured drink and beverage ware popularized in the late 1960s and into the early 1970s. Designated #2832, Sorrento was initially produced in Blue, Green, Brown, and Plum (gone are the poetic names used with Pebble Beach in 1970). The offering included only six drinking vessels and one size of plate. By 1976, Sorrento had been reduced to only four forms.

Fostoria Hawaiian pattern #2737, Amber with Brown accent: #126 basket, 9" (no handles), $20–26; #500 handled candy, 8", $22–30; and large shallow bowl 14½" (not shown in catalog), $30–38.

Fostoria Hawaiian pattern #2737, Amber with Peacock Blue accent: #568 cracker plate, $30–38; and footed dip bowl, #388, Amber only, $12–18. 14" d..

HAWAIIAN PATTERN

No. 2737 Line

Made in Amber with Brown Accent Color

Made in Amber with Peacock Blue Accent Color

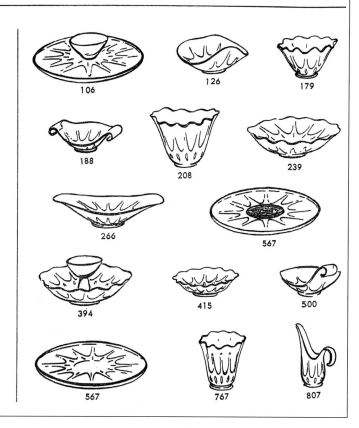

				Retail Price Ea.
2737/106			Appetizer Set	$12.50
			Height 3¾ in. - Diam. 14 in.	
			Consisting of:	
			1 Only 2737/568 Cracker Plate	
			1 Only 2737/478 Sauce Dish, Amber only	
2737/126	9	in.	Basket	5.00
			Height 3½ in.	
2737/179	8	in.	Ruffle Bowl	5.00
2737/188	9	in.	Handled Bowl	5.00
			Height 3 in.	
2737/208	8	in.	Deep Bowl	9.50
2737/239	11½	in.	Shallow Bowl	9.50
			Height 2¾ in.	
2737/266	15	in.	Oval Bowl	9.50
			Height 4 in.	
2737/369			Cheese and Cracker Set	12.50
			Diam. 14 in.	
			Consisting of:	
			1 Only 2737/568 Cracker Plate	
			1 Only 2737/226 Cheese Block (Walnut)	
2737/394			Shrimp and Dip Set	12.50
			Height 5⅝ in.	
			Consisting of:	
			1 Only 2737/248 Shrimp Bowl	
			1 Only 2737/388 Footed Dip, Amber only	
2737/415	8	in.	Flower Float	5.00
			Height 2 in.	
2737/500	8	in.	Handled Candy	5.00
			Height 3½ in.	
2737/567	14	in.	Torte Plate	9.50
2737/767			Ruffle Vase	5.00
			Height 6¾ in.	
2737/807			Pitcher Vase	5.00
			Height 8⅞ in.	

Fostoria Hawaiian pattern, line #2737, as illustrated in the Fostoria catalog dated July 15, 1961.

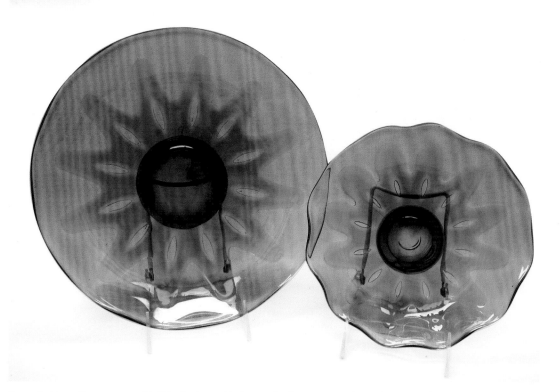

Fostoria Hawaiian pattern #2737, Amber with Peacock Blue accent, plates, $20–28. These are not on the 1961 piece listing and are distinguished from the torte plate by not having a turned-up edge.

Fostoria Pebble Beach #2806, Lemon Twist color. Front left to right: #72 One the Rocks/wine, 8 oz., 4⅛" h., $3–5; #421 dessert bowl, 2¼" h. x 4¾" w., $3–6; #7 sherbet (footed), 2¾" h., $3–5; #680 cream (footed), 3¼" h., $6–8. Back left to right: #550 plate, 8", $4–6; #84 juice, 7 oz., 4" h., $3–5; #58; ice tea, 5¾" h., $5–7.

Fostoria Hawaiian pattern #2737, handled candy, 8": #500 Amber with Peacock accent, $24–34; and Amber with Brown accent, $22–30.

PEBBLE BEACH PATTERN

No. 2806 Line

Made in Crystal Ice, Black Pearl, Lemon Twist, Pink Lady Mocha and Flaming Orange

				Retail Price Ea.
2806/2	10 oz.	Goblet	Crystal	$3.50
			Black Pearl, Lemon Twist, Pink Lady, Mocha	3.75
			Flaming Orange	4.25
		Height 6 in.		
2806/7	7 oz.	Sherbet	Crystal	3.50
			Black Pearl, Lemon Twist, Pink Lady, Mocha	3.75
			Flaming Orange	4.25
		Height 2¾ in.		
2806/72	8 oz.	On the Rocks/Wine	Crystal	3.50
			Black Pearl, Lemon Twist, Pink Lady, Mocha	3.75
			Flaming Orange	4.25
		Height 4⅛ in.		
2806/58	14 oz.	Ice Tea	Crystal	3.25
			Black Pearl, Lemon Twist, Pink Lady, Mocha	3.50
			Flaming Orange	4.00
		Height 5¾ in.		
2806/84	7 oz.	Juice	Crystal	3.25
			Black Pearl, Lemon Twist, Pink Lady, Mocha	3.50
			Flaming Orange	4.00
		Height 4 in.		
2806/211	10 in.	Salad Bowl	Crystal	9.00
			Black Pearl, Lemon Twist, Pink Lady, Mocha	9.50
		Height 4⅝ in.		
2806/421		Dessert	Crystal	3.25
			Black Pearl, Lemon Twist, Pink Lady, Mocha	3.50
			Flaming Orange	4.00
		Height 2¼ in. - Diam. 4¾ in.		
2806/454		Qt. Pitcher	Crystal	9.75
			Black Pearl, Lemon Twist, Pink Lady, Mocha	10.25
		Height 7⅛ in.		
2806/550	8 in.	Plate	Crystal	4.00
			Black Pearl, Lemon Twist, Pink Lady, Mocha	4.25
			Flaming Orange	4.50
2806/558	11 in.	Cake Plate	Crystal	6.00
			Black Pearl, Lemon Twist, Pink Lady, Mocha	6.25
2806/567	14 in.	Torte Plate	Crystal	9.00
			Black Pearl, Lemon Twist, Pink Lady, Mocha	9.50
2806/600	9 qt.	Punch Bowl	Crystal	26.50
		Height 7¾ in - Diam. 11½ in.		
2806/615	6½ oz.	Punch Cup	Crystal	3.25
		Height 3$\frac{5}{16}$ in.		
2806/622		3-Part Relish	Crystal	13.75
			Black Pearl, Lemon Twist, Pink Lady, Mocha	15.25
		Height 2½ in. - Diam. 10 in.		
2806/652		Shaker & Chrome Top E	Crystal	2.25
			Black Pearl, Lemon Twist, Pink Lady, Mocha	2.50
		Height 2⅞ in.		
2806/676		Sugar and Cover	Crystal	7.00
			Black Pearl, Lemon Twist, Pink Lady, Mocha	7.50
		Height 4 in.		
2806/680		Cream	Crystal	6.00
			Black Pearl, Lemon Twist, Pink Lady, Mocha	6.25
		Height 3¼ in.		

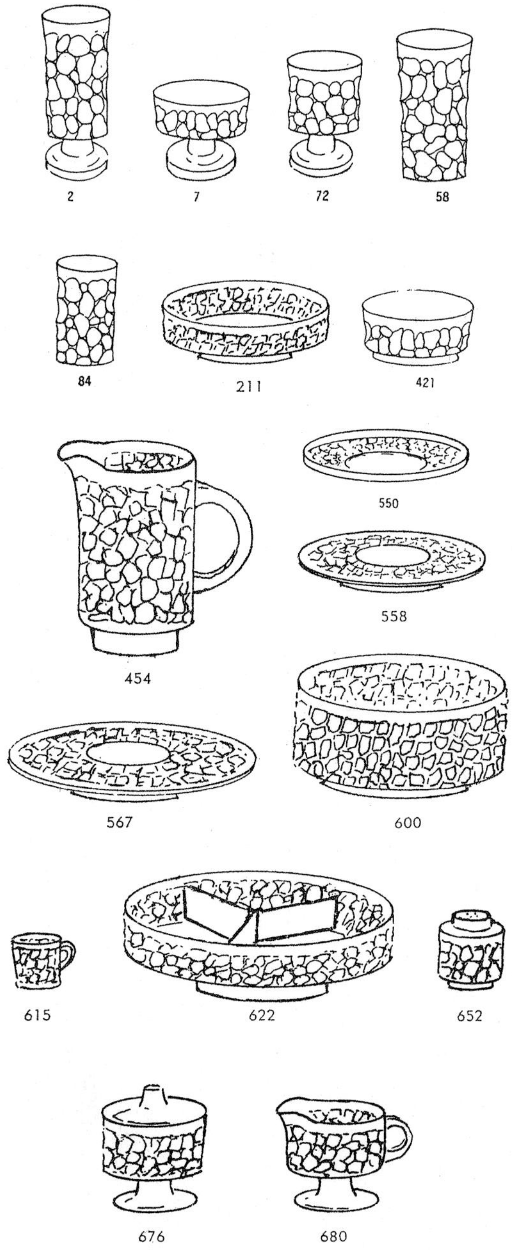

Fostoria company catalog page, January 1, 1970, featuring the then newly released Pebble Beach pattern, sixteen different shapes were available.

Fostoria Pebble Beach, #2806, Mocha (brown) color: #2 goblet (footed), 10 oz., 6" h., $3–5; #7 sherbet, 2¾" h., $2–5.

Fostoria Pebble Beach, #2806, Flaming Orange color: #7 sherbet, 2¾" h., $6–8; #84 juice, 7 oz., 4" h., $4–6; #421 dessert, 4¾" d., $6–8.

Fostoria Pebble Beach #2806, Black Pearl (smoky blue gray) color: Goblet #2806/2 (footed), 10 oz., 6" h., $10–14; #2806/84 juice, 7 oz., 4" h., $7–10; #2806/7 sherbet, 2¾" h., $5–8; #2806/550 plate, 8", $10–14.

Fostoria Sorrento, Pink: #2832/7 sherbet 6½ oz. 3⅝" h., $5–8; #2832/26 wine, 6½ oz., 5" h., $8–12; #2832/13 luncheon goblet/ice tea, 13 oz., 6¾" h., $10–18; uncataloged flat tumbler, $7–9. Juice glasses were not made in this pattern, but are aftermarket pieces created by removing and grinding the stem and foot from a wine.

Fostoria Sorrento, Blue: #2832/2 goblet, 9 oz., 6" h., $6–10; #2832/7 sherbet, 3⅝" h., $5–8; (top center) #2832/26 wine, 6½ oz., 5" h., $5–8; #2832/63 luncheon goblet/ice tea, 13 oz., 6¾" h., $8–12.

Fostoria Sorrento, Green: #2832/2 goblet, 9 oz., 6" h., $6–10; #2832/26 wine, 6½ oz., 5" h. $5–8; #2832/550 plate, 8⅜" d., $9–12; #2832/7 sherbet, 6½ oz., 3⅝" h., $5–8: luncheon goblet/ice tea, 13 oz., 6¾" h., $8–12.

Fostoria Sorrento, Plum: #2832/63 luncheon goblet/ice tea, 13 oz., 6¾" h., $10–14; #2382/64 tumbler/highball, 11 oz., 5⅝" h., $14–18; #2382/2 goblet, 9 oz., 6" h., $10–14.

SORRENTO PATTERN
No. 2832 Line
Made in Blue, Green, Brown and Plum

				Retail Price Ea.
2832/2	9	oz.	Goblet	$ 3.50
			Height 6 in.	
2832/7	6½	oz.	Sherbet	3.50
			Height 3⅝ in.	
2832/23	10	oz.	Double Old Fashioned	3.50
			Height 4 in.	
2832/26	6½	oz.	Wine	3.50
			Height 5 in.	
2832/63	13	oz.	Luncheon Goblet/Ice Tea	3.50
			Height 6¾ in.	
2832/64	11	oz.	Tumbler/Highball	3.50
			Height 5⅝ in.	
2832/550	8	in,	Plate	3.50

2   7   23   26

63   64   550

Fostoria Sorrento #2832. Catalog page from January 1, 1972.

Fostoria Sorrento, Brown: #2382/7 sherbet, 6½ oz., 3⅝" h., $5–8; #32382/2 goblet, 9 oz., 6" h., $6–10; #2382/550 plate, 8⅜" d., $8–10; #2832/63 luncheon goblet/ice tea, 13 oz., 6¾" h., $8–12; #2832/26 wine 6½ oz., 5" h., $5–8.

Fostoria Horizon Cinnamon. Top center: Sandwich plate, 10¾ in., $30–34. Second tier left to right: water/soda with colorless foot, 5" h. $6–10; ice tea with colorless foot, 7", $10–12; sherbet with colorless foot, 3¾" h., $6–8; three-part divided relish with open tab handles, 12½", $15–20; salad plate, 7½", $6–8. Front row: cup with handle (when with 5¾" saucer), set $7–9); mayonnaise underplate, 7½", $12–15; juice with colorless foot, 3⅜" h. $5–8; and mayonnaise bowl.

Fostoria Horizon Spruce (green) with Crystal foot, left to right; ice tea, water/soda, sherbet, juice. Price and dimensions in group photograph above.

Fostoria Horizon Spruce. Top center Sandwich plate 10 ¾" $32–38; Second tier two handled open sugar bowl 3 ¼" h. $9–14 ; salad bowl 8 ½" d. $22–28; salad plate 7 ½" $7–9; Front row: cup and saucer $8–10; sherbet with colorless foot $5–8; candy with lid $18–24.

JANUARY 1, 1960		MOUNDSVILLE, WEST VIRGINIA			23
4166/151	5 in. Ftd. Bowl	Silver Mist,			
		Silver Mist-Spruce	3.00	3.25	
4166/199	9 in. Ftd. Bowl	Silver Mist			
		Silver Mist-Spruce	6.00	6.50	
4166/757	6 in. Bud Vase	Silver Mist			
		Silver Mist-Spruce	2.00	2.25	

4166/151   4166/199   4166/757

Fostoria Silver Mist #4166. Catalog page from January 1, 1960.

Fostoria Silver Mist #4100 line: candle stick (not shown in catalog or Felt candlestick books), 5½" h., $12–16 each; #4166/199 footed 9" bowl, $12–18.

Fostoria Casual Flair: Blue (Sky), #4180 juice, 4" h., $8–14.

Fostoria Tiara #6044. Top center: Cinnamon flat-footed ice tea, 5⅞" h. $6–8; Cinnamon old fashion, 3¼" h., 4–6. Bottom rows, left to right: Spruce Green old fashion, 3¼" h., $4–6; Spruce Green sherbet/dessert bowl, 4½" w., $7–9; Spruce Green juice, 3⅜" h., $5–7; Crystal juice, 3 ⅜" h., $2–4; Crystal ice tea 5⅞" h., $3–5.

FOSTORIA GLASS COMPANY

GLASS COMBINATIONS WITH BRASS

2702/753	6¾ in.	Candleholder/Vase, Brass	$6.75
2702/756	8 in.	Candleholder/Vase, Brass	7.50
2702/784	9½ in.	Candleholder/Vase, Brass	8.25
2708/325	8 in.	Candleholder/Brass	3.75
2708/334		Duo Candleholder & Base/Brass	5.25
		Height 10 in.	
2708/384		Shallow Comport & Base/Brass	5.00
		Height 8⅜ in. - Diam. 8⅞ in.	

2702/753   2702/756   2702/784   2708/325   2708/334   2708/384

Fostoria Glass Combinations With Brass catalog from July 15, 1961.

Fostoria Glass Combinations, all with brass threaded connectors, #2700 line, left to right: 2702/753 without optic in base, 6" h., $16–20; #2708/384 shallow comport & base 8⅜" h., $22–30; #2702/753 candleholder/vase with optic inside base, 6¾ h., $20–28 each; #2702/784 candleholder, 9½" h., $22–30. Collection of Jaime Robinson.

Fostoria #2692/388 comport, Teal Green, 10" w., $10–16.

Fostoria Venture #6114: goblet, Smoke, four-winged foot, colorless bowl, 6⅞" h., $16–22. Photo used by permission, Replacements, Ltd.

34	FOSTORIA GLASS COMPANY	JANUARY 1, 1965

DECORATOR COLLECTION

Made in Teal Green, Lavender and Ruby

			Retail Price Ea.
2424/179	Ftd Petal Bowl	Teal Green	$4.00
		Lavender	4.00
		Ruby	4.50
	Height 4½ in. Diam. 6¾ in.		
2424/795	Footed Basket	Teal Green	5.00
		Lavender	5.00
		Ruby	5.50
	Height 6¼ in. Length 10 in. Width 6 in.		
2497/787	Flying Fish	Teal Green	3.00
		Lavender	3.00
		Ruby	3.25
	Height 8 in.		
2517/135	Handled Bon Bon	Teal Green	2.00
		Lavender	2.00
		Ruby	2.25
	Height 2½ in. Length 5 in.		
2560/767	Ruffled Vase	Teal Green	3.00
		Lavender	3.00
		Ruby	3.25
	Height 6 in.		
2666/807	Pitcher Vase	Teal Green	3.00
		Lavender	3.00
		Ruby	3.25
	Height 10 in.		
2692/388	Footed Comport	Teal Green	4.00
		Lavender	4.00
		Ruby	4.50
	Height 4 in. Length 6½ in.		
2700/152	Hanky Bowl	Teal Green	2.00
		Lavender	2.00
		Ruby	2.25
	Height 3 in. Diam. 6 in.		
2718/828	Footed Bud Vase	Teal Green	3.00
		Lavender	3.00
		Ruby	3.25
	Height 12 in.		

2424/179 2424/795 2517/135 2497/787 2560/767 2692/388 2666/807 2700/152 2718/828

Fostoria Decorator Collection from the January 1, 1965, catalog. Includes the footed comport above.

Fostoria Catalina Chartreuse #6046: ice tea, 5" h., $6–8; water/scotch/soda, 4³/₈" h., $5–8; champagne/sherbet, 3" h., $4–7; fingerbowl, 4 ³/₈" h., $7–10.

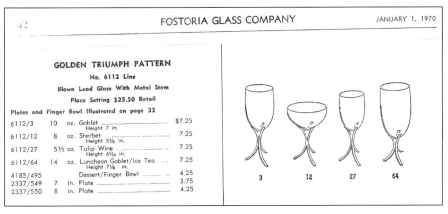

Fostoria Golden Triumph appearing in the January 1, 1970, catalog.

Fostoria Triumph. Golden Triumph 6112/3, goblet, 7" $14–18; Caribbean gift ware line footed jar w/o lid, 11¼" h., $45–55 with lid.

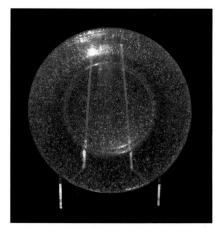

Fostoria Roulette made in 1968 only. #2739/208, Star bowl, Ebony w/Crystal, $30–38.

Fostoria sand glass. crystal sandwich plate. Contrast to snow glass made by Paden City. Note it has been suggested that, once Paden City glass closed in the mid–1950s, Fostoria was exploring the possibility of making the snow ware or a similar product. Courtesy of the collection of the Museum of American Glass in West Virginia.

Fostoria sand glass, #489 8/100 sand sandwich plate label on reverse of plate. Courtesy of the collection of the Museum of American Glass in West Virginia.

Fostoria sand glass. Top: Green bowl and Crystal plate; bottom: 489 8/100 sandwich plate and footed Green bowl. No value established. All items from the Fostoria factory morgue. Courtesy of the collection of the Museum of American Glass in West Virginia.

SCULPTURE PATTERN

Made in Lead Crystal, Gray Mist

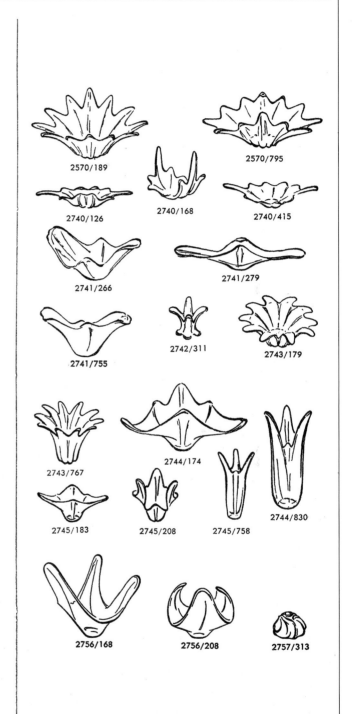

			Retail Price Ea.
2570/189	Shell	Crystal	$9.50
		Gray Mist	10.00
	Height 7¼ in. - Length 14 in. - Width 9½ in.		
2570/795	Basket	Crystal	9.50
		Gray Mist	10.00
	Height 5½ in. - Length 17 in. - Width 8 in.		
2740/126	Oblong	Crystal	4.75
		Gray Mist	5.00
	Height 3¼ in. - Length 13½ in. - Width 4½ in.		
2740/168	Spire Bowl	Crystal	4.75
		Gray Mist	5.00
	Height 5½ in. - Length 8 in. - Width 6 in.		
2740/415	Float	Crystal	4.75
		Gray Mist	5.00
	Height 2⅜ in. - Length 14¼ in. - Width 7 in.		
2741/266	Oval Bowl	Crystal	7.50
		Gray Mist	8.00
	Height 6½ in. - Length 14 in. - Width 6⅝ in.		
2741/279	Lineal Bowl	Crystal	7.50
		Gray Mist	8.00
	Height 4¼ in. - Length 18 in. - Width 5½ in.		
2741/755	Pinch Vase	Crystal	7.50
		Gray Mist	8.00
	Height 6 in. - Length 11½ in. - Width 3 in.		
2742/311	Candleholder	Crystal	3.00
		Gray Mist	3.25
	Height 3½ in.		
2743/179	Petal Bowl	Crystal	4.75
		Gray Mist	5.00
	Height 3¼ in. - Diam. 10¾ in.		
2743/767	Star Vase	Crystal	4.75
		Gray Mist	5.00
	Height 7¼ in.		
2744/174	Tricorne	Crystal	9.50
		Gray Mist	10.00
	Height 5⅝ in. - Width 13½ in.		
2744/830	Swung Vase	Crystal	9.50
		Gray Mist	10.00
	Height 12½ in.		
2745/183	Trindle Bowl	Crystal	6.00
		Gray Mist	6.50
	Height 4 in. - Width 8½ in.		
2745/208	Ruffle Bowl	Crystal	6.00
		Gray Mist	6.50
	Height 5¾ in. - Width 5¾ in.		
2745/758	Florette Vase	Crystal	6.00
		Gray Mist	6.50
	Height 8¼ in.		
2756/168	Cosmic	Crystal	4.75
		Gray Mist	5.00
	Height 8½ in.		
2756/208	Triton Bowl	Crystal	4.75
		Gray Mist	5.00
	Height 5¾ in.		
2757/313	Candle Twist	Crystal	3.00
		Gray Mist	3.25
	Height 2 in.		

2570/189   2570/795   2740/126   2740/168   2740/415   2741/266   2741/279   2741/755   2742/311   2743/179   2743/767   2744/174   2745/183   2745/208   2745/758   2744/830   2756/168   2756/208   2757/313

Fostoria Sculpture, 1961–1970; all pieces in this line came in Crystal and Gray Mist. From January 1, 1965, catalog.

Greenwich Flint Glass

Dunkirk, Indiana
1969–1972

Good   *Better*   *Best*

Greenwich Flint Glass was a distinctly identified and marketed line of glass within the larger company structure of Indiana Glass of Dunkirk, Indiana. The glass was designed by Tom Connally specifically for the Indiana Glass company, as they sought to expand into the art or décor glass market. Indiana had long been a producer of practical and utility glass. Connally was hired as an assistant glass designer at Indiana in 1961, and they produced his Greenwich line in 1969 through 1972 only. His wife later recalled that he produced a "total of 70 designs in five colors, for a total of 350 different pieces. 27 of those designs required stoppers. There are

some other glass pieces out there (from the Bischoff moulds) that carry a GFC sticker, but only Connally's design have a sticker of clear plastic with white ink reading "Greenwich Flint Craft." The use of Greenwich Flint name by Indiana spans more than the three years of Connally designs, but his designs are by far the most distinctively Modern. It could be argued that Connally's GFC designs are the most complete embrace of the modern aesthetic in American mid-century glass design.

Greenwich Flint labeled pieces in Amberina. Both shapes utilized previously by Bischoff glass. Tumbler, $12–18; vase, 17" h., $22–32.

Greenwich Flint Glass ,#1218 candle holder, Ruby, 7¾", $30–40. Courtesy of the Museum of American Glass in West Virginia collection.

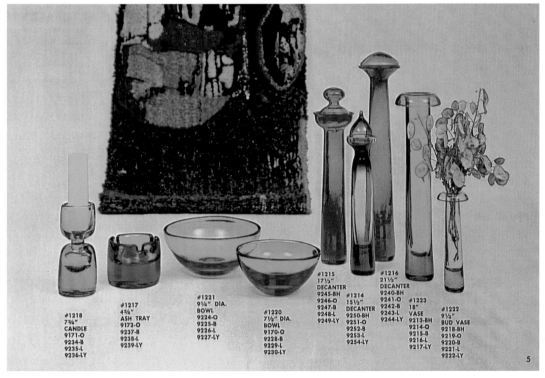

Greenwich Flint Glass catalog (accompanying price list dated December 2, 1968). Shared by Sandi Connally.

#1218
7¾"
CANDLE
9171-O
9234-B
9235-L
9236-LY

#1217
4¾"
ASH TRAY
9172-O
9237-B
9238-L
9239-LY

#1221
9¼" DIA.
BOWL
9224-O
9225-B
9226-L
9227-LY

#1220
7½" DIA.
BOWL
9170-O
9228-B
9229-L
9230-LY

#1215
17½"
DECANTER
9245-BH
9246-O
9247-B
9248-L
9249-LY

#1214
15½"
DECANTER
9250-BH
9251-O
9252-B
9253-L
9254-LY

#1216
21½"
DECANTER
9240-BH
9241-O
9242-B
9243-L
9244-LY

#1223
18"
VASE
9213-BH
9214-O
9215-B
9216-L
9217-LY

#1222
9½"
BUD VASE
9218-BH
9219-O
9220-B
9221-L
9222-LY

5

Greenwich Flint Glass catalog (accompanying price list dated December 2, 1968). Shared by Sandi Connally.

#1151 20½" L–DECANTER	#1147 12" S–DECANTER	#1148 16" M–DECANTER	#1202 7¼" DECANTER	#1203 7½" DECANTER	#1201 7" DECANTER	#1198 7½" DECANTER	#1199 8" DECANTER
9595-BH	9585-BH	9590-BH	9300-BH	9295-BH	9305-BH	9315-BH	9310-BH
9596-O	9586-O	9591-O	9301-O	9296-O	9306-O	9316-O	9311-O
9597-B	9587-B	9592-B	9302-B	9297-B	9307-B	9317-B	9312-B
9598-L	9588-L	9593-L	9303-L	9298-L	9308-L	9318-L	9313-L
9599-LY	9589-LY	9594-LY	9304-LY	9299-LY	9309-LY	9319-LY	9314-LY

Greenwich Flint Glass (accompanying price list dated December 2, 1968). Shared by Sandi Connally.

#1161 13" VASE	#1162 19" L–DECANTER	#1164 14½" S–DECANTER	#1163 17" M–DECANTER	#1167 14¼" VASE	#1168 13" VASE	#1165 14" BUD VASE	#1166 13" VASE
9535-BH	9530-BH	9520-BH	9525-BH	9505-BH	9500-BH	9515-BH	9510-BH
9536-O	9531-O	9521-O	9526-O	9506-O	9501-O	9516-O	9511-O
9537-B	9532-B	9522-B	9527-B	9507-B	9502-B	9517-B	9512-B
9538-L	9533-L	9523-L	9528-L	9508-L	9503-L	9518-L	9513-L
9539-LY	9534-LY	9524-LY	9529-LY	9509-LY	9504-LY	9519-LY	9514-LY

Greenwich Flint Glass #1198 decanter with mushroom stopper: Blue, 7½" h., $80–100. Courtesy of the Museum of American Glass in West Virginia collection.

Greenwich Flint Glass (accompanying price list dated December 2, 1968) Shared by Sandi Connally.

#1171 10" L–PITCHER 9480-BH 9481-O 9482-B 9483-L 9484-LY	#1172 8¾" S–PITCHER 9465-BH 9466-O 9467-B 9468-L 9469-LY	#1171 10" L–VASE 9475-BH 9476-O 9477-B 9478-L 9479-LY	#1172 8¾" S–VASE 9470-BH 9471-O 9472-B 9473-L 9474-LY	#1170 8½" S–DECANTER 9490-BH 9491-O 9492-B 9493-L 9494-LY	#1170 2¾" COCKTAIL 9173-BH 9174-O 9175-B 9176-L 9177-LY	#1169 10½" L–DECANTER 9485-BH 9486-O 9487-B 9488-L 9489-LY	#1169 9¾" MIXER 9495-BH 9496-O 9497-B 9498-L 9499-LY	#1178 7" S–DECANTER 9440-BH 9441-O 9442-B 9443-L 9444-LY	#1179 9" L–DECANTER 9435-BH 9436-O 9437-B 9438-L 9439-LY

#1188	#1189	#1192	#1182	#1183	#1185	#1186	#1185
12"	18"	19"	7"	13½"	11¼"	13"	12¾"
S—BOTTLE	L—BOTTLE	VASE	PITCHER	DECANTER	PITCHER	DECANTER	VASE
9385-BH	9380-BH	9365-BH	9425-BH	9420-BH	9405-BH	9395-BH	9400-BH
9386-O	9381-O	9366-O	9426-O	9421-O	9406-O	9396-O	9401-O
9387-B	9382-B	9367-B	9427-B	9422-B	9407-B	9397-B	9402-B
9388-L	9383-L	9368-L	9428-L	9423-L	9408-L	9398-L	9403-L
9389-LY	9384-LY	9369-LY	9429-LY	9424-LY	9409-LY	9399-LY	9404-LY
		22½"					
		DECANTER					
		9360-BH					
		9361-O					
		9362-B					
		9363-L					
		9364-LY					

Greenwich Flint Glass (accompanying price list dated December 2, 1968). Shared by Sandi Connally.

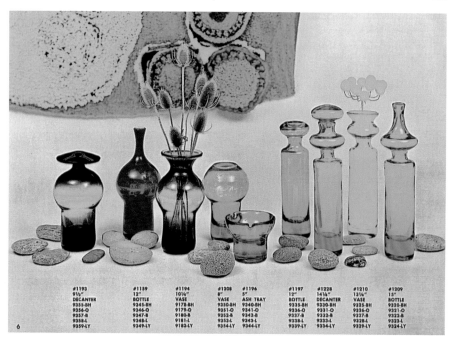

#1193	#1159	#1194	#1208	#1196	#1197	#1228	#1210	#1209
9½"	12"	10¼"	8"	5"	12"	14¼"	13¼"	15"
DECANTER	BOTTLE	VASE	VASE	ASH TRAY	BOTTLE	DECANTER	VASE	BOTTLE
9355-BH	9345-BH	9178-BH	9350-BH	9340-BH	9335-BH	9330-BH	9325-BH	9320-BH
9356-O	9346-O	9179-O	9351-O	9341-O	9336-O	9331-O	9326-O	9321-O
9357-B	9347-B	9180-B	9352-B	9342-B	9337-B	9332-B	9327-B	9322-B
9358-L	9348-L	9181-L	9353-L	9343-L	9338-L	9333-L	9328-L	9323-L
9359-LY	9349-LY	9182-LY	9354-LY	9344-LY	9339-LY	9334-LY	9329-LY	9324-LY

Greenwich Flint Glass (accompanying price list dated December 2, 1968). Shared by Sandi Connally.

#1143	#1224	#1142	#1225	#1225	#1154	#1224	#1227	#1226
12½"	8"	10½"	10"	8"	12½"	6¼"	9"DIA.	7"DIA.
L—DECANTER	S—VASE	DECANTER	M—VASE	L—PITCHER	L—VASE	S—PITCHER	L—BOWL	S—BOWL
9575-BH	9208-BH	9570-BH	9203-BH	9198-BH	9565-BH	9193-BH	9183-BH	9188-BH
9576-O	9209-O	9571-O	9204-O	9199-O	9566-O	9194-O	9184-O	9189-O
9577-B	9210-B	9572-B	9205-B	9200-B	9567-B	9195-B	9185-B	9190-B
9578-L	9211-L	9573-L	9206-L	9201-L	9568-L	9196-L	9186-L	9191-L
9579-LY	9212-LY	9574-LY	9207-LY	9202-LY	9569-LY	9197-LY	9187-LY	9192-LY

Greenwich Flint Glass (accompanying price list dated December 2, 1968). Shared by Sandi Connally.

Greenwich Flint Glass, all Green and with original labels. Left to right: #1148 decanter (missing lid), 16", $120–150 with lid; #1227 bowl, 9 " d., $30–45; #1228 decanter (missing lid), 14", $140–165 with lid; unknown form, $40–55.

Gunderson
Glass Works

New Bedford, Massassachutes

1939–1952

Good

Gunderson Glass Works was the continuation of Pairpoint Corporation (1894–1937). Pairpoint survived the Depression, but failed to fully recover and was sold "to a salvage company," according to glass authors Felt & Stoer. Robert Gunderson had been an employee of Pairpoint and led a team of investors who acquired the glass house in New Bedford, Massachusetts. Gunderson served as manager until his death in 1952. Upon his death the firm became a part of the National Pairpoint Co., and was then known as the Gunderson-Pairpoint Glass Works. It operated under this structure until closing in 1957. While a glass-making facility called Pairpoint GlassWorks continues to operate at the time of writing, the Gunderson chapter ended in 1957.

To Learn More:

Felt, Tom. *Gunderson Glass Works 1939-1952*. Monograph Number 55. 2006. Weston, West Virginia: West Virginia Museum of American Glass.

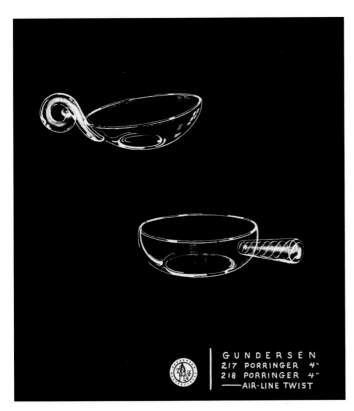

Gunderson company catalog illustrating two porringers (or servers/
handled nappies), both showing strong mid–century modern
influences. The item #217 resembles similar forms by Tiffin,
Steuben, Imperial, and others.

Gunderson company catalog illustrating three heavy, Mid–century
Modern designs.

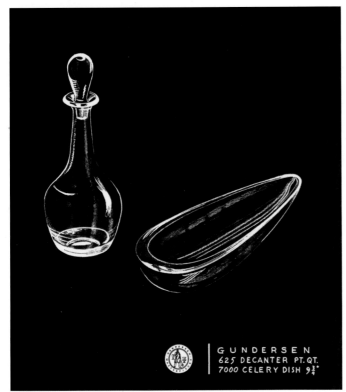

Gunderson company catalog. The 3625 decanter is modern–like
but the #7000 celery, strongly related to the thick,
asymmetrical Swedish glass of that era, is very much in the manner
of Mid–Century Modern.

A. H. Heisey & Company

Newark, Ohio
1896–1957

Good

Established in Newark, Ohio, the A. H. Heisey & Co. Inc. began producing glass in 1896 and continued until closing in December 1957. Founder Augustus H. Heisey (1842-1922) had worked at both Ripley & Co. and Cascade Glass (later King & Sons) in Pittsburgh, Pennsylvania, before marrying Susan Duncan, daughter of George Duncan. George, at that time, was a principal in Ripley & Co. and later established his own glass house. Thus, A. H. Heisey was well connected to and surrounded by others engaged in the glass industry. At the end of World War II and into the mid-20th century, Heisey struggled to remain relevant to the emerging markets and styles. Eva Zeisel, hired in 1954, brought new designs to the firm that won critical acclaim, but did not fare as well with sales.

Heisey's efforts at AMCM included Lodestar, Heisey's line #1632, which used basically the same shapes as Satellite but was made in a color Heisey dubbed "Dawn," a charcoal gra,y transparent glass with highlights of purple. Lodestar was introduced in 1952 for a short time and then again in production from 1955–1957.

Town & Country was an Eva Zeisel design for Heisey produced from 1954 to 1957. It was made in the gray-purple color Dawn. Its limited availability today suggests it was a commercial failure, although it was acclaimed upon introduction. It was given the Good Design award from the Metropolitan Museum of Modern Art. It was Heisey's line #1637A.

In addition to the pattern Town & Country, Heisey introduced three other Eva Zeisel designs in 1954: Hourglass #6006; Crystal Buds #6007A; and Roundelay #6009A. These were drinking vessel lines only and remained in production a very short time.

The shape known as Satellite was produced in 1956 only. Many of the Satellite forms were the same as those used in Lodestar, but not all shapes were produced in both colors of glass. Satellite was available in crystal and in crystal with a satin star base. It was pattern #1620.

For sixty-one years, Heisey engaged in hot glass production. The company ceased production with the Christmas vacation of 1957 and never produced hot glass again. The Heisey assets were acquired by Imperial Glass of Bellaire, Ohio. and many of the moulds later were acquired by the Heisey Collectors of America, Inc.

To Learn More:
Bredehoft, Neila & Tom. *Heisey Glass: 1896-1957*. Paducah, Kentucky: Collector Books. 2001.
Coe, Debbie & Randy. *The Colors of Heisey Glass*. Atglen, Pennsylvania: Schiffer Books. 2006.

LODESTAR by Heisey

8

LODESTAR—Pattern No. 1632
In "Dawn" Color

No.	Size	Item	Price Dozen	Each
1-1632	11 in.	Crimped bowl..	$83.40	$6.95
2-1632	12 in.	Deep fruit, floral or salad bowl...	78.00	6.50
3-1632	8 in.	Bowl..........	51.00	4.25
4-1632	7½ in.	Crimped vase...	33.00	2.75
5-1626	8 in.	Vase..........	33.00	2.75
6-1626		Jar & cover....	71.40	5.95
7-1632	1 lt.	Candle centerpiece..........	19.80	1.65
8-1632	2 lt.	Candlestick (pr.)	87.00	7.25
9- 500	12 in.	4-cpt. tray....	78.00	6.50
10-1632	5 in.	Mayonnaise and #7 crystal ladle.	31.80	2.65
1632	5 in.	Mayon. bowl....	23.40	1.95
11-1632	10 in.	Celery tray....	39.00	3.25
12-1632	5½ in.	Ash tray.......	28.20	2.35
13-1632	14 in.	Party plate.....	78.00	6.50
14-1632	2 pc.	Sugar & cream..	28.20	2.35
15-1632	5 in.	Candy & cover..	37.80	3.15
16-1632	7½ in.	3-cpt. relish..	57.00	4.75
17-1626	1 qt.	Pitcher........	39.00	3.25
18-1632	6 oz.	Cocktail, juice or old fashion...	13.20	1.10
19-1632	4½ in.	Dessert or sauce dish (nappy)....	16.20	1.35
20-1487	13 oz.	Ice tea, flared..	14.40	1.20
21-1487	10 oz.	Tumbler, flared.	12.00	1.00

MISCELLANEOUS ITEMS IN "DAWN" COLOR

No.	Size	Item	Price Dozen	Each
22-1565	6¾ in.	Jelly or nappy...	12.00	1.00
23-1485	2 pc.	Salt & pepper—dawn, #59 top...	28.80	2.40
24-1485	3 oz.	Oil & crystal stopper........	30.60	2.55
1485	3 oz.	Oil, dawn, no stop	23.40	1.95
25-1415	12 oz.	Ice tea........	14.40	1.20
26-1415	8 oz.	Tumbler.......	10.80	.90
27-1415	5 in.	Sherbet........	10.80	.90
28-1415	5 oz.	Juice.........	9.60	.80
29-1415	18 oz.	Juice pitcher...	27.00	2.25

"DAWN" GLASS BY HEISEY IS A VERSATILE "SMOKE" OR "CHARCOAL" COLOR THAT BLENDS WITH ANY COLOR SCHEME.

TOWN AND COUNTRY—Pattern No. 1637A in "Dawn" Color
"GOOD DESIGN" AWARD FOR 1955
Designed by Eva Zeisel

No.	Size	Item	Price Dozen	Each
30-1637A	12 oz.	Tumbler or ice tea...........	14.40	1.20
31-1637A	8 in.	Plate...........	23.40	1.95
32-1637A	5 in.	Dessert or sauce dish, flared.....	13.20	1.10
32a-1637A	8 in.	Round relish or serving dish...	35.40	2.95
33-1637A	14 in.	Sandwich plate..	47.40	3.95
34-1637A	11 in.	Salad bowl.....	45.00	3.75
99	2 pc.	Wood servers...	12.00	1.00

Made in America by Hand

A. H. HEISEY & CO., NEWARK, OHIO

Heisey company 1956 catalog page, illustrating the Lodestar and Town and Country lines. For reasons unknown, Heisey printed their catalogs of this era in blue ink.

Heisey catalog page with listing of pieces made and prices for Lodestar and Town and Country, accompanying the illustrated page from the same original company catalog.

Heisey Lodestar pattern was produced for market only in the color Dawn. Shown here are a pair of one light "candle centerpiece," #7–1632, $50–60 each, and the 12" d. "deep fruit, floral or salad bowl," #2–1632, $125–170.

Heisey Town and Country line #1637A, Eva Zeisel design, illustrated are the 14" salad plate #34–1637A in Limelight and the 11" salad bowl #34–1637A in the color Dawn.

No.	Size	Item, crystal	Price Dozen	Each
-1632	14 in.	Party plate....	$102.00	$8.50
1632	8½ in.	Torte plate....	60.00	5.00
-1626	8 in.	Crimped vase..	48.00	4.00
-1632	4 in.	Cupped bowl...	33.00	2.75
-1632	12 in.	Deep fruit or		
		floral bowl.....	102.00	8.50
1632	8 in.	Bowl..........	60.00	5.00
1632	5 in.	Bowl or nappy..	27.00	2.25
3-1632	11 in.	Crimped bowl..	102.00	8.50
1632	7½ in.	Crimped bowl..	60.00	5.00
1632	6 in.	Crimped bowl..	39.00	3.25
2-1543	1 lt.	Star candleblock	39.00	3.25
6-1632		Sugar..........	24.00	2.00
7-1632		Cream.........	24.00	2.00
8-1632	5 in.	Candy box & cov.	51.00	4.25
9-1632	7½ in.	3-part relish...	72.00	6.00
0-1632	10 in.	Celery tray....	54.00	4.50
1-1632	2 pc.	Mayonnaise &		
		glass ladle.....	44.40	3.70
1632	5 in.	Mayonnaise bowl	36.00	3.00
2-1632		Cigarette urn...	24.00	2.00
3-1632	5¼ in.	Ash tray........	42.00	3.50
4-1632	6 oz.	Juice or Cocktail	24.00	2.00
5-1632	1 qt.	Juice or cocktail		
		pitcher.........	57.00	4.75

Frosted Star Appears to be Carved from Solid Glass...

A. H. HEISEY & CO.
NEWARK, OHIO

Heisey company 1956 catalog page illustrating the Satellite pattern. Satellite was always colorless glass.

NEW HORIZONS AT HEISEY

It's the New Hourglass!

This latest of "new horizons at Heisey" is bound to intrigue those with a flair for things modern. Eva Zeisel has lent her fresh, deft touch to a thrilling new line of hollow bottom glasses we've christened Hourglass. Shown above are the ice tea, goblet, claret and cocktail in this exciting line.

And this is just one of several new patterns designed for Heisey by Eva Zeisel. You'll want to cash in on the proven appeal of these designs.

One of four Eva Zeisel designs introduced by Heisey in 1954 was Hourglass #6006. It never appeared in a Heisey catalog, was not marked with the diamond H logo (being a hand blown line). Itis shown here in a 1954 trade journal ad. Uncommon, it often attains individual prices in excess of $100 per piece. Courtesy of Neila and Tom Bredehoft.

J. H. Houze Glass Company

Point Marion, Pennsylvania
1914–2004

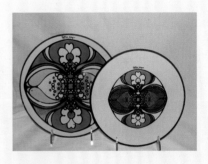

Good

From their factory located in Point Marion, Pennsylvania, the J. H. Houze Glass Company began operation in 1914. Early production focused on making flat window glass into convex glass forms. Production and clients varied greatly over time. Their 1930s and 1940s production included immense amounts of colored slag glass used as components in electric lamps, smoking stands, ash tray bases, and more. In 1952, the firm was engaged in producing colored glass for use as lenses in sunglasses. They used the smoke colored glass from the sunglass lenses to expand and develop a very successful "smoked glass" product line of screen printed items. At one time a line of formal dinnerware under the "Houze Art" trade name was produced.

Over time, the range from Houze went from bent glass to pressed novelties, lighting components, diverse pressed ware, and on to include extensive decorating of glass. While not modern in design, a very modern idea marketed by Houze was the creation of small glass trays with birthday, holiday, and greeting card slogans and art. These were sold in small boxes ready to mail. They were very popular. Houze success later in their history came to be tied to decorating glass. Hot glass production ceased in the late 1960s.

Houze did contract work for a large number of yet-unidentified glass designers. Some of the most recognized pieces are their smoke-colored trays and ash trays, which can be found with hundreds of varying decorations, commemorative events, souvenirs, and advertisements. In the 1960s, pop artist Peter Max came to Point Marion and was in residence there while Houze worked to refine a number of plates that bear the work of the then-popular artist. Max, a German-born American (b. 1937), is an illustrator and graphic artist best known for psychedelic designs and exuberant colors.

Houze Giftware and Accessories
Houze Glass production was predominately giftware during the AMCM period. The use of their smoke glass from sun glass production was adapted and adopted to an amazing variety of other applications. See the Imperial Glass chapter for use of Houze smoke glass at Imperial.

Houze red, white and blue with Gold floral decoration on a smoke slumped form, $12–18.

Houze glass oval plate, designed and signed by Peter Max, circa 1962, $30–35. Photo by John Houze.

Houze glass round 7" plate, designed and signed by Peter Max, circa 1962, $30–35. Photo by John Houze.

Houze glass triangular plate, 7" per side, designed and signed by Peter Max, circa 1962, $30–35. Photo by John Houze.

Houze glass round 7" plate, designed and signed by Peter Max, circa 1962, $20–25. Photo by John Houze.

Houze glass octagonal 9½" plate ,designed and signed by Peter Max, circa 1962, $34–38. Photo by John Houze.

Houze glass octagonal 9½" plate, designed and signed by Peter Max, circa 1962, $36–42. Photo by John Houze.

Houze glass square plate, designed and signed by Peter Max, circa 1962, $34–40. Photo by John Houze.

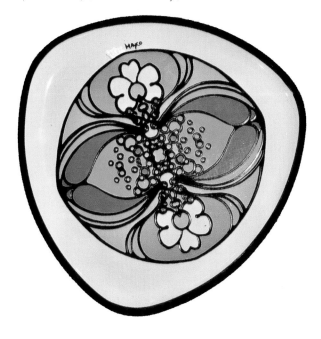

Houze glass triangular plate, 7½" per side, designed and signed by Peter Max, circa 1962, $25–30. Photo by John Houze

Houze glass five-part divided relish, smoke glass with white decoration, $12–16.

Imperial Glass Corporation

Bellaire, Ohio
1902–1984

Good   *Better*   *Best*

Opening in 1902 in Bellaire, Ohio, the Imperial Glass Company was successful for many decades. Their success allowed them to acquire the assets of other glass houses that had failed, including Central Glass of nearby Wheeling, West Virginia, and A.H. Heisey & Co and Cambridge Glass Co., both of Ohio. Imperial, like their competitor Fenton Glass, tried a few modern designs, but their client base preferred tradition. Imperial's Mid-century Modern products were few and met with limited success. Imperial glass ceased production in 1984.

Their Twist line appears in a 1943 Imperials Glass catalog cited by Measell (*Imperial Encyclopedia Vo. III* page 601). That early reference includes a small compote. Ten pieces of stemware, four tumblers, and a flat fingerbowl, lacking the distinctive twist motif, are illustrated in catalog 53 (arguably 1953). It was line #100 and remained in production into the 1960s, as it appears in the 1962

catalog as "Imperial Twist." The creator of Twist was Carl Uhrmann.

The lines Flame #680, Pinch #675, and Flare #670 were the designs of popular mid-century designer Russell Wright. The three designs were all limited to flat tumblers. The Flare line has a wee surface texture, the result of a small amount of vermiculite or mica.

Some interesting Imperial products from the 1950s united pressed Imperial glass with shaped or slumped pieces of "Charcoal" sheet glass produced by Houze Glass in Point Marion, Pennsylvania. Glass from the two firms were glued together at the Imperial factory and marketed as Imperial. This ware, called Elysian, was produced from 1958 into the early 1960s.

Imperial Glass Twist promotional literature

Imperial Twist. Top: sherbet 4³/₈" h., $5–8; goblet, 6³/₈" h., $12–16. Bottom: wine, 4½" h., $7–9; cordial, 3⁵/₈" h., $7–10.

Imperial Twist creamer made after the line was converted to a more economically produced pressed pattern on left, $8–12, and the original handblown creamer on the right, with hand applied and shaped foot and handle, $12–18.

IMPERIAL GLASS CORPORATION, BELLAIRE, OHIO

IMPERIAL TWIST

110
9 oz. Goblet

110
6 oz. Sherbet

110
12 oz. Footed Ice Tea

110
5 oz. Claret

110
3 oz. Cocktail

110
14 oz. Pilsener
10 oz. Pilsener

110
5 oz. Footed Juice
or
Whiskey Sour

110
3 oz. Wine

110
1 oz. Cordial

110
7 oz. Parfait

110/5D
8½" Plate

110/680
14 oz. Tumbler

110/680
12 oz. Tumbler

110/680
6 oz. Juice Tumbler

110/680
8 oz. Sherbet

110
26 oz. Decanter & Stopper

Imperial Twist company catalog page showing the stem–less tumblers, handblown stemware and the #110 decanter.

Imperial Twist decanter in uncommon Jonquil with crystal hollow stopper. Featured in the 1959 Imperial catalog, the Jonquil color was used in that year only, made in thirteen shapes. The shape was listed only as #110 line in Twist but was cataloged as #50/6, when produced as Jonquil. $200–250.

Imperial Twist candleholders, $10–14 each.

Imperial Pinch #675 tumblers, Charcoal Brown, 6 oz., $6–10, and 11 oz., $18–24.

Imperial Pinch #675 tumbler, Ruby, 6 oz., $18–26.

RUSSEL WRIGHT "PINCH"
65*

14 oz. Tumbler	11 oz. Tumbler	6 oz. Tumbler	6 oz. Tumbler	11 oz. Tumbler	14 oz. Tumbler

Charcoal Brown   Verde

14 oz. Tumbler	11 oz. Tumbler	6 oz. Tumbler	6 oz. Tumbler	11 oz. Tumbler	14 oz. Tumbler

Pink   Forest

Imperial catalog page, circa mid–1960s, showing "Russel Wright Pinch" in Charcoal Brown, Verde, Pink, and Forest colors and in 14-, 11- and 6 oz. sizes.

IMPERIAL...

Flare

Made expressly for color harmony with currently popular colored pottery and linens . . . . . Colors on tables are no longer seasonal . . . . . Smart tumblers are fast replacing colored stemware in the minds of most hostesses everywhere! . . . . . . PINCH design is #675 . . . . . . FLARE design is #670 . . . . . FLAME is #680 . . . . . Color descriptions: "Seaspray" is the palest aqua . . . . . . "Hemlock" is a deep forest green . . . . . "Ripe Olive" is a deep brown . . . . "Verde" is a green gold.

Pinch

Flame

IMPERIAL GLASS CORPORATION
BELLAIRE, OHIO

Member Glass Crafts of America

Imperial original announcement for the lines Flare, Pinch, and Flame. The colors available were Seaspray which was described as "the palest aqua," Hemlock, "a deep forest green," Ripe Olive, "a deep brown," and Verde, "a green Gold."

Imperial Twist, smoke colored flat tumbler, 12 oz., $12–18.

Imperial Kallaglas advertisement describing it as "New! Designed by Erwin Kalla." Colors offered were Heather, Green, Brown, and Turquiose. Ten different shapes were made in the line.

Imperial catalog page illustrating the Svelte line. Catalog 53A, circa 1952.

Imperial Svelte. Note that Svelte is a two tone glass, a colored bowl on a colorless foot. Introduced circa 1952 and illustrated in the 53A catalog, the colors were Violet Heather, Forest Green, and Driftwood Brown. By 1957 the colors offered had been expanded to include Champagne, Clover Pink, and Dresden Blue.

Imperial Kallaglas: #990, 12 oz. footed tumbler, Brown, $8–12; 6 oz. sherbet, Heather, $6–10; 5½" nappy, Heather, $8–10; and 12 oz. footed tumbler, Turquiose, $8–12.

Imperial Dawn pattern. These are the shapes of the earlier Svelte, but issued in the late 1960s as line #3300 and called Dawn, with only five shapes available. Shown here are the Nut Bown ice tea, $6–8; footed Blue Haze on–the–rocks, $6–8 , Nut Brown wine, $5–7; and Blue Haze sherbet $4–6. Not shown are the goblet and the colors Verde and Crystal. All discontinued prior to 1973.

The Symmetry line was introduced by Imperial in 1958. It was a smoky, charcoal-colored glass product made by Houze Glass of Pt. Marion, Pennsylvania, and sent to Bellaire, Ohio, where Imperial marketed and shipped it. The glass was slumped by Houze into simple forms and shapes, fourteen of them appearing in the catalog #62 (circa 1961–62). Five-part, 9 x 13" relish #1955/5. $12–18.

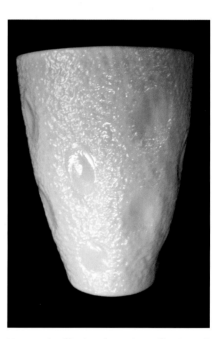

Textured milk glass from the collection of the National Imperial Glass Museum, $10–14.

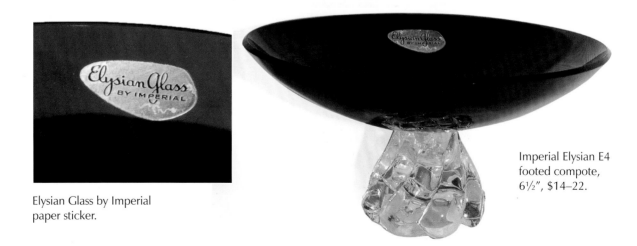

Elysian Glass by Imperial paper sticker.

Imperial Elysian E4 footed compote, 6½", $14–22.

ELYSIAN

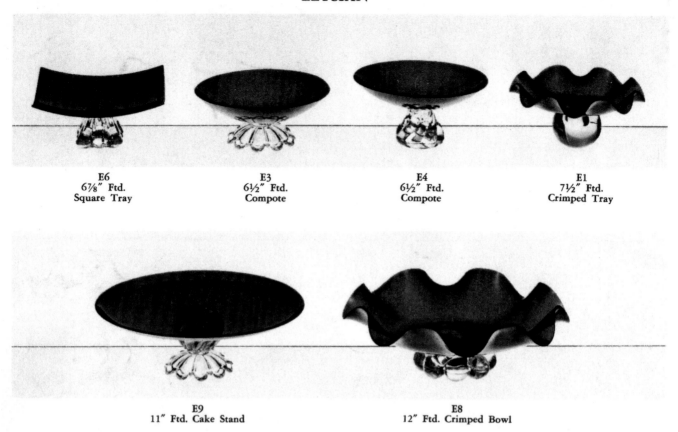

E6
6⅞" Ftd.
Square Tray

E3
6½" Ftd.
Compote

E4
6½" Ftd.
Compote

E1
7½" Ftd.
Crimped Tray

E9
11" Ftd. Cake Stand

E8
12" Ftd. Crimped Bowl

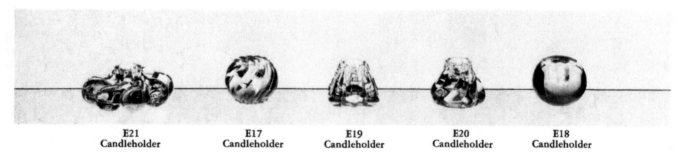

E21
Candleholder

E17
Candleholder

E19
Candleholder

E20
Candleholder

E18
Candleholder

The Elysian line was related to the Imperial Symmetry line and dvertised in 1958 as "a wedding of Crystal and Charcoal Imperial's New Elysian Glass." Utilizing the smoky flat glass produced and slumped into shape by Houze Glass, it was glued onto crystal bases . The bases, pressed into old Heisey glass moulds after Heisey closed, were sold as candleholders to complement the two colored bowls and compotes.

Imperial Burnt Orange #607 deep bowl, 9" d., produced in 1959 as one of several bold colors that year. None were widely sold. No value determined.

Imperial Jonquil #50/600 shallow bowl, 9" d., produced in 1959 $100–140. Collection of the National Imperial Glass Museum.

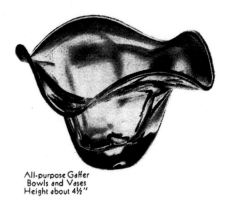

All-purpose Gaffer
Bowls and Vases
Height about 4½"

HANDLED BON BON

Casual Crystal by Imperial

CRIMPED IVY VASE

SINGLE REST ASH TRAY

Beautiful to Own . . .

These exquisite bowls, trays and vases add a 'touch of the artistic'; they're at home in any home. Casual, beautiful, versatile; you'll find any or all of them indispensable.

OLIVE OR TIDBIT SERVER

PINCH & FLAIR VASE

Lovely to Give . . .

Always a welcome gift! A gift selection of distinctive design; a reflection of your very good taste. Shower the bride, gift your hostess, or give a special occasion significance with these lovely pieces.

HANDLED PECAN TRAY

So Very Useful . . .

Vases that 'do things' for flowers, servers that invite guests to enjoy tasty tidbits, ash trays and bowls that glorify tables with smart, modern, crystal design. They beautify, yet serve in so many attractive ways!

BUD FLOAT BOWL

2-HANDLED SMOKERS BOWL

Inexpensive Too! . . .

They look like they're 'out of reach' but surprisingly, they're priced for you, your home, your friends and everyday living. From $1.50 to $6 at gift and department stores near your home.

BLOSSOM VASE

Casual Crystal Servers
and Trays, six styles
(6" Wide)

IMPERIAL GLASS CORPORATION
Bellaire, Ohio

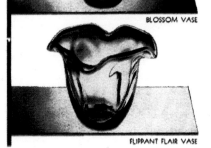

FLIPPANT FLAIR VASE

Imperial Casual Crystal includes some forms reminiscent of Swedish modern forms utilized by a number of other American Modern glasshouses.

Imperial Spangled Bittersweet vase produced in 1959. The glass has small "spangles" or metallic flakes that do not appear in the photograph. No value determined. Collection of the National Imperial Glass Museum.

Imperial glass vase #970 in Charcoal, 18". Collection of the National Imperial Glass Museum. $80–95.

Imperial Glass spangled glass bottle vase, circa 1959.

Heather No. 969
18" vase.

Verde No. 968
16" vase.

Company photos of mid-1960s large Imperial vases #969 and #968.

Stiegel Green No.
967 16" vase.

Charcoal No. 970
18" vase.

As seen in a company photograph these large Imperial vases #967 and #970 were produced in the mid–1960s in Stiegel Green, Charcoal, Heather and Verde. The pieces in this offering were 16"-18" h..

Indiana
Glass Company

Dunkirk, Indiana
1907–2002

Cover art from the undated Indiana Handcraft catalog.

Indiana Glass Company began in 1907 and was known for mass-produced utilitarian glass. Around the year 1962, Indiana Glass became a part of the Lancaster Colony Corporation. From 1969 until 1972, Indiana produced a line under the name of Greenwich Flint in an effort to gain market share in the more upscale and prestigious handmade glass sector. Indiana's hand-formed production began when they acquired Bischoff Glass of Culloden, West Virginia, and briefly operated it as a subsidiary of Lancaster Colony Corporation, the parent organization for Indiana Glass. the operation that briefly produced glass as Indiana Handcraft evolved from that purchase.

Indiana Handcraft label appearing on the green bowl shown on page 170.

Indiana Handcraft undated catalog page.

Indiana Handcraft wheat pitcher with applied handle, Concord #6524; Blue, 9½", $28–34; Red, $30–36.

Indiana Glass decanter. Designer Wayne Husted wrote the authors saying "the design (shown here) which I named 'Kingston' was made in two sizes. One is 16.5 inches tall and the other is 21.5 inches tall. All of the designs on the three pages from the first catalog, I designed, before Tom Conally took over designing." Kingston Honey decanter with stopper, 21½", $80–95.

A Kingstown #6541
8" Decanter
9117-G
9118-B
9119-H

B Kingstown #6541
12" Decanter
9127-G
9128-B
9129-H

C Concord #6511
7½" Pitcher
8106-O
8107-G
8108-B

D Concord #253
7½" Water Bottle
8466-O
8467-G
8468-B

E Kingstown #714
6½" Crimp Bowl
9507-G
9508-B
9509-H

F Concord #980
6" L-Swan
8456-O
8457-G
8458-B

G Concord #980
5" M-Swan
8446-O
8447-G
8448-B

H Concord #980
4¼" S-Swan
8436-O
8437-G
8438-B

I Kingstown #6537
8½" S-Pitcher
9217-G   9219-H
9218-B

J Kingstown #6537
12½" M-Pitcher
9227-G
9228-B
9229-H

K Kingstown #6537
16½" L-Pitcher
9057-G
9058-B
9059-H

L Concord #6523
20" Decanter
8026-O
8027-G
8028-B

M Concord #6520
15½" Vase
8166-O
8167-G
8168-B

N Concord #658
10" S-Decanter
8076-O
8077-G
8078-B

O Concord #659
16" L-Decanter
8086-O
8087-G
8088-B

P Kingstown #6550
P-Pitcher
9177-G
9178-B
9179-H

Q Kingstown #6550
M-Mug
9187-G
9188-B
9189-H

R Kingstown #407
11½" Crimp Bowl
9287-G
9288-B
9289-H

S Concord #6521
9" Vase
8176-O
8177-G
8178-B

T Kingstown #947
8" Handled Vase
9567-G
9568-B
9569-H

U Concord #819
7" Pitcher
8366-O
8367-G
8368-B

Indiana Handcraft undated catalog page.

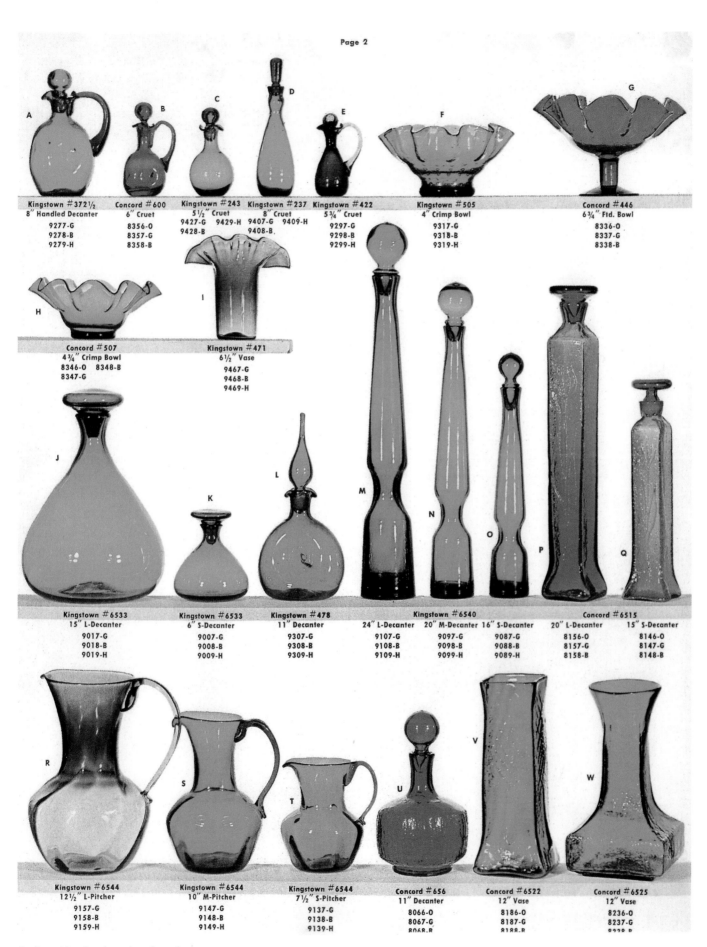

A
Kingstown #372½
8" Handled Decanter
9277-G
9278-B
9279-H

B
Concord #600
6" Cruet
8356-O
8357-G
8358-B

C
Kingstown #243
5½" Cruet
9427-G   9429-H
9428-B

D
Kingstown #237
8" Cruet
9407-G   9409-H
9408-B

E
Kingstown #422
5¾" Cruet
9297-G
9298-B
9299-H

F
Kingstown #505
4" Crimp Bowl
9317-G
9318-B
9319-H

G
Concord #446
6¾" Ftd. Bowl
8336-O
8337-G
8338-B

H
Concord #507
4¾" Crimp Bowl
8346-O   8348-B
8347-G

I
Kingstown #471
6½" Vase
9467-G
9468-B
9469-H

J
Kingstown #6533
15" L-Decanter
9017-G
9018-B
9019-H

K
Kingstown #6533
6" S-Decanter
9007-G
9008-B
9009-H

L
Kingstown #478
11" Decanter
9307-G
9308-B
9309-H

M
Kingstown #6540
24" L-Decanter
9107-G
9108-B
9109-H

N
20" M-Decanter
9097-G
9098-B
9099-H

O
16" S-Decanter
9087-G
9088-B
9089-H

P
Concord #6515
20" L-Decanter
8156-O
8157-G
8158-B

Q
15" S-Decanter
8146-O
8147-G
8148-B

R
Kingstown #6544
12½" L-Pitcher
9157-G
9158-B
9159-H

S
Kingstown #6544
10" M-Pitcher
9147-G
9148-B
9149-H

T
Kingstown #6544
7½" S-Pitcher
9137-G
9138-B
9139-H

U
Concord #656
11" Decanter
8066-O
8067-G
8068-B

V
Concord #6522
12" Vase
8186-O
8187-G
8188-B

W
Concord #6525
12" Vase
8236-O
8237-G
8238-B

Indiana Handcraft undated catalog page.

Brief Histories of AMCM Hot Glass Manufacturers

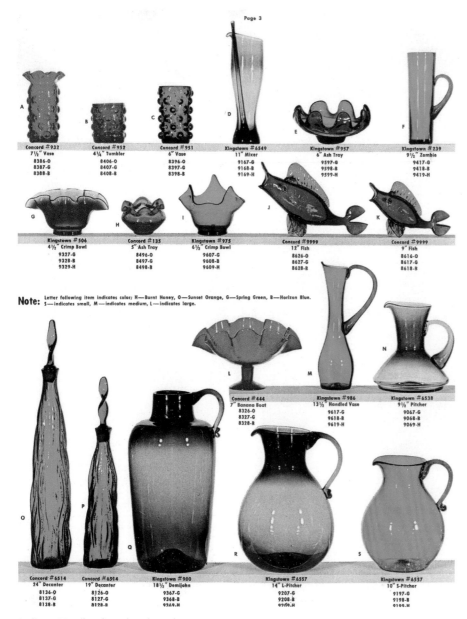

Page 3

A	B	C	D	E	F
Concord #932	Concord #952	Concord #951	Kingstown #6549	Kingstown #957	Kingstown #239
7½" Vase	4¼" Tumbler	6" Vase	11" Mixer	6" Ash Tray	9½" Zombie
8386-O	8406-O	8396-O	9167-G	9597-G	9417-G
8387-G	8407-G	8397-G	9168-B	9598-B	9418-B
8388-B	8408-B	8398-B	9169-H	9599-H	9419-H

G	H	I	J	K
Kingstown #506	Concord #135	Kingstown #975	Concord #9999	Concord #9999
4½" Crimp Bowl	5" Ash Tray	6½" Crimp Bowl	12" Fish	9" Fish
9327-G	8496-O	9607-G	8626-O	8616-O
9328-B	8497-G	9608-B	8627-G	8617-G
9329-H	8498-B	9609-H	8628-B	8618-B

Note: Letter following item indicates color; H—Burnt Honey, O—Sunset Orange, G—Spring Green, B—Horizon Blue.
S—indicates small, M—indicates medium, L—indicates large.

L	M	N
Concord #444	Kingstown #986	Kingstown #6538
7" Banana Boat	13½" Handled Vase	9½" Pitcher
8326-O	9617-G	9067-G
8327-G	9618-B	9068-B
8328-B	9619-H	9069-H

O	P	Q	R	S
Concord #6514	Concord #6514	Kingstown #900	Kingstown #6557	Kingstown #6557
24" Decanter	19" Decanter	18½" Demijohn	14" L-Pitcher	10" S-Pitcher
8136-O	8126-O	9367-G	9207-G	9197-G
8137-G	8127-G	9368-B	9208-B	9198-B
8138-B	8128-B	9369-H	9209-H	9199-H

Indiana Handcraft undated catalog page.

Green crimped bowl with pontil and Indiana Handcraft paper label, Kingston #506, 4", $15–20.

Kanawha
Glass Corporation

Dunbar, West Virginia
1955–1983

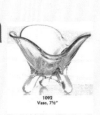  

Good   *Better*   *Best*

Kanawha operated as Kanawha Glass Specialties Co. from 1955 until 1960, when it was reorganized as Kanawha Glass Corporation. Kanawha Glass was one of the many handmade glass plants that dotted the corridor of old U.S. Rt. 60 between Huntington and Charleston, West Virginia. The area, historically referenced as the Teays Valley, shared the brightly colored, handmade and mouth-blown styles of glass that easily embraced crackle glass and often organic forms.

Kanawha Glass is best known for their pressed and mould-blown shapes, but there is much more to the story than is commonly acknowledged. Products from Kanawha that have the distinctive Teays Valley pontil mark or scar on its base were probably produced at their second factory in Scott's Depot, West Virginia. Kanawha Glass was predominately blown into an iron mould and handled by a snap or mechanical tool and not attached to a hot punty—thus, no punty scar or pontil. But Kanawha hired glass master Robert Hamon and engaged his small, hand production factory to make the pontiled, mouth-blown, free-formed glass sold as Kanawha. This arrangement lasted several years and Kanawha catalog show two distinct lines: the traditional, formed pressed ware, and the AMCM-styled, freehand ware created under the hand of Hamon.

Kanawha closed in 1983, and today the factory site is occupied by a parking lot and retail stores.

Kanawha Glass #214 tall jug with hand applied handle, Orange-red, smooth base, $28–40.

Kanawha Glass vases: #228, Amberina, $24–34; and #229, Green, $20–28. A moulded piece had a hot glass trail or wrap applied, then, held by the marie (small foot indention at base), was swung while hot. The result was a different form for every vase made, and heights that varied greatly.

Kanawha Glass catalog, two-page, centerfold spread. 1965.

Kanawha Glass decanter #1045. 13" Kanawha joined forces with glass master Robert "Bob" Hamon and used the nearby, smaller Hamon factory to produce hand-blown and pontiled products. Kanawha's production from their main factory was largely pressed ware. Amberina crackle bottle with colorless foot and riggaree. $80–100.

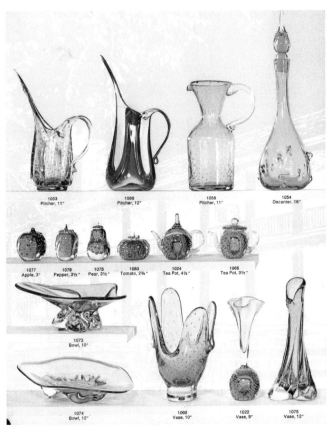

Kanawha Glass catalog page, 1968

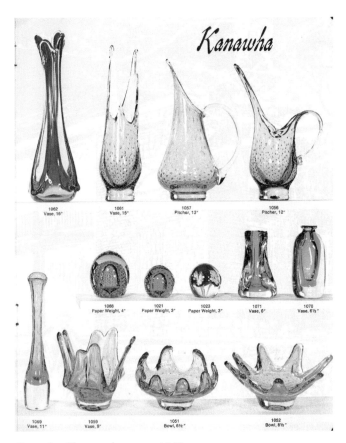

Kanawha Glass catalog page, 1968.

Kanawha Glass #1051 bowl, light Amber, pontiled 6½″ d., $28–38.

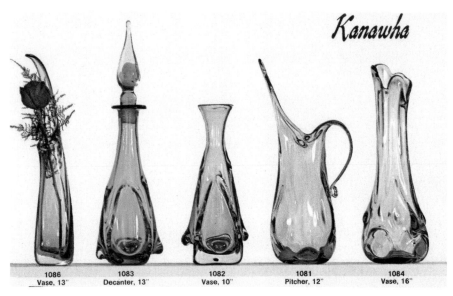

1086
Vase, 13"

1083
Decanter, 13"

1082
Vase, 10"

1081
Pitcher, 12"

1084
Vase, 16"

Kanawha Glass catalog supplement page, 1969.

817
Ash Tray, 5"

831
Holder,
2½"

832
Lighter,
3¼"

848
Ash Tray, 4¾"

715
Decanter, 13½"

716
Decanter, 10½"

714
Decanter, 13½"

1045
Decanter, 13"

713H
Decanter, 11"

713R
Decanter, 11"

710R
Decanter, 9"

710H
Decanter, 9"

Kanawha Glass catalog page, 1970. Illustrated is the #1045 decanter shown on page 172.

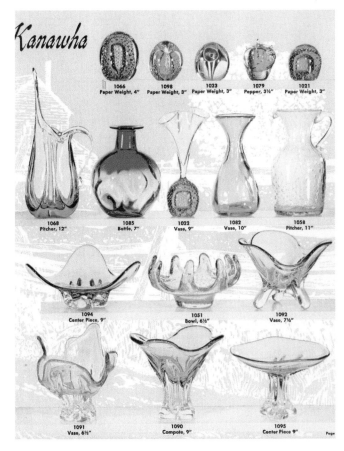

Kanawha Glass catalog page, 1970.

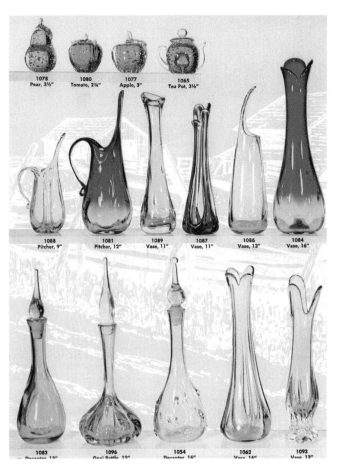

Kanawha Glass catalog page, 1970.

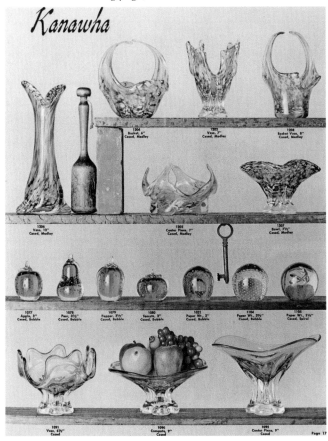

Kanawha Glass catalog page, 1971. Note the intriguing juxtaposition of very modern, organic form glass placed next to an antique, wooden potato masher, an antique key, and a used brick.

Kanawha Glass catalog page, 1971.

Kanawha Glass catalog page, 1973.

Kanawha Glass made this pitcher form, one of the most widely found AMCM shapes today. It is seen in Amberina crackle in at least half of the antique malls across America. $20–28, the same form in Amber is less common and less desired. $14–26.

Libbey
Glass Company

Toledo, Ohio
1888–present

The New England Glass Co., of Cambridge, Massachusetts, relocated to Toledo, Ohio, and became W.L. Libbey & Son Company in 1888. They continued to produce hot glass from their new factory in Ohio, and became Libbey Glass Co. in 1892.

In 1942, Libbey issued a catalog titled *Modern American Glassware*. The objects were designed by Edwin W. Fuerst and included controlled air bubbles, heavy optics, and cog-like bases. In many ways, these Libbey Modern American items foresaw the visual elements of Modernism in American Glass. Restrictions on materials for production were lifted at the close of World War II, but Libbey did not reinstate the items from the Modern American line. In fact, Libbey turned to mass-produced, machine-made glass. Over the following decades, Libbey grew to be a giant international and global firm, using the ideas and machinery of inventor Michael Owen to manufacture massive quantities of machine-made products. The company has adapted to changes in trends, market place, and style. Today it continues to operate a number of glass factories around the world, making glass and numerous other products.

Libbey Glass, a mass produced machine-made glass house, utilized its vast resources to enter the AMCM market by adding decoration to the surface of colorless glass they produced. Sometimes attached metal and wood handles, bases, etc., would further add to the modernist appeal. Some of the most popular Libbey lines for many years included Golden Foilage and Silver Foilage. This adaptation of those patterns add Turquoise to the silver, making a 1950s color statement. It was likely marketed as a juice pitcher, $12–20. Collection of the Museum of American Glass in West Virginia.

Morgantown Glass Works

Morgantown, West Virginia
1899–1971

Good

Better

Best

Opening in 1899, the Morgantown Glass Works produced handmade glass in Morgantown, West Virginia. It operated under a number of names including Economy Glass Works, Economy Tumbler Company, and Morgantown Glassware Guild, but always at the same site and often using the same labors, moulds, and clints. The wares produced were largely handmade, mouth-blown tableware, barware, and giftware. This factory was far from the only glass factory in the Morgantown community, but it alone bears the common title of Morgantown Glass. Today, wares made under the changing ownership arrangements are generally all referenced as "Morgantown Glass." Morgantown American Mid-century Modern designs include Russel Wright's design for American Modern and Ben Seibel's Raymor Modern.

In 1958, Morgantown issued their first color catalog and the line debuted inside was named Décor by Morgantown. It featured bold colors, simple forms, and often slanted tops. The original 1958 color selections were Steel Blue, Peacock Blue, Evergreen, Ruby, Burgundy, Lime, Pineapple, and Crystal.

With time, the line grew to incorporate a number of elegantly simple forms in both the bold and earth tones of the period. Moss Green (1964), Gypsy Fire (1962), and Thistle (1962) were among the numerous colors added over the years.

Humans first set foot on the moon in 1969. It is little wonder that American glass would acknowledge that historic event. Morgantown Moonscape was introduced in 1970 and is one such nod to the historic moment. By that time, Fostoria Glass had a controlling interest in Morgantown and was making the decisions. Moonscape was the final collaborative project for the two firms. Thin, blown lids and thin bowls on the objects were blown at Morgantown. The thick, pressed glass bases were made at Fostoria in Moundsville, and, later, the components were joined by gluing. The line was short-lived as Morgantown's assets were liquidated by June 1971.

We can only address Morgantown's most popular textured glassware production at mid-century as "the quandary of LMX."

In 1933, the popular tableware trade journal *China, Glass, and Lamps* wrote about a new, rough hewn line of tumblers, flat and footed, in semi-transparent crystal and green. The El Mexicano line, in name and appearance, addressed the interest in the 1930s for Mexican folk pottery and casual patio-smart tableware. This historical note is significant in that it was 1962 when the shapes of El Mexicano (abbreviated as LMX at the factory) re-appeared from the Morgantown factory in a new selection of colors, then all transparent, whereas the earlier had been all opaque. However, the forms are the same for both lines. In the marketplace, these re-introduced Morgantown textured objects were intended to challenge Bryce's El Rancho (introduced in 1955) and Seneca's Driftwood (introduced in 1953).

The quandary is simple: if a line was produced in the 1930s as El Mexicano, and re-introduced in the 1960s in the same forms but with different colors pallet and name, Crinkle, is that 1960s product an AMCM product? I would suggest that it is not. Crinkle sold well, but was retro and not modern in the hands of Morgantown.

Morgantown introduced a line called Swirl in the 1950s (per author Gallagher). It included both a 64 oz. and 32 oz. pitcher, as well as five sizes of tumblers. Production of pitchers ended in 1966 while tumblers were continued for several years. The line was numbered #9844.

Appearing in the 1966 catalog only, line #3000, Festival, was the most extensive Morgantown tableware line during the Décor era. Festival was Morgantown's effort to enter into the then-successful era of textured glass tableware. The short production time makes it challenging to find pieces today. Produced in the Festival line were a 64 oz. pitcher, a plate, and a berry bowl. Tumblers included tea, hi-ball, water, juice, and old fashion (all flat based). Stemmed and footed pieces included sherbet, cocktail wine, footed ice tea, and goblet glasses.

Perhaps the most recognized American Mid-century Modern design from Morgantown was American Modern, designed by Russel Wright. Richard Haden, plant manager and member of the family that owned the factory recalled, "My Dad developed a line with him (Wright) in the middle or late forties. It was almost in the height of its popularity when I went to the plant in 1949, and continued in popularity for a number of years after I got there." Wright designed the glass not to have the usual small button where a handmade stem attached to the hand cast foot. This was a production challenge that Morgantown overcame. The initial line included five stemmed shapes and four flat shapes. Colors were crystal, coral (pink), seafoam (blue-green), chartreuse (topaz), and granite gray (changed to smoke in later years). The colors were not usual Morgantown production but special tones developed to fulfill Wright's desire to match his American Modern ceramic tableware produced by Steubenville Pottery.

While Morgantown produced American Modern for Wright, it was never a Morgantown product. It did not appear in Morgantown catalogs and the line always remained the sole property and under control of Wright.

Morgantown Glass closed in 1971.

To Learn More:

Gallagher, Jerry. *A Handbook of Morgantown Glass. Volume I: A Guide to Identification and Shape.* Privately published. 1995.

Snyder, Jeffery B. *Morgantown Glass: From Depression Glass Through the 1960s.* Atglen, Pennsylvania: Schiffer Publishing, Ltd. 1998.

Morgantown company brochure. The message is that Morgantown is the glass for swinging young people who are hip and cool folk. It is driven home by this line drawing of the loafer- and blazer-clad young man with his high-heeled, skirted and flip-haired girl. Use this glass and you are cool like them. The reverse reads "Décor. A new elegance for the young originals by Morgantown. Décor, the touch of difference… by which the young originals are known. A fascinating and highly individual group of handcrafted pieces in sophisticated shapes and qui vive colors: Gypsy Fire, Peacock Blue, Ruby, Burgundy, Steel, Golden Moss and Crystal… "

CONSOLE SETS

80—6½"
CANDLE

9928
FLOWER LITE

12—4", 6", 8"
COMPOTE

GENUINE
Old
Morgantown
Lead Crystal
HANDMADE IN U.S.

121—5"
CANDLE

101
BOWL

9935
CANDLE

9922
FLOWER LITE

81—4½"
CANDLE

9922
FLOWER LITE

ASH TRAYS

130—8"
AMETHYST

130—8½"
GLORIA BLUE

129—4½"
STEEL BLUE

129—4½"
AMBER

10

Morgantown Glassware Guild company catalog, circa 1965–67, showing console sets and textured ashtrays. Everyone making AMCM had to produce an ash tray, it seemed. We were then a nation of smokers.

Morgantown introduced a line of free form shapes in the late 1960s. Similar forms date easily back to the 1950s from Italy and American firms like Tiffin. Called simply "Free Forms" the line included a large and small vertical vase a similar shape, a large and small bowl, and a large and small tray (like the bowl but less deep). They came in Moss Green, Crystal, Ebony, and Amberina as well as some two-tone colors as shown here. Ruby and Gypsy Fire, 13¼" long, $30–45; Cobalt and Crystal, 12" long, $25–40.

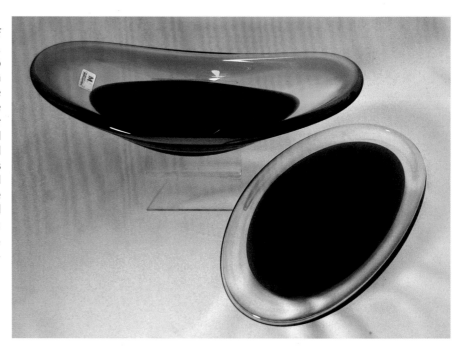

Morgantown Guild produced a number of candleholders, and hurricane and candle lamps. Shown here is the two-part #9923 hurricane lamp, oddly called Colonial. The form looks like nothing in Williamsburg, but the appeal to the early 1960s colonial home décor market was apparent. Evergreen color, 8½", $24–32 each piece.

Morgantown Guild undated catalog supplement page showing "Free–Forms." Circa late 1960s.

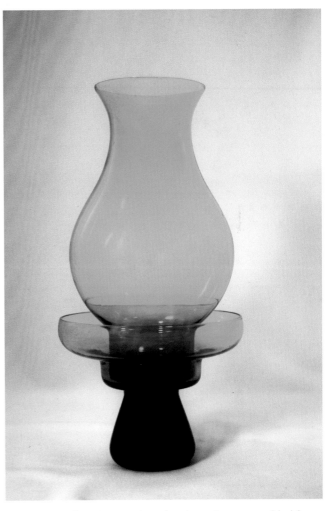

Morgantown #9923, two-piece, hurricane lamp assembled for use. Same as nearby image showing the two distinct pieces.

Morgantown Guild Ebony (black) and Opal (white) two-piece medium mushroom box #1412, circa 1970, $40–50.

Morganton Guild catalog, circa 1968. Ebony and Ebony with Crystal combination forms in a selection of modern and mid–century objects.

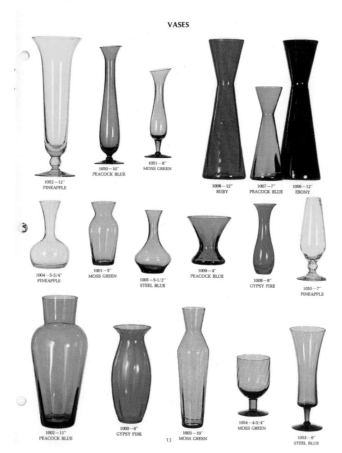

What were the people at Morgantown Guild thinking? The 1970 catalog featured these interesting ideas for a drinking glass that hung around one's neck. The chain version was for men, the pearl one for women. You could not lose your drink and need not hold it at all times, as it swung freely from the necklace and against your chest. Novel idea. One wonders why it did not catch on. Today, these are most uncommon. Image from the 1970 Morgantown Guild catalog, the only year they were offered.

Morgantown Guild catalog page, circa 1968, illustrating 18 distinct AMCM vase forms. Slant tops and bold colors are the defining characteristics for most.

Morgantown Guild catalog, undated, early 1960s. Noted is the bottom row vase $9942–6" shown in Steel Blue, a strong example of AMCM.

Morgantown Guild, selection of Décor line items made 1958–1971. Left to right: #9902–7" slant top vase in Steel Blue, $10–16; snack bowl with slant top, Evergreen $16–24; #1404 candy box (apple–like) with lid, Moss Green, 6", $12–20; #9002–7" slant top vase in Amethyst, $8–14; #82 slant top candleholder, Peacock Blue, 7", $16–24.

Morgantown Guild Gypsy Fire color was introduced in 1962. All Gypsy Fire Décor line, top: Crinkle footed sherbet $10–16. Middle, left to right: straight-sided box #9953 covered box (missing the colorless pressed lid), 8" (one of three sizes made), $20–28 with lid; #9941½ flowerlite (discontinued in 1963), came with a colorless glass flower holder/frog insert to hold the floral arrangement in place, $20–26. Bottom, left to right: #1161 urn, 8½", $26–34; #12 flower arranger (compote) came in three sizes, as footed bowls for floral arrangements, $22–30; #104 or #1300 candle light, 8¾", $20–28 each.

BAUBLES

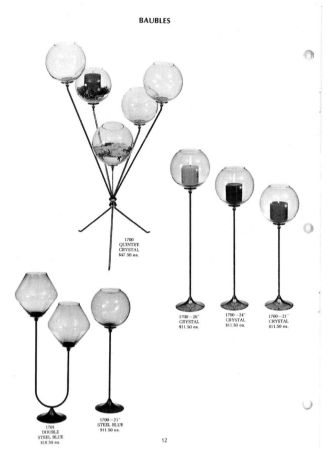

1700
QUINTET
CRYSTAL
$47.50 ea.

1700—26"
CRYSTAL
$11.50 ea.

1700—24"
CRYSTAL
$11.50 ea.

1700—21"
CRYSTAL
$11.50 ea.

1701
DOUBLE
STEEL BLUE
$18.50 ea.

1700—21"
STEEL BLUE
$11.50 ea.

12

Morgantown Guild, c. 1969, catalog page featuring glass and wire creations called Baubles. They appear on the cover of the 1969 catalog and remained in the line for about one year.

AVAILABLE IN
CRYSTAL OR STEEL BOWL
MIST OR SILVER BASE

MOONSCAPE

3033—CANDY BOX & COVER
$12.75 ea.

3037—CANDY JAR & COVER
$12.75 ea.

3045—16" PATIO LIGHT
$12.75 ea.

3036—7½" BOWL
$12.75 ea.

3042—COVERED CANDY
$10.50 ea.

3041—8" BOWL
$12.75 ea.

3044—10" HURRICANE
$10.50 ea.

3034—11" VASE
$10.50 ea.

3043—7" VASE
$10.50 ea.

3035—9½" BOWL
$18.00 ea.

9

Morgantown Guild Moonscape line, as illustrated in the 1970 catalog.

Morgantown Guild #9844 Swirl line, introduced in the 1950s. Amber, 9 oz. old fashion, $6–10 : Burgundy, 6 oz. juice, $5–8; Ruby, 6 oz. juice, $8–12, colorless crystal, 4 oz. cocktail, $4–6; Evergreen, 14 oz. water tumbler, $6–10. All discontinued by 1970.

Morgantown Guild Moonscape, blown, #3033 candy box and cover Steel Blue attached to the pressed, colorless base, $30–40.

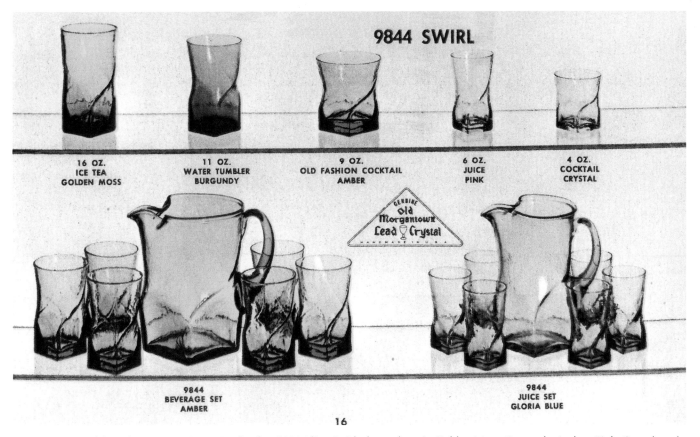

Morgantown Guild catalog page, c. 1965–67, for the #9844 line Swirl, shown here in Golden Moss, Burgundy, Amber, Pink, Crystal, and Gloria Blue. Five sizes of beverage tumblers and two sizes of pitchers appear.

Russel Wright American Modern glassware made by Morgantown Glassware Guild. Note that the stemware lacks the usual button of glass found where the hand pulled stem is attached to the foot. Wright demanded a production process that eliminated the button. Left front: two cordials, $10–14 each; three cocktails $10–16 each, and one sherbe,t $12–20. Second tier (l to r): footed goblets in all four colors produced, $18–24 each. Second from top row: two 5 oz. juice tumblers, $12–16 each. Top row: 10 oz. water $12–20; 14 oz. ice tea, $14–22.

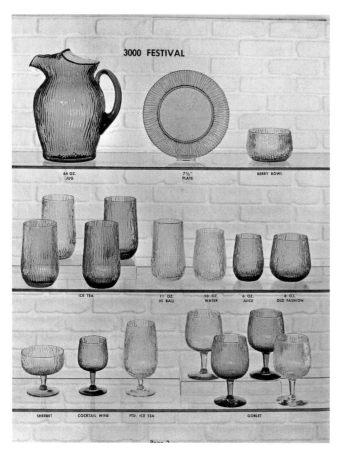

Morgantown Guild catalog page, 1966. The line shown is #3000 Festival in the colors Crystal, Gloria Blue, Moss Green, and Amber.

Morgantown Guild #3000 Festival, colorless crystal goblet, 5³/₈" h., $6–12.

Morgantown Guild #3000 Festival, two Moss Green wines, 4½" h., $8–14; sherbet, 3½" h. $6–10; 8¼" h. pitcher with hand-applied handle, $28–38.

Morgantown Guild #3000 Festival Amber sherbet, 3½" h., $6–10; goblet, 5³/₈" h., $8–12, wine, 4½" h., $6–10.

Morgantown Guild, #2008 martini set in Seville Gold. Tumblers, $10–14 each; pitcher with applied handle, $40–50. Interest in cocktail serveware at the time of this writing has been stirred by the television show *Madmen* and impacted prices. This may or may not be a sustained interest and market.

Morgantown Guild, #2001 martini set in Seville Gold. Pitcher, $30–45; tumblers, $10–14 each.

Morgantown Guild, #2002 Martini set in Steel Blue, diamond optic, unattached, inverted, hand-applied handle. Tumblers, $8–10; pitcher, $35–48.

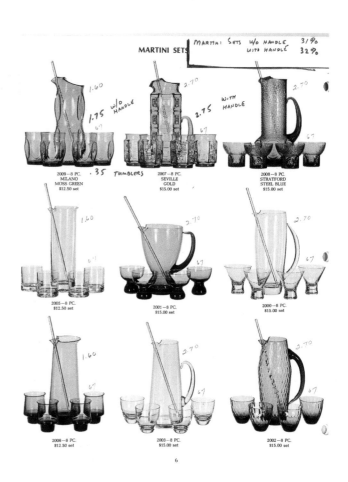

Morgantown Guild catalog page, circa 1969, for Martini sets in Moss Green, Seville Gold, and Steel Blue.

Morgantown Guild, Martini set #2008, handleless pitcher with #2001 tumblers in Steel Blue and colorless stirring rod. Pitcher, $25–35; tumblers, $12–16 each.

Brief Histories of AMCM Hot Glass Manufacturers

Morgantown Guild #3010: bowl, Ebony with Opal (white) foot, 5", $45–55; Martini pitcher, Ebony with colorless crystal foot $55–70. Jaime Robinson collection.

ODD BALLS 3010

8-1/2 OZ. OLD FASHIONED
13.00 4 pc. set

6 OZ. COCKTAIL
11.00 4 pc. set

MARTINI S
17.50 6 pc. s

5" BOWL
6.50 ea.

8" BOWL
12.75 ea.

HANG UPS 3029

SNACK BOWL
12.75 ea.

COCKTAIL PITCHER
7.50 ea.

ON THE ROCKS
16.00 4 pc. set

BLOODY MARY
16.00 4 pc. set

5

Morgantown Guild 1970 catalog page. Shown is the popular, odd-ball, #3010 line and the short lived Hang Ups beverage sets.

1970

M
lead crystal by
MORGANTOWN

MORGANTOWN GLASSWARE GUILD, INC.

Morgantown Guild catalog cover, prominently dated 1970. Shown are Moonscape vase and candle lamp and a Hang Ups, three-toed on-the-rocks, along with other lines.

Morgantown Guild #3029 Hang Ups colorless crystal and Steel Blue, three-toed foot, $20–30.

Morgantown Manor, Blue: goblet, 6″ h., $12–18; iced tea, 6¼″ h., $14–22; sherbet, 4³⁄₈ h., $8–14

Morgantown Manor iced tea, Steel Blue and Crystal, 6¼″ h., $16–22.

Morgantown Malta, Steel Blue: iced tea, 5 ⁵⁄₈″, $14–18; goblet, 4¾″, $10–16; wine, 3⁷⁄₈″, $8–12; and dessert bowl, 2½″ h. x 4³⁄₈″, $6–10.

Paden City Glass

Paden City, West Virginia
1916–1951

Paden City produced one line that was Mid-century Modern. The Russel Wright-designed "Snow" pattern, or line, was made by Paden City Glass Co. from 1948 to 1953 for Justin Tharaud. The line was never marketed as Paden City Glass. The Metropolitan Museum of Art has one piece in their collection, a gift of the artist. After Paden City Glass closed in 1951, it is possible that Fostoria Glass attempted to continue production of the line. See the Fostoria section of this book to explore that possibility.

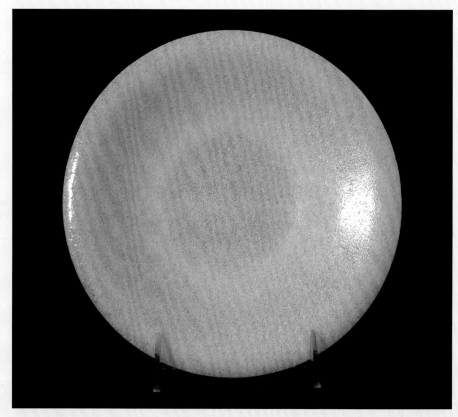

Paden City Glass-made, Russel Wright design, Snow plate. Shown is an 8½" luncheon plate. $24–32.

Paden City, Russel Wright's Snow plate in profile. The plate's profile is the easiest way to verify the Wright design from similar patterns.

Pilgrim Glass Corporation

Ceredo, West Virginia

1948–2001

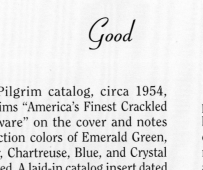

Good   *Better*   *Best*

This company shipped its handmade glass from its Ceredo, West Virginia, factory beginning in 1948. Alfred Knobler purchased the existing Tri-State Glass Company from Walter Bailey in 1948 and relocated it from Huntington, West Virginia, to Ceredo shortly after acquiring the firm. Knobler, initially a factory representative for diverse product lines, became a successful importer of international products for his company Knobler, Inc., but Pilgrim was his passion, as he indulged in making, marketing, and exploring glass. Pilgrim was one of the leading producers of colorful glass in the Teays Valley, the geographic area ranging from Huntington to Charleston, West Virginia.

In the 1960–70s, Pilgrim glass artisans crafted small, popular pieces meant to be set on window sills and ledges to add bright color as the sun came through the window. These small pitchers and vases were produced by the thousands in a diverse selection of colors, and in plain, satin, and crackle finishes. While the small objects dominated their production, Pilgrim also produced massive glass forms in hand blown, colored, and mid-century styles.

A Pilgrim catalog, circa 1954, proclaims "America's Finest Crackled Glassware" on the cover and notes production colors of Emerald Green, Amber, Chartreuse, Blue, and Crystal Crackled. A laid-in catalog insert dated January 10, 1955, is titled "Important Changes" and reads, "Available in new Real Ruby and note new Charcoal Smoke and Pilgrim Pink added to long accepted colors: Blue, Emerald Green, Amber & Crystal." Removed from the color offering was Chartreuse.

The arrival, in the mid-1950s, of Italian glass masters Alessandro and Roberto Moretti, brothers, brought modern designs and Italian skills to Pilgrim. Alessandro and Roberto were joined at Pilgrim by their brother-in-law Mario Sandon who added his skills to the host of skilled artisans at Pilgrim.

Pilgrim's focus and predominant sales for many years were in the small colorful vases, pitchers, etc., collectively called window vases. These were under 5 inches in height and exhibited great, bold color, but little that can be catalogued as modern mid-century. However, the presence of three Italian glass artists on the Pilgrim factory floor did much to introduce mid-century designs and sensibilities.

In the 1968 Pilgrim glass catalog, page three is dedicated to "the sculptured beauty" of glass. Shown are nine shapes of "completely handmade, without moulds" glass that combines Blue, Topaz and Crystal in several forms. The hand-manipulated surface treatments are fully reminiscent of Italian glass of that era.

The 1968 catalog pieces were largely the work of the three Italian men. In addition to the objects shown early in the catalog, a second selection, found on page 19 of the same year, shows four shapes in three color treatments, titled only "cased ware." The catalog describes the objects: "layers and layers of glass flow in hearty curves, Crystal over a combination of Blue and Topaz, Crystal over Avocado Green, Crystal over Ruby. Each piece is blown into simple, unaffected shapes." Produced for only one year, these four forms indeed capture Mid-century Modern in their heavy, bold directness.

Fire Island was a line of textured drinking vessels produced by Pilgrim and shown in the trade magazine *Giftwares*. The Fire Island line appears in no known Pilgrim catalog.

Pilgrim closed in 2001.

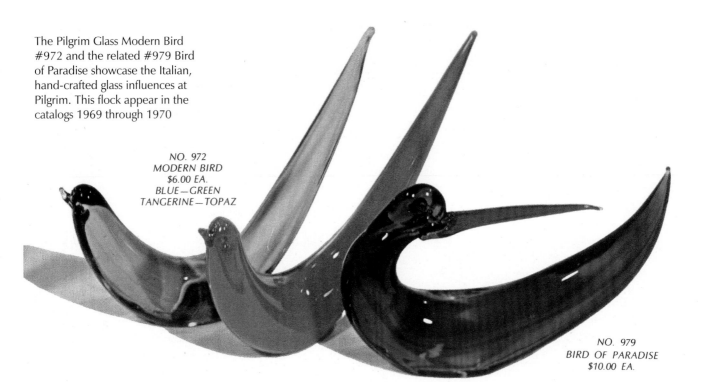

The Pilgrim Glass Modern Bird #972 and the related #979 Bird of Paradise showcase the Italian, hand-crafted glass influences at Pilgrim. This flock appear in the catalogs 1969 through 1970

NO. 972
MODERN BIRD
$6.00 EA.
BLUE—GREEN
TANGERINE—TOPAZ

NO. 979
BIRD OF PARADISE
$10.00 EA.

Pilgrim Orange optic vase with rolled rim, 5¹/₈" h. x 5" d., rough pontil, $30–38.

Pilgrim Glass, Ruby and Purple–Blue optic decanters with blown spire stoppers: 13¼" Ruby, $50–75; 14" Purple–Blue, $45–65; both with rough pontils.

HANGING PLAQUES

HANGING BIRD PLAQUES—5" TO 6"
NO. 633
$1.25 EA.
(PACK: 1 DZ. ASSTD. SHAPES)
AVAILABLE: BLUE—CRYSTAL—GREEN—TOPAZ
ORDER: 1 DZ. OF A SINGLE COLOR, OR
1 DZ. ASSORTED COLORS

Hanging Bird Plaques appeared in the 1970 catalog in four colors, 5–6" long, sold individually, $14–22 each.

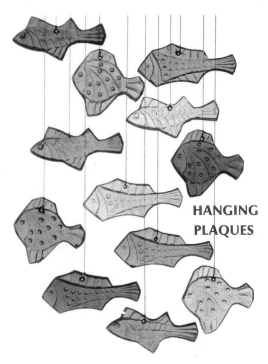

HANGING PLAQUES

HANGING FISH PLAQUES—5" to 6"
NO. 630
$1.25 EA.
(PACK: 1 DZ. ASSTD. SHAPES)
AVAILABLE: BLUE—CRYSTAL—GREEN—TOPAZ
ORDER: 1 DZ. OF A SINGLE COLOR, OR
1 DZ. ASSORTED COLORS

Hanging Fish Plaques appeared in the 1970 catalog in four colors. 5–6" long, sold individually, $12–20 each.

Pilgrim TALL, TALL, TALL, VASES

Giant Vases in Decorator Shapes and Colors, as listed.

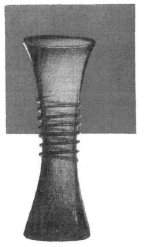

◆ 62—12"
$3.00 Each
In Choice of
TANGERINE, TOPAZ

◆ 64—12"
$3.00 Each
Choice of LEMON-LIME,
SEA GREEN, TANGERINE
In Real RUBY — $3.25

◆ 92—15"
$3.25 Each
Choice of SEA GREEN,
SKY BLUE, TANGERINE

◆ 93—20"
$3.75 Each
Choice of SEA GREEN
SKY BLUE, TANGERINE

Pilgrim glass produced larger crackle glass pieces for their 1964 New York World's Fair catalog. Shown here are pieces 12" to 20."

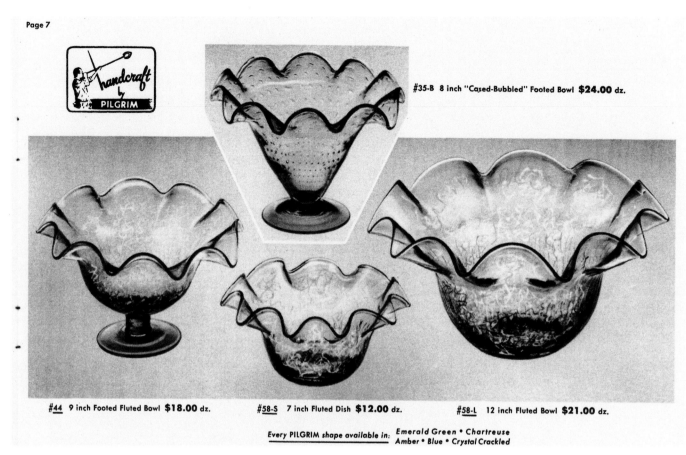

Page 7

#35-B   8 inch "Cased-Bubbled" Footed Bowl **$24.00** dz.

#44   9 inch Footed Fluted Bowl **$18.00** dz.   #58-S   7 inch Fluted Dish **$12.00** dz.   #58-L   12 inch Fluted Bowl **$21.00** dz.

Every PILGRIM shape available in: Emerald Green • Chartreuse
Amber • Blue • Crystal Crackled

Pilgrim Glass catalog circa 1954 showing crackled, crimped bowls and the #35–B, 8", "cased bubble" footed bowl. The page notes these forms were available in Emerald Green, Chartreuse, Amber, Blue, and Crystal Crackle.

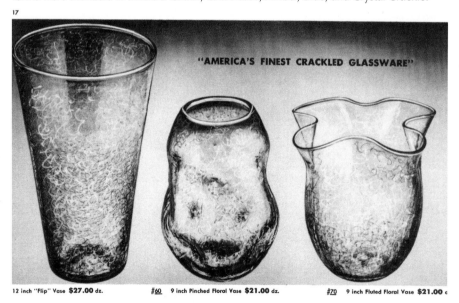

17

"AMERICA'S FINEST CRACKLED GLASSWARE"

12 inch "Flip" Vase **$27.00** dz.   #60   9 inch Pinched Floral Vase **$21.00** dz.   #70   9 inch Fluted Floral Vase **$21.00** d

Pilgrim Glass catalog, circa 1954, 9–12" crackle forms.

#76 Small Ash Tray
$6.00 dz.

#82-C Multi-rest "Cased Glass"
Bubble Ash Tray **$30.00** dz.

#79-C 3-rest "Cased Glass"
Bubble Ash Tray **$30.00** dz.

#103 "Cased Glass" Paper Weights
$12.00 dz.

Address orders and correspondence to:

THE PILGRIM GLASS CORPORATION

225 FIFTH AVENUE, NEW YORK 10, N. Y.

PILGRIM HANDCRAFT available in your choice of:

Emerald Green
Amber
Chartreuse
Blue
Crystal Crackled

KEEP THIS CATALOG . . .

Use it to help receive, identify and price PILGRIM HANDCRAFT.

Use it as a handy guide between calls by our salesmen.

Use it to re-order PILGRIM HANDCRAFT. Save time and your good disposition—refer to our ware numbers and color range.

DEALER'S NOTE:

All prices shown are wholesale.
Terms: 1%-15 days, net 30.
Shipment: FOB, Huntington, West Virginia.
Packing: A 3% packing charge is added to the net amount of invoice.

PRINTED IN U.S.A.

Pilgrim Glass, circa 1954 catalog, illustrating their "cased bubble" ware in ash trays and paperweights.

Pilgrim Glass Fire Island line shown in trade magazine. The offering was Amber, Green, Blue, and Crystal.

Pilgrim Glass Fire Island tumbler, Amber Satin, 4½" h. x 4" d., $8–12.

SMOKER'S CORNER
Colorful Ashtrays for home, office or den. Sizes 6" to 8".

NO. 78
$18.00 DZ.
ASSTD. COLORS

NO. 80
$36.00 DZ.
ASSTD. COLORS

NO. 76/OWL
$18.00 DZ.
BLUE—TANGERINE

NO. 76/FLORAL
$18.00 DZ.
BLUE—TANGERINE

Pilgrim Glass 1970 catalog shows these 6" to 8" ashtrays in cased glass and with applied color owl or floral prunts.

Pilgrim Glass circa 1968 or 1969 catalog. The back cover illustration shows "massive, bold pieces of cased glass combining Blue, Topaz and Crystal…the ultimate in the glass blower's art." Often attributed to Murano and not recognized as AMCM with strong Italian influences.

CRANBERRY SCULPTURED VASES

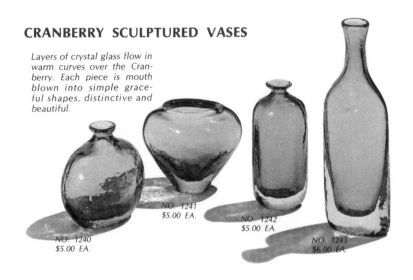

Layers of crystal glass flow in warm curves over the Cranberry. Each piece is mouth blown into simple graceful shapes, distinctive and beautiful.

NO. 1240
$5.00 EA.

NO. 1241
$5.00 EA.

NO. 1242
$5.00 EA.

NO. 1243
$6.00 EA.

Pilgrim Glass, Cranberry Sculpted Vases. Cranberry heavily cased in crystal. Undated 1960s catalog.

Pilgrim Glass sculpted vase #1240 in Blue, Topaz and Crystal, smooth ground base, 5⅝" h., $55–75.

Pilgrim Glass #209 cordial decanter with hand-pulled decoration, Crystal cased over Blue, $70–90.

Pilgrim Glass cased bowl #201, Blue, Topaz, and Crystal. Four-lobe, ground base, $45–65.

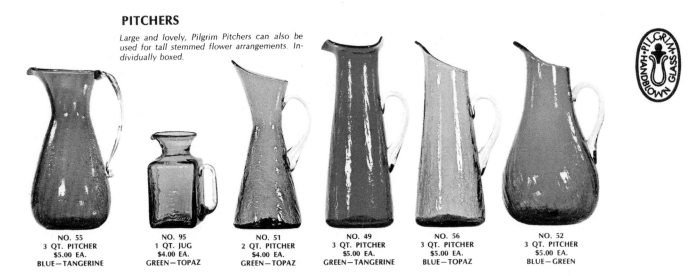

PITCHERS

Large and lovely, Pilgrim Pitchers can also be used for tall stemmed flower arrangements. Individually boxed.

NO. 55
3 QT. PITCHER
$5.00 EA.
BLUE—TANGERINE

NO. 95
1 QT. JUG
$4.00 EA.
GREEN—TOPAZ

NO. 51
2 QT. PITCHER
$4.00 EA.
GREEN—TOPAZ

NO. 49
3 QT. PITCHER
$5.00 EA.
GREEN—TANGERINE

NO. 56
3 QT. PITCHER
$5.00 EA.
BLUE—TOPAZ

NO. 52
3 QT. PITCHER
$5.00 EA.
BLUE—GREEN

Pilgrim Glass catalog illustration for "large and lovely" pitchers. Shown are six forms/sizes. The circa 1968–69 catalog offered only four of these forms. Pitchers 49 and 52 were not in the prior illustration.

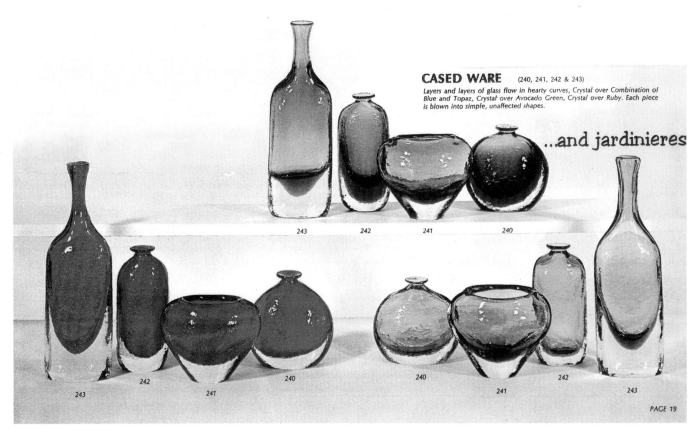

CASED WARE (240, 241, 242 & 243)

Layers and layers of glass flow in hearty curves, Crystal over Combination of Blue and Topaz, Crystal over Avocado Green, Crystal over Ruby. Each piece is blown into simple, unaffected shapes.

...and jardinieres

PAGE 19

Pilgrim Glass catalog, circa 1968–69. The sculpted line of cased glass included four forms available in three colors combinations: Blue and Topaz with Crystal; Crystal and Avocado Green; and Crystal with Ruby.

Famous PILGRIM Crackled Glassware. Easy-to-hold, lovely to look at. Universally popular for casual and formal entertaining. The loveliest of hostess gifts. Available in choice of CRYSTAL, LEMON-LIME, SEA GREEN, SKY BLUE, TANGERINE, and TOPAZ.

* 613—HB
14-oz. Hiball
$5.00 Set of 8, boxed
In Real RUBY—$6.00 Set

Also Available:
* 613—DHB
Jumbo 18-oz. Double Hiball
$9.00 Dozen Glasses

* 613—J
5-oz. Juice Glass
$4.50 Set of 8, boxed
In Real RUBY—$5.50 Set

* 613—OF
7-oz. Old Fashioned
$5.00 Set of 8, boxed
In Real RUBY—$6.00 Set

* 613—W
10-oz. Water Tumbler
$5.00 Set of 8, boxed
In Real RUBY—$6.00 Set

* 47
2 Quart Pitcher
$2.50 Each
In Real RUBY — $2.75

Pilgrim 1964 World's Fair catalog, showing their "Pinched Drinkware" in four sizes of tumblers, plus the 18 oz. size, not shown, and a 2-quart pitcher. Colors offered in 1964 were Crystal, Lemon–Lime, Sea Green, Sky Blue, Tangerine, and Topaz.

DRINKWARE

NO. 613-OF
9 OZ. OLD FASHIONED
$7.50 SET OF 8
NO. 613-OF/RUBY
$8.00 SET OF 8

NO. 613-J
5 OZ. JUICE
$6.00 SET OF 8
NO. 613-J/RUBY
$6.50 SET OF 8

NO. 613-W
10 OZ. WATER
$7.50 SET OF 8
NO. 613-W/RUBY
$8.00 Set of 8

NO. 47
2 QT. PITCHER
$3.50 EA.
NO. 47/RUBY
$4.00 EA.

NO. 613-HB
14 OZ. HI-BALL
$7.50 SET OF 8
NO. 613-HB/RUBY
$8 Set of 8

Pilgrim Glass catalog illustration for pinched, crackled drinkware. Note that the forms are different at their base, where the edge rolls under, than crackle pinched forms by others. 1960s catalog; offered in Ruby only.

Pilgrim Glass cased ashtray/bowl. Green and Blue in heavy, cased crystal. Ground base, polished pontil, 5" d., $35–48.

CRANBERRY SCULPTURED ART WARE

Massive, bold pieces of Cased Glass, Crystal over Cranberry, in a delightful collection of decorative and utility art pieces.

NO. 1208
$10.00 EA.
HEIGHT 12"

NO. 1206
BASKET
$10.00 EA.
DIAMETER: 9"

NO. 1209
DECANTER
$8.50 EA.
HEIGHT: 11"

NO. 1212
FRUIT BOWL
$10.00 EA.
DIAM. — 13

NO. 1202
CENTERPIECE
$10.00 EA.
DIAM. 13"

Genuine
Cranberry
Glass
By
Pilgrim

Pilgrim Glass catalog, dated 1970. A five-piece selection of Cranberry Sculptured Art Ware.

Rainbow Art Glass Company

Huntington, West Virginia
1954–1973

Good   *Better*   *Best*

In its earliest days, Rainbow Art Glass Company operated strictly as a decorator of glass blanks produced by others. By 1954, it had begun to melt and form its own glass at their plant in Huntington, West Virginia.

Rainbow was a mouth-blown, handmade factory that predominately blew hot, molten glass into iron moulds to impart a pattern or form. Their wares usually bear a pontil mark on the base and may include multiple colors, air-traps, and large ornamental stoppers.

By the mid-1960s, Rainbow had joined with Viking Glass of New Martinsville, West Virginia, and Viking handled the marketing of Rainbow glass. A Rainbow catalog states that they were "affiliated" with Viking. In 1974, Rainbow had ceased to exist and the factory was known as "Viking Plant II."

Among the most interesting forms from Rainbow are the open-sided candle lamps shown on the following pages.

Rainbow Glass Company catalog, circa 1963.

Rainbow Glass, Sutton shaped pitcher #767, pontiled with encased bubble/air-trap, 9½" to 10". Left, Orange with applied Amber handle, $32–40; right, all Amber, $28–36.

Rainbow Glass round bottle vase, pontiled, Amber with encased bubble/air-trap, $30–38.

Brief Histories of AMCM Hot Glass Manufacturers

Page 12

Rainbow Glass Company catalog, early 1960s.

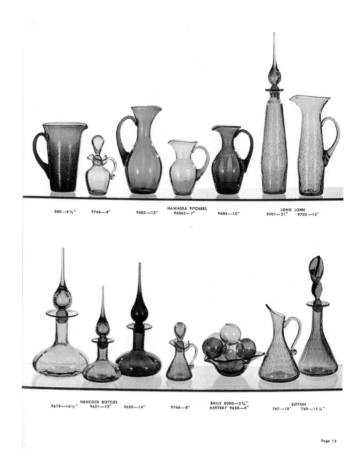

Page 13

Rainbow Glass Company catalog, early 1960s. Note the Sutton air-trap/bubble pieces on the bottom row.

Rainbow Glass Catalog, circa late 1960s.

Rainbow Glass Twinkle-Light #748 with smiling or sun face: Green, 7", $20–28.

Rainbow Glass "Twinkle–Lights," each with one side/window cut open. Green, #745, 5½", $20–28; Amethyst, $22–30; Blue, #747, 7", $22–30; and Amber (amber unknown in this line, may not be Rainbow), $18–22.

Rainbow Glass catalog page, undated, circa late 1960s. Twinkle–Light candle lamps.

Rainbow Glass catalog page, circa early 1960s.

Rainbow Glass smiling heads. Left to right: #872, Green with Blue features, 13½", $140–185; #871, Amber with Red features, 10", $120–145; #872, Amber with Red features, 14¼", $165–210

Rainbow Glass tall, stoppered bottle, Amberina with Red stopper, pontiled, 14", $40–55

Rainbow Glass Duo–Tone #D–219, Amber with Ruby applied looped handle, 13", $30–42. Same mould/shape as the bottle shown at left.

Rainbow Glass Duo–Tone line. Green bottle with air-trap/controlled bubble, pontiled. Blue tear drop stopper and applied leaf prunt, $100–125.

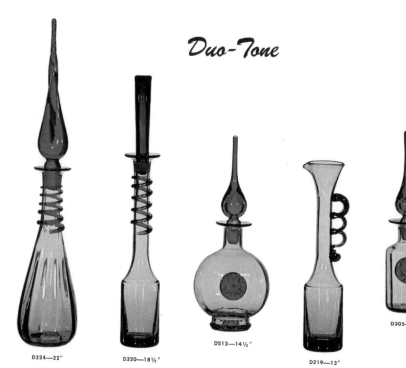

Duo-Tone

D324—22"   D320—18½"   D312—14½"   D219—13"   D305—12½"

Rainbow Glass catalog page, circa 1965–67. Duo–Tone line.

Rainbow Glass catalog page, circa 1965–67. Duo–Tone line.

Rainbow Glass 1966 catalog. Duo–Tone line.

Rainbow Glass Duo–Tone line. Green vase with applied Blue leaf prunt,10", $40–48;
#D–316 Green bottle with Blue applied wrap and hollow stopper, 12", $55–70;
#D–214 Green pitcher with Blue applied handle, 6¼", $20–28. All pontiled.

The influence of Viking Glass and its later ownership of Rainbow Glass is shown in this image. The left bottle bears a Rainbow paper label; it has a flared lip and is of thick and pontiled green glass. The right bottle/decanter bears a Viking paper label, has a optic diamond pattern, and is thin blown. Both were made in the same Huntington factory, under different ownership, at different times. Rainbow, $30–40; Viking, $28–35. The absence of the flared lip and presence of a traditional optic makes the Viking rendition less AMCM.

Rainbow Glass catalog cover. 1971. The two-piece candle lamps wtih the crackle glass globes, on the left, were in the line a short time.

Rainbow Glass catalog page, circa 1967. Bottles.

Rainbow Glass catalog page, giving this line a distinctly "colonial American" name (The Middleburg), but the colors and forms are anything but. Left to right, they measure 16½", 10½" and 12½".

Bottles

Rainbow Glass catalog page, circa 1967.

Rainbow Glass, #9621 Hancock bottle with tear-drop stopper, Blue, 12", $30–45; #306 Ruby bottle with tear-drop stopper, 10½", $30–45. Both pontilled.

Rainbow Glass tall, hour glass bottle w/ stopper, crackle, Amber, $30–45.

Rainbow Glass #311 Green bottle with stopper, 10", $20–28; #303 Orange bottle with stopper, 7¼", $20–28; #301 Amethyst square bottle with stopper, 6¼", $18–24. No pontils.

Rainbow Glass catalog page featuring the cylinder crackle bottles with stoppers, called elsewhere The Middleburg, but here with a fourth shorter size. Also shown are the bottle with lid and the pitcher shown earlier.

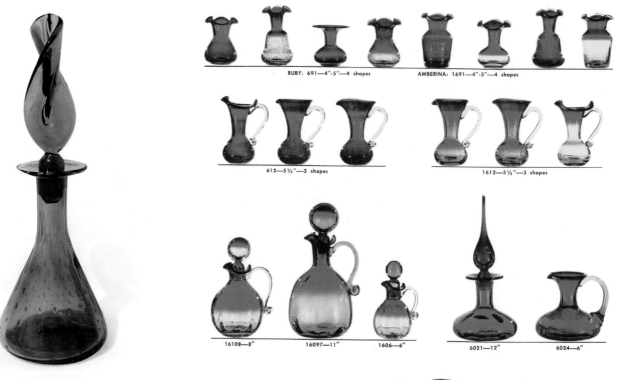

RUBY: 691—4"-5"—4 shapes   AMBERINA: 1691—4"-5"—4 shapes

612—5½"—3 shapes   1612—5½"—3 shapes

16108—8"   16097—11"   1606—6"   6021—12"   6024—6"

Rainbow Glass #769 air-trap decanter, Amber with large flame twist stopper. The decanter is shown in the catalog illustration above. The twisted stopper alone is 8¾" h.; the overall height is 16¼". $95–120.

Rainbow Glass catalog page, early 1960s. Note that the small, colorful window vases are prominent parts of the company line. Amberina, crackle, bulbous, and exaggerated tear drop stoppers are mid-century design elements entering into Rainbow designs at that time.

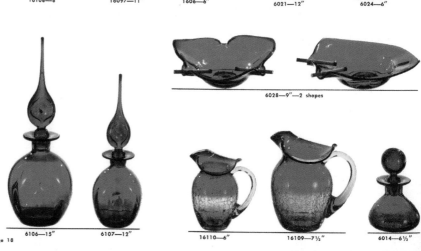

6028—9"—2 shapes

6106—15"   6107—12"   Page 18   16110—6"   16109—7½"   6014—6½"

Seneca
Glass Company

Morgantown, West Virginia
1891–1983

Good   *Good*

Opening in the town of Fostoria in Seneca County, Ohio, in 1891, Seneca Glass Company relocated to Morgantown, West Virginia, in 1896. Seneca was Morgantown's first glass factory, and it operated there until it was sold in 1982. It then operated as Seneca Crystal for an additional two years before closing forever. Seneca's main product line across time was high-quality, hand-cut, lead crystal. Colored glassware began to be produced by Seneca in the 1930s. By the 1950s, Seneca began to explore more casual, colorful and, at times, modern design themes.

Seneca Glass products were sold for decades in the best jewelry and department stores in North America. It was a luxury item. While best known for colorless crystal, Seneca produced a number of colored glasses throughout their history.

To Learn More:

Page, Bob and Dale Frederiksen. *Seneca Glass Company 1891-1983: A Stemware Identification Guide.* Greensboro, North Carolina: Page-Frederiksen Publishing Company. 1995.

Lindbeck, Jennifer A. and Jeffrey B. Snyder. *Elegant Seneca: Victorian, Depression, Modern.* Atglen, Pennsylvania: Schiffer Publishing, Ltd. 2000.

Seneca Glass catalog, 1973. Cascade was introduced by Seneca in 1972 and produced then in Crystal, Green, Grey, Peacock Blue, and Yellow.

When introduced in 1952, Seneca's Driftwood pattern was a symmetrical, round design that had the letters "DW" worked into the textured surface design. It was redesigned to make it more "contemporary" by removing the letter and making the glass and other forms with irregularly spaced angles for the sides, base, and lips. Original design tumbler, Smoke, $10–16; and redesigned tumbler, Cobalt, $12–18.

Seneca Cascade, Ruby, introduced after 1973, dessert /cereal bowl (shown twice), $12–18 each; old fashion, 3¾" h., $10–16.

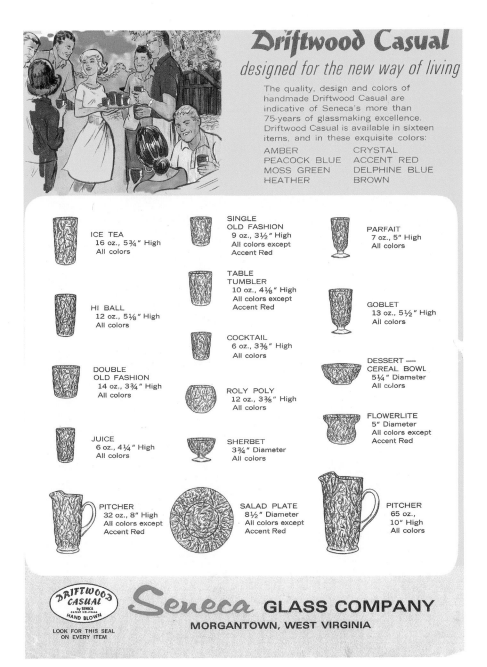

Driftwood Casual

designed for the new way of living

The quality, design and colors of handmade Driftwood Casual are indicative of Seneca's more than 75-years of glassmaking excellence. Driftwood Casual is available in sixteen items, and in these exquisite colors:

AMBER · CRYSTAL
PEACOCK BLUE · ACCENT RED
MOSS GREEN · DELPHINE BLUE
HEATHER · BROWN

ICE TEA
16 oz., 5¾" High
All colors

HI BALL
12 oz., 5⅛" High
All colors

DOUBLE
OLD FASHION
14 oz., 3¾" High
All colors

JUICE
6 oz., 4¼" High
All colors

SINGLE
OLD FASHION
9 oz., 3½" High
All colors except
Accent Red

TABLE
TUMBLER
10 oz., 4⅛" High
All colors except
Accent Red

COCKTAIL
6 oz., 3⅜" High
All colors

ROLY POLY
12 oz., 3⅜" High
All colors

SHERBET
3¾" Diameter
All colors

PARFAIT
7 oz., 5" High
All colors

GOBLET
13 oz., 5½" High
All colors

DESSERT ——
CEREAL BOWL
5¼" Diameter
All colors

FLOWERLITE
5" Diameter
All colors except
Accent Red

PITCHER
32 oz., 8" High
All colors except
Accent Red

SALAD PLATE
8½" Diameter
All colors except
Accent Red

PITCHER
65 oz.,
10" High
All colors

DRIFTWOOD CASUAL by SENECA PATENT NO.170644 HAND BLOWN

LOOK FOR THIS SEAL ON EVERY ITEM

Seneca GLASS COMPANY
MORGANTOWN, WEST VIRGINIA

Driftwood Seneca company flier page, circa 1966. Note the illustration showing the mid–1960s attire and casual entertaining. Colors offered then were Amber, Crystal, Peacock Blue, Accent Red (red with colorless foot), Moss Green, Delphine Blue, Heather, and Brown. 16 shapes were then available.

Seneca Cascade pattern cocktail/juice pitcher #1972, colorless crystal, 10", $14–22.

Seneca Ingrid pattern, four-lobe, colorless stem and foot with Smoke bowl. Note the Ingrid lines included all Crystal, Crystal with Smoke stems, and other possible color combinations. With this wide bowl, it is line #526. With a more conical bowl, it is line #520. The Ingrid line emulates a Scandinavian line with the identical four-lobe stem, thus the pattern name. As shown, $10–16.

Seneca Driftwood, salad or fruit bowl, 9" d., Charcoal, $30–45; and Driftwood look-alike small tumblers. Note the slight color variance and greater transparency. Easily confused, but this is not a known Seneca shape.

Seneca Driftwood Casual factory literature sheet, circa 1960s. The word "casual" was later dropped from the name.

Seneca Driftwood. Top: Plum (Amethyst) 32 oz., 8" pitcher, $28–34; second row (left to right) Amber 65 oz., 10" pitcher, $32–44; Heather (pink) uncommon handled ice tea, $18–26; Red Accent, 10" pitcher, $60–80; bottom row (left to right): Delphine Blue ice tea, 5¾", $6–8; Crystal table tumbler, 4⅛", $4–6; Moss Green juice, 4¼", $3–6; Peacock Blue roly poly, 3⅜", $4–6; Charcoal salad plate, 8½", $8–12; Plum desert/cereal bowl, 5¼" d., $6–8; Delphine Blue footed parfait, 5", $6–8; Brown footed sherbet, 3¾" d., $3–6; Amber footed goblet, 5½" h., $5–8.

Silverbrook Art Glass Works

Riverhead, New York
c. 1946–c. late 1960s

Good

The four Kreutz brothers—John, Joseph, Frank, and Henry—came to the United States from Czechoslovakia to make glass, but their path was not direct. Fleeing their home in fear of the approaching German invasion, they worked hot glass in Argentina, Bolivia, and Uruguay before coming to the United States in 1943. They worked at Tiffin Glass, in Ohio, before beginning their own firm near Riverhead, New York, around 1946.

Little is currently known about this small firm, but their designs are noteworthy for Mid-century Modern designs. All Silverbrook production seen to date or illustrated in the scant available literature, shows only colorless crystal glass.

It is evident that design influences run between Silverbrook and Tiffin, as the common forms of the two companies, the controlled bubble and off-hand pheasants, are so similar. Noted also is the striking similarity between the vase-bookends shown in Silverbrook images and a similar form made at Eriksen glass. Several other Silverbrook forms found are reminiscent of other American mid-century producers and more research is needed about this little known glasshouse.

To Learn More:
Rouche, Berton. "A Reporter at Large." *The New Yorker.* February 11, 1950.
Melvin, Jean S. *American Glass Paperweights and Their Makers.* Camden, New Jersey: Thomas Nelson, Inc. 1967.
Jones, Helen. "Silverbrook Art Glass." *All About Glass.* Vol. VII. No. 4. January 2010.

Silverbrook Art Glass candleholders with controlled air-trap bubbles, 2½" d., $14–20 each; bowl with air-trap and two applied surface columns, 3⅛" h. x 9⅞" l., $34–42.

Silverbrook Art Glass vase with four petal-like applied leaves. Colorless with air-traps. Hand-signed on the base with either "J" or "F" Kruetz in a cursive script, $100–125.

Silverbrook Art Glass advertisement that appeared in *Crockery and Glass Journal*, February, 1948.

Silverbrook Art Glass pheasant figurine, 5" h x 6⅝" l., $25–35; a pair of pinched old fashion tumblers, 3¼" h. x 3¾" d., $12–20 each.

Silverbrook paper label as it appears on the pheasant.

L.E. Smith
Glass Company

Mt. Pleasant, Pennsylvania
1907–2010

Good   *Better*   *Best*

L.E. Smith Glass began in Mt. Pleasant, Pennsylvania, in 1907, and produced pressed glass from their factory there until closing in June, 2010. Production for Smith was, at times, large, often diverse, and predominately not modern in design or style.

Smith, like others, proclaimed their glass to be a line of authentic reproductions of classic earlier ware. It was a dramatic departure when, in the fall of 1958, they introduced a line of "striking, handcrafted, modern vases and pitchers." The new line was called Soft Simplicity, but that was later shortened to just Simplicity. Swung vases were a popular element in the line as they soared and thrust colorful asymetrical and organic necks to near towering heights. The initial offering included four colors. (*China, Glass & Tableware*, August 1958).

The vases in elongated swung forms were predominantly in the 10- to 24-inch range. A few, made from punch bowls, were as large as 60 inches tall. In this size they competed with the monumental pieces made during the same era, such as the "floor" pieces crafted at Blenko. Simplicity/Soft Simplicity remained in production from 1958 through 1976. A few swung vases were made at Smith after that time, but they were not specifically a part of the Simplicity line. Simplicity, much like Viking Epic, was a line and not a single pattern. The Viking Epic line predates Smith's Simplicity by about one year. There are many shapes and colors in the two lines that are hauntingly similar. Both Epic and Simplicity developed into eclectic lines with glass animals, ash trays, vases, bowls, candlesticks and more. The Simplicity line remained in production at Smith until 1976.

The most common colors for Smith Simplicity are the opaque color Bittersweet (an orange milk glass), Green, Amber, Amethyst, and Flame (an Amberina-like, heat sensitive Amber-red color). Transparent blue became Peacock Blue in the hands of Smith glass, in a manner similar to the way Viking gave their blue the snazzy color name of Bluenique. Less common, but not rare, Simplicity colors include Milk Glass/White Opaque, Ruby Red, Yellow, and Crystal. Found, but much less so, is the opaque color Lilac, a light purple milk glass. It was produced in 1961 only, per Smith author Tom Felt.

To Learn More:

Felt, Tom L.E. *Smith Glass Company: The First One Hundred Years.* Paducah, Kentucky: Collector Books. 2007.

Felt, Tom. *L.E. Smith Encyclopedia of Glass Patterns & Products.* Paducah, Kentucky: Collector Books. 2011.

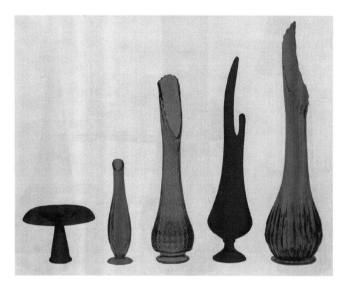

Smith Glass introduced their line of modern shapes called Simplicity in the fall of 1958, one year after Viking introduced the Epic line. Swung vases, elongated to exceptional heights, were a staple in both Simplicity and Epic.

Smith Glass, Simplicity line, circa 1959 catalog. Note the three cone-based pieces, each offered in two sizes.

Smith Glass, Simplicity line, all with 3¾" base, but varying in height from 8" to 17½", per Smith author Tom Felt. Left to right: #2501 candle pitcher, Bittersweet, $24–28; hurricane candle holder, unknown line number, Amethyst, $12–18; candle pitcher, Peacock Blue, $18–24.

Smith Glass #1504 scoop hurricane candleholder, Peacock Blue, $18–26.

Smith Glass catalog illustration for Simplicity line, circa 1959. Note the #1504 scoop hurricane candleholder and #2501 candle pitcher.

Smith Glass, Simplicity line in a early 1960s catalog, featuring 6" bowl, 14" to 18" vases, and 6" flared bowl, all from the same mould.

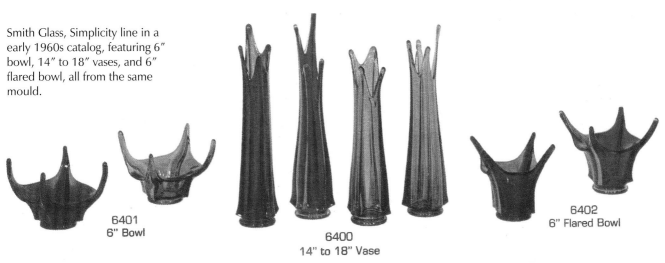

6401
6" Bowl

6400
14" to 18" Vase

6402
6" Flared Bowl

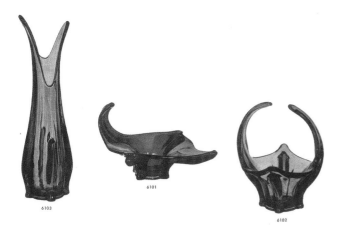

6103

6101

6102

Smith Glass, Simplicity line, #6100 series in a circa 1961 catalog. Left to right: #6103 tall vase; #6101 jack–in–the pulpit bowl form; and #6102 basket.

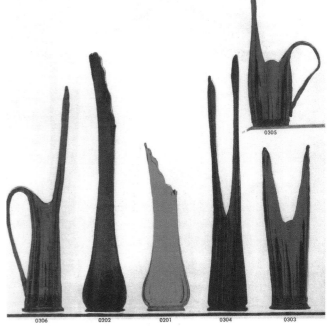

0305

0306   0202   0201   0304   0303

Smith Glass, Simplicity line catalog page, circa 1959. Swung vases of varying forms and line numbers.

Smith Glass, Simplicity line 1967–68 catalog page.

Smith Glass Simplicity line #6101 bowl, circa 1967–68, produced in Peacock Blue, Amber, Flame, and Green. As shown, $12–18.

Smith Glass, Simplicity line, Bittersweet. Left to right: #4805 covered candy, $34–40; #4702 low compote, small, $20–30; #4802 low compote, large, $30–40.

Smith Glass, Simplicity line vases. Left to right: #952 swung vase, Lilac, 44", $250–350; #0201 Flame (Ruby) swung vase, 17¾", $16–24; and Bittersweet #602 swung vase with Fayette Glass sticker, 46" h., $240–300 (Fayette was marketing division of Smith). West Virginia Museum of American Glass collection.

Soft Simplicity

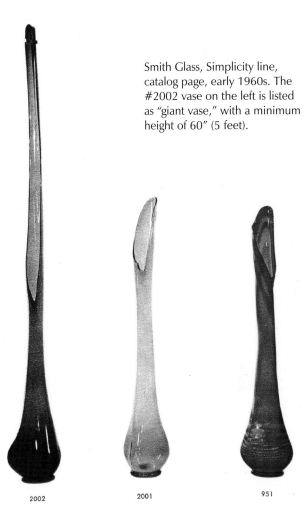

Smith Glass, Simplicity line, catalog page, early 1960s. The #2002 vase on the left is listed as "giant vase," with a minimum height of 60" (5 feet).

Smith Glass, Soft Simplicity line in a 1966 brochure. Swung vases were offered at over 40", as was item #5403, and in decreasing size ranges down to 20–26". Note we are not certain what distinguishes the Simplicity line from the Soft Simplicity line.

2002   2001   951

Smith Glass, Simplicity line pieces, all in Bittersweet, circa 1963–1970. Left to right: swung vase, 20", $24–32; large crimped compote, 6⅞" h., $22–30; small crimped compote 5½" h.; $18–24; compote (flat), 4" h. x 11" d., $18–22; #3804 candy with lid, 10" h., $16–22.

Smith Glass, Simplicity line, #1912 handled candleholder with foot, each approximately 12" h. Left to right: Peacock Blue $20–30; Bittersweet $28–38; Lilac $35–45.

Smith Glass, Simplicity line, #3804 footed candy with lid, Green, 10" h., $18–26.

Smith Glass, Simplicity line bird #3901, approximately 12" h. Strikingly similar to Viking Epic bird, but Viking never made an opaque orange (Bittersweet). To distinguish other colors, note that Smith birds have apparent feathers, Viking has no feathers. As shown $14–22.

Smith Glass cigarette lighter, Bittersweet, $10–18.

Smith Glass, large ashtray, Flame colored, $14–22.

SANDSCROLL

6594
Cigarette Box and
Butane Lighter
Combination
Hgt. - 6 1/2"

6593
Double Old Fashion
9 oz., Hgt - 3 1/2"

THE L. E. Smith Glass COMPANY

MOUNT PLEASANT, PA.
15666

"Over a Half Century
of Fine Handcrafted Glass"

The Smith Glass Sandscroll line was introduced in 1968 as a line
of ashtrays, which grew over the next few years before being
discontinued in 1970. Author Tom Felt quotes the April 1969
issue of *House & Garden,* saying, "Sandscroll looks contemporary
at first glance. Put it with your favorite heirloom, and it becomes
traditional. Its surface derives from the actual texture of wet,
green sand." In this advertisement from Smith company
literature, circa late 1960s, Sandscroll is a limited line designed
for drinking and smoking.

As seen in this company catalog page, circa 1969-70, the Smith
Glass Sandscroll line expanded into these forms.

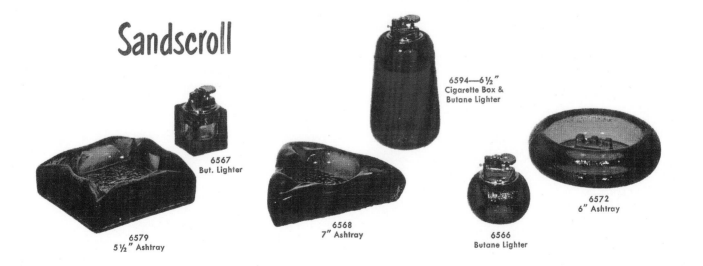

Smith Glass Sandscroll line smoking accessories circa 1968, from a company catalog illustration.

Steuben

Corning, New York
1903 –2011

Good   *Better*   *Best*

Steuben Glass Works began in 1903, when English glassmaker Frederick C. Carder partnered with Thomas G. Hawkes of Corning, New York. Hawkes owned a large glass cutting firm and sought a supplier for quality blanks. Carder remained the artistic genius behind the colorful and endlessly diverse Steuben products until it was sold to Corning Glass Works, where it became the Steuben Division. Color production ceased in about 1932, when Carder was replaced and the focus shifted to thicker, colorless, and more modern creations.

Arthur A. Houghton, Jr., just out of Harvard University, was the force leading Steuben into the heavy, thick colorless crystal. His family owned Corning Glass and controlled Steuben. He advocated going modern in design, using clear glass only. Houghton showcased the new glass at the Chicago World's Fair of 1933–34, where Steuben's first modern designs were widely shown. New York architect John Monteith Gates had joined with sculptor and designer Sidney Waugh to pioneer Steuben's modern movement. The new ware was so popular that Steuben had its own futuristic pavilion at the New York's World Fair of 1939-40. These modern designs remained the hallmark of Steuben until the last few years.

In 2008, Corning Inc. sold Steuben to Schottenstein Stores Corp., owners of a number of discount retail stores and other ventures. In the fall of 2011, Schottenstein announced it was closing Steuben, ending 108 years of exceptional glass production.

Steuben signature appearing on the base of the twist stem shown nearby.

Steuben, both signed in script. Left: large #8008 ashtray, 6¾", $40–75; right: medium #8028 ashtray, 5¼", $35–60. David Hill, designer.

Steuben Floret bowl #8059 with three loop base, signed, 7¾" d., $120–170. First found by us in the Spring 1956 catalog.

Steuben Spiral bowl #8060, circa 1954, signed, 7" d., $150–180. Donald Pollard designer.

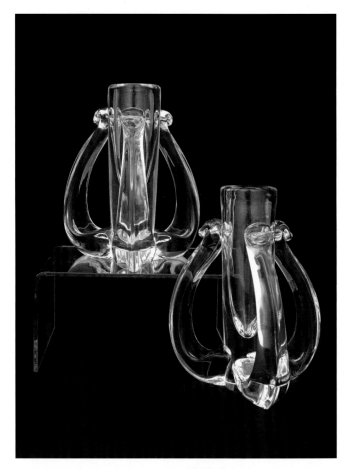

Steuben candlesticks, low scrolled, signed, $120–160 each.

Steuben Versailles candlesticks, #SP978, Circa 1962; air-trap base, applied decoration, signed, 8½" h., $150–200 each. Donald Pollard, designer.

Steuben Star Spangled vase #8098 and SP949F, signed. 8¾" h., $120–180. First found by us in the Spring 1960 catalog.

Teays Valley Glass Companies

**Corridor between Charleston
and Huntington, West Virginia
1920s–1970s**

Within the glass belt of West Virginia–Pennsylvania–Ohio, there was a smaller area that fostered and grew a distinctive style of handmade glass. Roughly defined as the geographic area spanning Huntington, West Virginia, on the Kentucky-Ohio border and running to Charleston, West Virginia, is a region dubbed The Teays Valley.

When, in the 1990s, the author was trying to gain an understanding of the handmade, often pontiled, brightly colored glass crafted in this region, a conversation seeking to define the area was had with glass author Tom Bredehoft. Tom has academic roots that lie in the study of geography. He identified the long, wide valley that joins Huntington and Charleston as the bed of an ancient post-glaciatic river, the Teays. It is that long abandoned river bed that left the expanse of flat land that became U.S. Route 60 and later I-64, both corridors that helped define the region's handmade glass industry. No singular community within the Teays Valley is, in fact, called Teays Valley, but in the context of this glass discussion, it is the region and ancient river bed of approximately 50 miles in length that we make reference to here.

The quest to understand why such a large number of often small glass houses rose up in the relatively small geographic area, and mostly within a period of a few decades is intriguing and interesting. Few survived long; even fewer are remembered today. The towns that have been home to glass production in the 50-mile long Teays Valley of West Virginia include Barboursville, Ceredo, Charleston, Culloden, Dunbar, Huntington, Kenova, Milton, Scott Depot, and St. Albans.

The hot glass producers that have operated here are many. Some grew, survived and thrived; others did not. These firms earn their places in a survey of American Mid-century Modern because some of the most striking examples of this type of American glass hail from this relatively small community. Names like Blenko, Rainbow, and Bischoff are significant players in the explosion of form and color closely associated with American Mid-century Modern. Their neighbors, the lesser known firms, made similar products in several cases. Few stretched to the boldness of a Blenko floor vase or the enthusiastic designs of Bischoff, but they had in common bold colors and hand blown, often pontiled glass, in organic and modern shapes.

Why was there this divergence from then successful American glass style and why here in the Teays? While the core and seeds of this concentration of glass style are yet unknown, it is the appearance of a number of glass men from Sweden, and specifically from Swedish families with generations of work in the hot glass industry, that seems to be the origin of the Teays Valley style. Famed glass families like Berquist, Eriksen, and Muller brought their Scandinavian artistic sensibilities to the small glass houses of the Teays Valley. An undated letterhead from Tri-State Glass Manufacturing Company (circa 1940) boldly states, "Swedish Crackle Handcrafted." It appears that there was a self-awareness of their style, historical tradition, and marketability.

One significant feature is the concentration of Swedish glass makers in the valley by the 1930s, the eve of the Mid-century Modern period. It is not for lack of a reason that the term Swedish Modern came to be, or that an American, West Virginia glass company, when striving to convey an image of bold modern glass, would assume for itself the name Viking. By the 1940s, the designs and influences of Scandinavia were making a major impact on American material culture.

KING GLASS
"Crowned with Success"

Exciting addition to our showrooms—hand made American glass in colors of charming subtlety — Smoke (which we call Dawn Grey), Lime, Green, Amethyst, Amber, Crystal.

No. 106 — French Chalice, 8″ high, $30.00 doz.

No. 121—Bowl with large tear drop bubble, 11″ diam., $30.00 doz.

No. 110—Covered Candy Dish, 9″ high, $39.00 doz.

F.O.B. Kenova, West Va.

King Glass offers a wide selection of pitchers, decanters, vases, highballs, candy dishes, bowls, apothecary jars, etc., in crackle, bubble or plain finish.

See King Glass in our showrooms and at:
National China and Glass Show, Hotel New Yorker, Room 618-619
Chicago Gift Show, Palmer House, Room 728-729

Exclusive and national distributors of King Glass

soovia **JANIS** • ROOM 739 • 225 FIFTH AVENUE, NEW YORK 10, N. Y.

Western Representative: The Grant-Jacoby Company, Room 302 — Brack Shops, Los Angeles, Calif.

King Glass, of Ceredo, was one of the several dozen smaller glass factories operating in the 20th century in the Teays Valley of West Virginia. This advertisement, appearing in *Crockery & Glass Journal* in July 1953, shows a the Scandinavian influence in the air-trap #121, 11-inch bowl.

Emch Glass salesman's or catalog photo. Pinched side, heavy crystal #1041 decanter, circa 1950. Original photo in the collection of Clark and Mary Ann Emch, son and daughter–in–law of the original factory owner.

Emch Glass relocated from Morgantown West Virginia (denoted by the star on this West Virginia shaped label) to the Teays Valley in the late 1940s. Emch operated there until circa 1954.

Emch Glass salesman's or catalog photo, circa 1950. Many of the Teays Valley companies produced their versions of pinched lines of glassware. Original photo in the collection of Clark and Mary Ann Emch, son and daughter–in–law of the original factory owner.

Emch Glass salesman's or catalog photo, circa 1950. This thick, heavy Swedish looking #3087 "footed vase, twisted stem" resembles the ware made at the time by Tiffin Glass and others. Original photo in the collection of Clark and Mary Ann Emch, son and daughter–in–law of the original factory owner.

Emch Glass salesman's or catalog photo, circa 1950. Heart Candy Dish strikingly similar to products from Gunderson, Steuben, Imperial, and others. Original photo in the collection of Clark and Mary Ann Emch, son and daughter–in–law of the original factory owner.

Tex Glass, Inc.

Decatur, Texas
1941–1979

Tex Glass produced these handblown textured tumblers and jug/pitcher in Amber. The pattern is often confused with Bryce El Rancho, Seneca Driftwood and Morgantown Crinkle. Tumblers, $10–14 each; jug, $30–45.

Herman and Bertha Rosenzweig were the founders of Tex Glass, Inc., in Decatur, Texas. Tex Glass operated from 1941 until its closing in 1979. Herman died in 1965 and Bertha continued to run the firm after his death. He had started his own factory in Vienna, Austria, before fleeing the Nazis. He worked in Canada and Mexico, then opened a glass factory in Athens, Texas. After Athens, they relocated to Decatur and remained there until closing.

To date, only the deep thumbnail beverage line of heavily textured glass has been positively identified as Tex Glass. It is certain that other glass will be identified as the product of this small factory that remained in production for roughly three-and-one-half decades.

Tex Glass tumblers in Blue, Amethyst, Amber, and Green, $10–14 each.

Tiffin Glass / U.S. Glass

Tiffin, Ohio 1938–1984

Good.   *Better*   *Best*

Tiffin air-trap, swirl vase, Desert Red, c. 1963–1966, $60–80.

U.S. Glass was formed in 1893 by a large number of successful American Glass firms, as a way to regulate glass prices. In 1938, U.S. Glass Co. offices were moved from Pittsburgh to Tiffin, Ohio. The Tiffin location was the last of the U.S. Glass sites in use when it closed in 1984, nearly a century after its founding.

Tiffin glass claims a place of high esteem in American Mid-century Modern discussions, as it embraced the "Swedish" style of modern to a degree that few other American glass manufacturers did. Heavy, colorless crystal began at Tiffin with the 1940 introduction of Tiffin's Swedish Optic line. The Cellini line came in 1947, incorporating hand-formed, open work stems crafted by highly skilled artisans. In 1959, Tiffin began production of the Empress line. Empress pieces are large, organic, color-filled forms that often twist, sprawl, and embrace large spaces with fluidity. The Empress line came in 75 various forms: Ruby/crystal; Emerald Green/crystal; smoke and crystal; sapphire blue and crystal; twilight and smoke. Ruth Henninger's book, *Tiffin Modern: Mid-century Art Glass,* reports that Twilight and Green replaced Emerald Green and Crystal in 1960, making the prior combination in production a very short time. Some of the Empress pieces are amazingly elegant, such as the low, long flower arranger. Some are indeed angry and twisted forms, like the ash tray #6599, which was not included in the 1959 catalog. It lacks the visual elements of MCM.

A single colored line of Tiffin was also produced in the same moulds as Empress. While the forms are often identical, this line does not have the cased, two-colored glass.

The bold period of modern designs at Tiffin ended in 1959 when company president Carlson retired, and new leadership lead the company away from the Mid-century Modern designs.

Tiffin's line #17430, called the pulled "Italian" foot line by collectors, is a very Swedish-looking form that exists in vases, bowls, and stemware. Both colorless and colored glasses were used. Other heavy Scandinavian styled forms were often employed in the Tiffin line. An example of the heavy rib optic, in the Amber-like Desert Red color, is shown at left. This piece embodies both the heavy rib optic pattern and the air-trap technique, creating a strong AMCM form. Air-trap at Tiffin was produced for a short time circa 1967.

Beginning with the sale of Tiffin glass in 1958, the company went through an amazing number of changes in ownership. It was sold again in 1961, declared bankrupt in 1962, and then sold in 1963 to operate as Tiffin Art Glass Co. In 1966, it was purchased by Continental Can Co., and sold again in 1968 to Interpace, parent company to many tableware manufacturers. Interpace produced glass marketed as both Tiffin and as Franciscan Crystal, the latter only in 1969–71. The factory was sold for the last time in 1979, prior to ceasing hot glass production in May of 1980.

To Learn More:

Henninger, Ruth, et al. *Tiffin Modern: Mid-century Art Glass.* Atglen, Pennsylvania: Schiffer Publishing, Ltd. 1997.

O'Kane Kelly. *Tiffin Glassmasters: The Modern Years.* Privately published. 1998.

Page, Bob and Dale Frederiksen, with Dean Six and Jaime Robinson. *Franciscan: An American Dinnerware Tradition.* Greensboro, North Carolina: Page-Frederiksen Publishing Company. 1999.

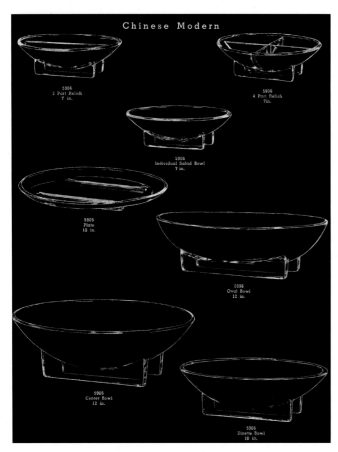

Chinese Modern

Tiffin Chinese Modern #5906 catalog page, c. 1949–1952. The serveware/gift ware in this line was made in crystal and crystal with platinum decoration. Chinese Modern was to compete in the same market as Cambridge Square, a colorless, geometric, and "modern" design.

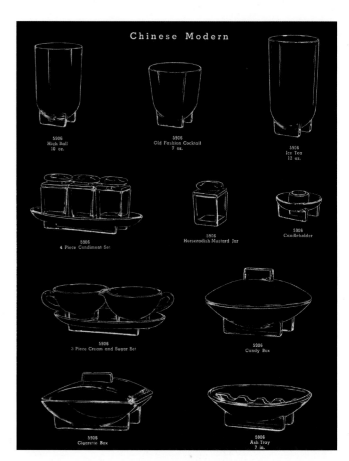

Chinese Modern

Tiffin Chinese Modern #5906 catalog page, circa 1949–1952.

Tiffin 8" footed rose bowl #6132, Plum, 7¾" h., $40–50.

Tiffin New Whirling Crystal catalog page, c .1950. Shown front left is #5986 flared bowl; right, #5966 vase, 10" h.; back vase unidentified.

Tiffin hurricane with Italian foot #17430 line, 11″ h. Company catalog photograph, circa 1959

Tiffin #6255 vase, 8″ h., $75–85. Discontinued before 1951.

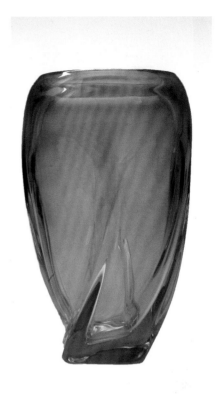

Tiffin #5511 twist vase, c.1955, Twilight color, 9½″ h., $120–140.

Tiffin #17430 line rose bowl, Wisteria, 7″, $40–55.

Tiffin #15 flip vase, c. 1967. Company catalog photograph.

Tiffin Modern catalog, c.1959, showing Whirling Crystal and other forms.

Tiffin Italian foot #17430 line. Left to right: Greenbrier vase, 12¾" h., $60–80; Desert Red (uncommon color), 12¾" h., $100–125; Greenbrier Sweet Pea vase, 6" h., $40–50. Jaime Robinson collection.

Tiffin bubble optic #14 rose bowl, c.1967, 7" h. Company catalog photograph.

Tiffin #17430 line centerpiece footed bowl. Company catalog photograph, circa 1959.

Tiffin #17430 line Italian
foot bowl, c.1950–1955,
in the color Pine with
controlled bubble, 8″ w.,
$75–85. Jaime Robinson
Collection.

Tiffin #17430 line Italian foot. Top:
Killarney Green urn vase, 10½″ h.,
$80–95; left, Killarney Green rose bowl,
8″ h., $50–60; right, Crystal hurricane,
11″ h., $50–60; bottom: Twilight low
compote, 8¼″ w., $70–80.

Tiffin #17430 line Italian foot vase, flared, Citron, 9" h., $90–110.

Tiffin #17430 line Italian foot vases in Wisteria. Left to right: Swirl optic, 12¾" h., $140–160; Teardrop, 10¼" h., $95–115; Flared vase, 9" h., $75–90.

Tiffin Holiday #17573 line. Top: Twilight ice tea, $24–30; middle row: Crystal sherbet ,$12–16; Crystal ice tea, $14–18; front: Wisteria with Crystal water, $20–25. All c. 1950

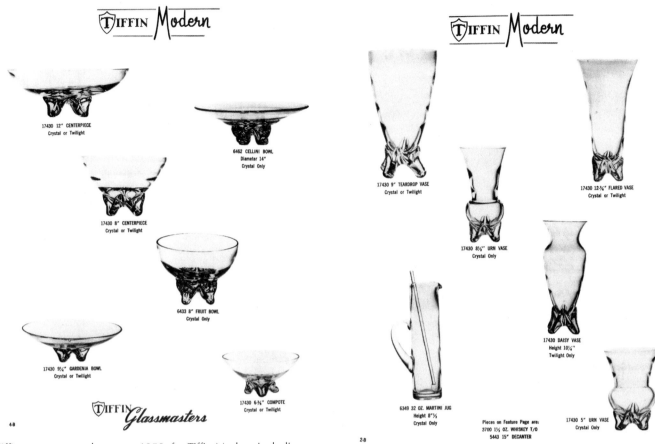

Tiffin company catalog page, 1959, for Tiffin Modern including items in the #17430 line and others.

Tiffin Italian foot 1959 catalog page.

Tiffin Holiday #17573 line water, Wisteria and Crystal, $20–25.

Original Tiffin factory photograph. Top row: four pieces #17430 line Italian foot and unidentified solid footed vase; bottom row: #5529 oval bowl, 14" l.; #5529 gardenia bowl, 12" w.; #5533 rose bowl, 6" h.

Brief Histories of AMCM Hot Glass Manufacturers

Tiffin #17423 comport in Wisteria, shown without lid, 5¾" h., $40–50 without lid, $90–100 with lid.

Tiffin Cellini line #17423 catalog page, c. 1951. Left to right: goblet 6¼" h.; champagne/sherbet, 4⅞" h.; liquor, 4½" h.; wine, 5⅛" h.

Tiffin Cellini line #6727 vase, c.1967, 9½" h.

Tiffin "Swedish Modern Crystal" table display. Original factory photograph.

17350 TALL FLARED VASE, SWEDISH OPTIC
Height—12¾"

17350 TUB VASE, SWEDISH OPTIC
Height—9¼"

17350 LOW FLARED VASE, SWEDISH OPTIC
Height—9"

5934 HURRICANE LAMP VASE
Blown Bowl with Blown Base
Swedish Optic
Height—10½"

Tiffin Swedish Optic catalog page, c. 1950s.

United States Glass Company

No. 525
Large Bowl
Swedish

No. 526.. Small Bowl
Kosta...

No. 526
Medium Bowl
Kosta

Tiffin Optic bowls. #525 large bowl Swedish; #526 small bowl Kosta; #526 medium bowl Kosta.

Tiffin Swedish Optic rose bowl in Copen Blue with colorless ball feet. Small rose bowl, $28–35; large rose bowl, $50–55.

Tiffin #6416 dahlia vase, swirling ball stem, 9½" h., $40–60.

Tiffin catalog photograph, #11 bonbon. This form is strikingly similar to pieces produced by Imperial, Steuben, and others.

Tiffin catalog photograph, #6280 gardenia bowl, 12 ¼″ w., two open handles.

Tiffin catalog photograph of #6722 vase, 7″ h., c.1967.

Tiffin catalog photograph, #6278 vase, 8″ h., with swirl base.

Tiffin vase #6727, c.1967, 9½″ h.

Tiffin catalog photograph, #6462 Da Vinci bowl.

Tiffin catalog photograph, two-handled fruit bowl.

Tiffin catalog photograph, #6420 candlestick, 10" h., produced in crystal only.

Tiffin catalog picture, #6270 bowl with applied foot and leaves, 9¼" w.

Tiffin #17437 crystal flared, footed vase with Swedish optic, 9", $38–50.

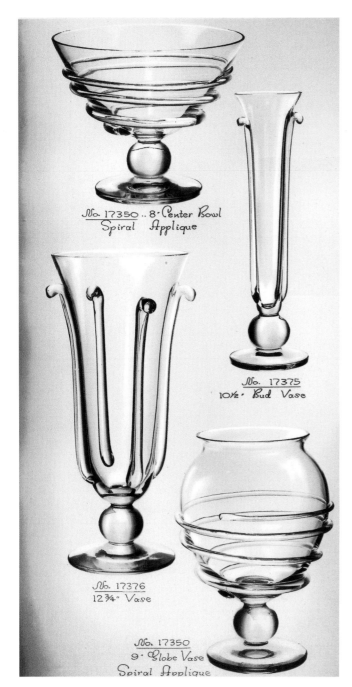

Tiffin undated catalog photograph of colored ribbon on a crystal optic vessel. Top row #5526 vase, 10" h.; #5539 vase, 12½" h.; #5527 vase, 20" h.; #5528 vase, 8½" h. Bottom row: #5532 plate 14" w.; #5530 ash tray; #5528 bowl, 14½" w.

Tiffin catalog page illustrating four items with applied surface decorations. Noted is Tiffin's place as a part of U.S. Glass Co.

Tiffin Green Fantasy line, Killarney Green ribbon on an optic, ten rib, oval crystal bowl, 14", $140–185.

Tiffin catalog photograph, #85 bud vase.

Tiffin #85 bud vase, Twilight (a color that shifts from blue to pink depending on the type of light), 11$\frac{1}{8}$" h., $75–95.

Tiffin catalog photograph, #20 open stem candlestick.

Tiffin Empress line, Ruby & Crystal
#6578 Vase, 12–14" with swung lips.
$120–145

introducing

Empress

All the beauty of the crown jewels... their fire and color in excitingly extravagant new lines of loveliness in motion... soaring flames of ruby red, plumes of emerald and sapphire, subtle shadings of twilight and smoke... a triumph for the Tiffin Glassmasters.

TIFFIN *Glassmasters*

Tiffin catalog cover "introducing" the Empress line, circa 1959. Shown is the #6580 large hurricane lamp or vase.

Tiffin Empress, c. 1959, catalog page 1–A. Items shown are in Smoke and Crystal, Emerald Green and Crystal, and Sapphire Blue and Crystal.

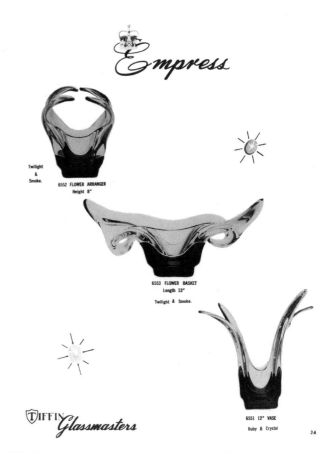

Tiffin Empress, c. 1959, catalog page 2–A. Includes an item in the color combination Twilight and Smoke.

Tiffin Empress catalog, circa 1959, page 3–A.

Tiffin Empress catalog, circa 1959, page 4–A

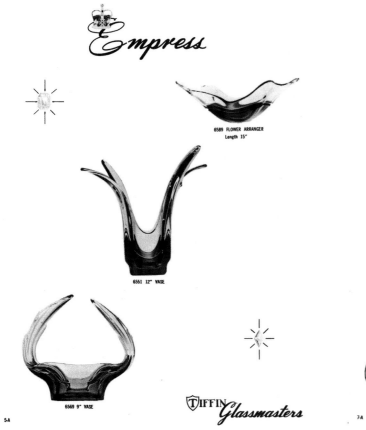

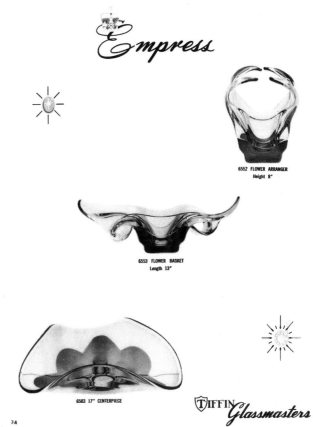

Tiffin Empress catalog, circa 1959, page 5–A

Tiffin Empress catalog, circa 1959, page 7–A

Tiffin Empress line. Top: #6608 flower arranger in Orange, 22" l. $45–65; bottom: #6553 flower basket, 13", Banana color, $40–55.

Tiffin Empress vase #6551, Twilight and Smoke, 12" h., $150–180.

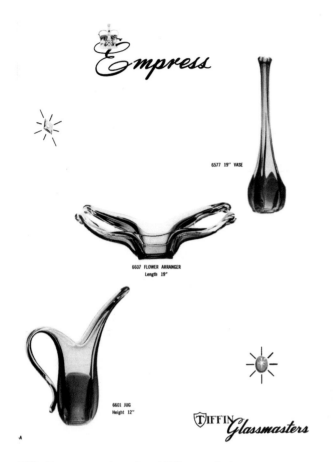

Tiffin Empress catalog, circa 1959, page 9–A

Tiffin Empress catalog, circa 1959, page 10–A

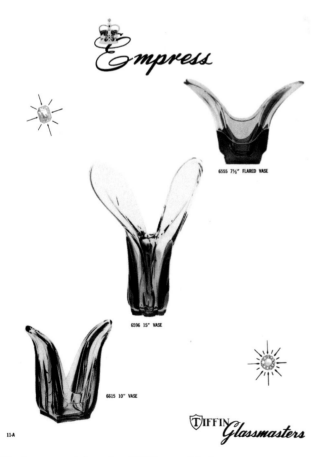

Tiffin Empress catalog, circa 1959, page 11–A

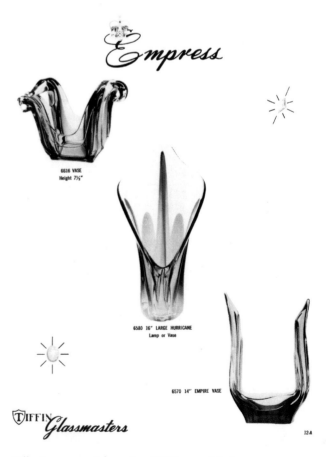

Tiffin Empress catalog, circa 1959, page 12–A

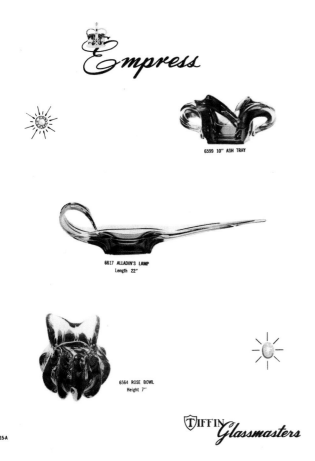

Tiffin Empress catalog, circa 1959, page 15–A

Tiffin Empress catalog page 18–A

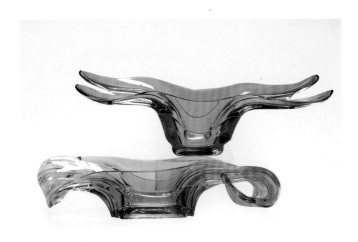

Tiffin Empress in Copen Blue & Crystal. Top: flower arranger#6550, 15½"l., $100–140; bottom: TV flower basket#6566, 15½" l., $120–160.

Tiffin Empress vase, Crystal and Ruby. 19" h. $85–120. Gift of the Tiffin Glass Collectors Club to the Museum of American Glass in West Virginia.

Tiffin Empress illustrated advertisement, circa 1960. "Tiffin Modern Breaks All Sales Records."

No. 6553. Flower basket—$10.00, retail.

No. 6551. Vase $10.00, retail.

No. 5466. Ash tray—$10.50, retail.

No. 6554. Ash tray—$6.50, retail.

No. 6559. Vase $12.00, retail.

No. 6560. Vase $12.00, retail.

No. 6557. 13½" plate—$10.00, retail.

Great things are happening at U.S. Glass!

TIFFIN MODERN

BREAKS ALL SALES RECORDS!

Introduced in January, Tiffin Modern has already proven to be one of the greatest successes in glassware history. Stores have re-ordered again and again *and again*. Many have called it their all-time best seller!

This is Tiffin's newest group of occasional accent pieces. The graceful shapes and the deep jewel-like radiance of unusual colors give any room, any decor new beauty and warmth.

Some of the pieces are shown here. There are several others in the line. They are available in: twilight and green, ruby and crystal, twilight and smoke, crystal and smoke, and smoke alone.

If Tiffin Modern isn't in your store now—see your Tiffin representative immediately.

UNITED STATES GLASS COMPANY
TIFFIN 15, OHIO • GLASSPORT, PENNA.
SINCE 1905

Tiffin Maderia pattern produced 1972 to 1978 only. The mug was introduced in 1973 and discontinued in 1975; it was made in Olive and Smoke only. Smoke mug, $9–12.

Tiffin Maderia. Front row, left to right: juice/wine, 6 oz., Plum, $6–8; double old fashion, 12 oz., Citron, $4–8; goblet, Apple Green, $8–12; mug, Brown, $8–12; juice/wine, Cornsilk, $4–6; goblet, Blue, $8–10. Back row, left to right: juice/wine, $4–6; ice tea, 10 oz., Rancho Ruby (made in 1973 only), $14–18; sherbet, 6 oz., Ice (crystal), $4–6; carafe (1973–75 only) $14–22; goblet, Twilight, $18–24; highball/tumbler, 14 oz., Rose (pink), $12–16.

Viking Glass Company

New Martinsville, West Virginia
1944–1987

Good *Better* *Best*

Viking Glass evolved from New Martinsville Glass (1900–1944) of New Martinsville, West Virginia. In 1944, New Martinsville Glass adopted heavy, colorless crystal glass in the European style. The firm was renamed Viking to reflect the style of glass they were then producing. New Martinsville Glass Manufacturing Co. had opened in 1900, and was struggling by the end of the Great Depression. An effort to embrace the new style of modern crystal at the factory went well, indeed, with a new name that evoked the new look.

Viking Glass made pressed glass—always pressed glass—and not hand blown or free form. Pieces that are blown or fully hand-formed with a Viking label were made when Viking had control of the Rainbow Glass factory in Huntington, West Virginia. The workers' skills at New Martinsville were as pressers, and the skills at the West Virginia Rainbow factory were in blown and hand-formed pieces. The Rainbow factory operated,

according to notes appearing in print in their catalogs as early as 1966, as being "affiliated with Viking Glass Co., New Martinsville, W.Va." From 1974–1979, Viking operated the Rainbow site as "Viking Plant II."

Viking was one of the largest and most prolific producers of American glass that embodied the Mid-century Modern aesthetic. While it has proven particularly difficult to identify designers for any line except Astra (Dick Schnake), the forms and colors are iconically modern. It is also true that Mid-century Modern was given an American dose of sensibility in the hands of Viking. While forms are colorful and exuberant, they refrain from being as rebellious and daring as similar forms in the hands of European designers.

The bulk of the AMCM glass made at Viking was lumped into one "line," titled Epic. The line included a number of patterns. The most dominant colors produced in Epic were Avocado (1964–

1970), Amber (1950 into the 1970s), Bluenique (1958–1970), and Persimmon (1958–1970). The Avocado and Amber were colors of the 1960s, omnipresent in everything from shag carpets to kitchen appliances. Bluenique was Viking's "unique blue," thus named Bluenique. Persimmon was Viking's bold orange, an exceptionally popular 1960s color. While Viking orange (Persimmon) and L.E. Smith's orange (Bittersweet) are often confused, it should be noted that there are similar forms between the two companies, but Persimmon is always transparent and Bittersweet is always opaque. Both companies made only the one orange color noted.

Within the Epic line was an entire Noah's ark of animals: from penguins to swans, cats to dogs, and many more. The only animals that seem to address the modern design aesthetic are the long-tailed birds and the egret. Both have elongated, graceful, and dramatic forms.

They have been seen paired with the low sculptural bowls as a center accent piece, or with two birds at the sides of another Viking object of the same color.

In late 1959, advertisements appeared in national magazines for Viking's new Flamenco line. It was thick, heavy crystal over color. It is known to have been produced in red, an opaque, jade-like green, and blue. This is a line reminiscent of ware from Tiffin Glass and Italian manufacturers.

The Viking line Tundra first appeared in trade journals at the end of 1965. A full page advertisement stated "Announcing a New Creation…A New Sensation By Viking. Tundra." The objects shown look like they have the pinched and pulled surfaces of handmade glass from Italy. However, Viking made these Tundra pieces in a hand-pressed mould, and then hand-tooled the top to give each piece a distinctive original character. While looking like handmade, imported modern Italian glass, Tundra was capable of being mass-produced to give a very similar visual appeal. In 1967, Tundra pieces were in the catalog, in the colors Avocado, Bluenique, Persimmon, and Honey. The line must not have been popular, as it is uncommon to find it today.

Other popular AMCM lines from Viking include an extensive line of ashtrays and smoking accessories;

smoking was big business in the 1945–1970 era. Swung vases that reach epic proportions—in excess of 36 inches—and a short line of objects with a rolled edge are also desired Viking AMCM items.

Scroll is a Viking line that is first found in a 1954 *Crockery & Glass Journal* advertisement featuring the seven-inch oval flowerlite/floral bowl. By December 1955, there is a note stating, "Viking Glass… is planning to add a number of new items to its Scroll line." Illustrated was a "new Oval Scroll" mayonnaise bowl with ladle. By 1956, Viking literature listed ten Scroll shapes, in "plain or crackled," and in nine colors, four of which are satin. No satin or crackle examples are known to this writer, suggesting limited production. Noteworthy tableware pieces include the cream and sugar and gravy boat. There are no plates, beverage glasses, or stemware, but a variety of other tableware forms exist. Scroll is not found in Viking literature after 1962.

Viking introduced a new tableware line at the end of 1960: Astra #6100. As Sputnik raced across the night sky and the media was driven by the start of the space race, patterns that turned to the sky were becoming popular. Astra has "a star motif in the base of each" piece and, when introduced at Atlantic City's trade show, was cited as a "new article"

with a "full assortment of table accessories, ashtrays and vases." It was made with a simple, unembellished body and a geometric, formed base. In visual appeal, it was related to the Square pattern made by Cambridge Glass. A four-leaf catalog from Viking titled "Viking's Newest Star ASTRA" states, in fine print, "Designed By Dick Schnacke." Schnacke was a local resident and this is his only known foray into glass design. The Astra line was originally offered only in crystal, but a few pieces were made later in the 1960s colors. A complete listing of pieces made is found in *Viking Glass 1944–1970*. The single candle block and ashtray are known to have been produced at a later date in color.

In 1987, Viking was sold. From 1987 until 1998, the Viking factory operated as Dalzell Viking, under the direction of David Dalzell, who was previously at Fostoria and came from a family with glass involvement spanning over a century. The factory ceased all hot glass production in 1998.

To Learn More:
Six, Dean. *Viking Glass 1944-1970.* Atglen, Pennsylvania: Schiffer Publishing, Ltd. 2003.

Viking epic line left #31190. Footed bowl with wave rim, Bluenique, 9", $22–32; low bowl with wave rim, $20–28; colorless footed bowl, Viking factory sample (gift to Museum of American Glass from the Cummings family, owners of Viking), $20–26.

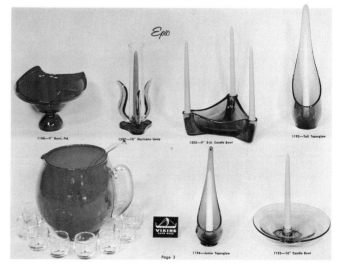

Viking Catalog page, 1960.

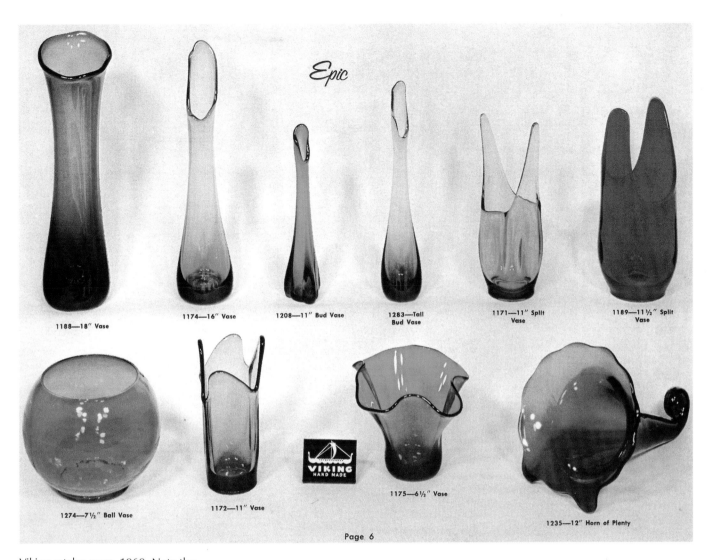

Epic

1188—18″ Vase

1174—16″ Vase

1208—11″ Bud Vase

1283—Tall Bud Vase

1171—11″ Split Vase

1189—11½″ Split Vase

1274—7½″ Ball Vase

1172—11″ Vase

VIKING HAND MADE

1175—6½″ Vase

1235—12″ Horn of Plenty

Page 6

Viking catalog page, 1960. Note the "split vases" in red and green with pinched sides and the smoke-colored wave rim, 11″ vase.

Viking Amethyst asymmetrical "scoop" bowl, $24–34.

Viking catalog page, 1960. Color and organic forms continue to hallmark the Epic items.

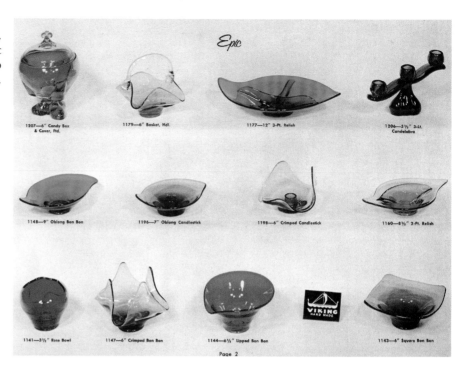

Viking catalog page, 1960, for the Epic line, showing noteworthy early shapes. #1182 crimped bowl, 12"; Epic three-toe footed bowl; large three-spire abstract bowl, 12"; modern basket #1163, 6"; oval deep bowl in imitation of numerous Italian forms, 20"; oblong shallow bowl #1186, 17"; and a square bowl with wave rim #1170, 8½".

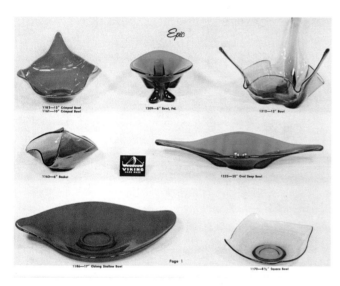

Viking Epic #1182 crimped bowl, 12". It is Lovingly referenced as "The Flying Nun" bowl, after a popular 1960s television show, because of its shape. Red, $40–55; Amber, $30–45.

Viking Epic candlesticks in Bluenique. Three light #1206 candelabra, shown in the 1960 catalog, $14–20 each; Epic three-toe candleblock #1210, made circa 1963 for a short time, $14–18 each

Viking Epic 6" footed candy box & cover, #1207, shown in the 1960s catalog. Persimmon color, $50–70.

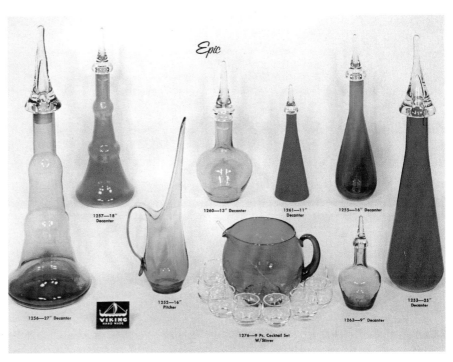

Viking catalog page, 1960. The line of tall spire stoppered "decanters" in sizes up to 27 inches are dramatic and desirable. The long-spout #1252 pitcher (shown here in green) remained in the line for several years..

Viking decanters with crystal spire stoppers as shown in the 1960 catalog. #1253, Ruby, 16", $50–75; #1261 in Bluenique, 11", $28–35.

Viking #1252 long-spout pitcher, shown in the 1960 catalog. Here in Persimmon, $35–50; Charcoal, $32–45; Green, $30–40; and Bluenique, $32–45 (varies 14½" to 16½").

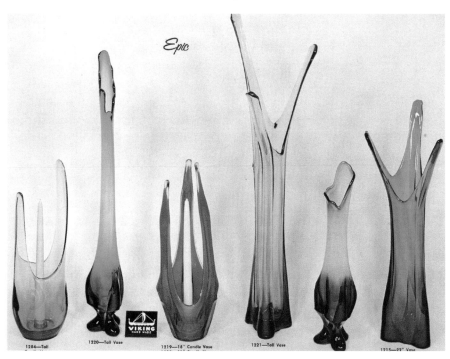

Viking catalog page, 1960. Shown are swung Epic vases and candle vases, with the larger two vases lacking height measurements and called only tall vases, while the far right vase is measured at 22".

Viking was famous for their tall swung vases in the Epic line. Here is an Epic three-toe, Amber swung vase, $20–28; open-footed, Persimmon bowl, $25–35; and an oddly shaped Bluenique swung vase, $48–60.

Viking Epic footed, covered candy, Green, $24–35; Amber footed shallow bowl with one side crimped up, one crimped down, $20–28.

Viking Glass stingray-shaped, Epic line three-part relish, Bluenique, $40–52; Charcoal, $38–48.

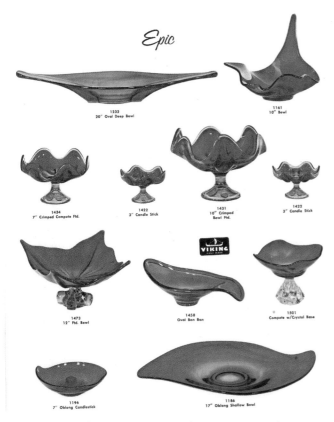

Epic

Viking Glass catalog page, 1964. Epic line pieces in Persimmon. Noted are the rolled edge.

Viking Glass Epic line twist forms. Avocado colored covered candy #1524, 8½" h. with lid, $18–24; small, crimped handkerchief, footed vase, 5½" h., $12–16. Items with this swirling foot were shown in a "Sparkling Designs for '65 from Viking" advertisement that appeared in *China, Glass & Tableware*, December, 1964.

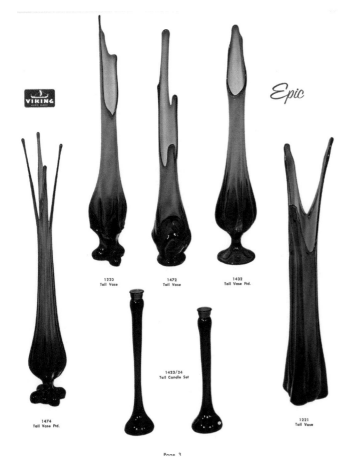

Epic

Viking Glass 1964 catalog page illustrating Epic line items in Bluenique.

Viking Epic #1212 bowl in green, 12", $30–45; and #1219 candle vase in Bluenique, $30–40. The candle vase is cataloged at 18" tall, but it varies greatly piece to piece.

Viking Glass stingray-shaped, Epic line three-part relish, close-up.
This is one of the exceptionally strong Viking AMCM designs.

Viking Glass Epic line forms made from the same mould. Left is
Thistle (uncommon color) #1405 vase 8" $25–35; right is
Persimmon #1251 pitcher vase 7" $18–28.

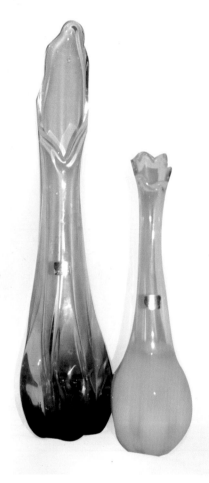

Viking Glass introduced a line in *China, Glass & Tableware*,
December 1959, that very much echoed the Ruby and crystal
cased line Empress made by Tiffin, which was introduced earlier
in 1959. Viking called the pieces Flamenco and described it as
"Two–Hue Crystal." Other colors made included Bluenique with
Crystal and Jade with Crystal, both shown here. Bluenique
Flamenco swung vase, 17¼", $70–85; Jade Flamenco swung
vase, 11½", $60–80.

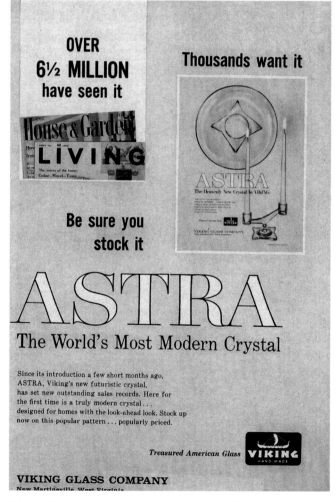

Viking Glass trade advertisement introducing the Astra line.
Appearing in 1961, it informed shop keepers noted that 6½
million people would see ads promoting Astra in *House and
Garden* and *Living* magazines. Launching Astra was an
exceptionally costly venture, but the line did not meet sales
expectations. Note the candlestick shown in the illustration, it
was very modern in its George Jetson appeal.

Viking Glass Epic line items. Left: Charcoal Epic "waves" footed bowl #1190, 10¾" d., $30–36 (this appeared in the 1960 catalog). Front: Epic "drape" footed bowl (comport), 7" w., $20–26/ Back: Epic "three foil" large, 22" swung vase#1215, $32–46. This vase form appeared in a national advertisement campaign in 1958 and in the 1960 catalog. Right: Epic "taperglow" hurricane lamp #1194 ,16", $30–40.

Viking Glass Epic line crimped bowl #6718. While successful in emulating freehand Italian glass of the same era, these Viking four-pointed bowls are pressed glass with hand tooling to their rims when yet hot. Persimmon $32–40; Amber $28–38.

Viking Glass Epic long-tailed birds, Persimmon. Left: #1316, the larger and less common bird, 11¼" h., $30–40; right: #1311, 10¼" h., $25–35. The smaller bird was produced in the tens of thousands, in multiple colors, over many years.

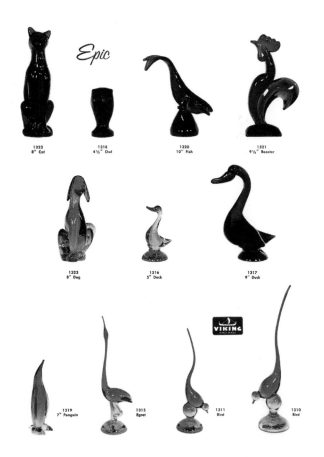

Viking Glass Epic line animals featured in the 1964 catalog. Note the two sizes of long-tailed birds, the egret, and the uncommon owl and penguin.

Brief Histories of AMCM Hot Glass Manufacturers

Viking Glass, Epic-like oblong shallow bowl #1186, 18",
Bluenique, $45–60. Also shown are the bowl mould in crystal,
$35–50 after heavy side columns were added to the form, and a
basket made post-1980 from the revised #1186 mould, $35–45.

Epic

Viking Glass, Epic line catalog page, circa 1962, showing items in
Green. Noteworthy are the #6609 oval basket and #6610
basket made from the same mould and tooled differently when
hot. The oblong shallow bowl #1186 was a Viking staple for
several years.

Tundra

Viking Glass catalog page. 1960 for the Tundra pattern vases and
bowls. Tundra was promoted in *Gifts & Decorative Accessories* in
December, 1965, as "Announcing a new creation… a new
sensation by Viking. Tundra." The pattern is intended to give the
appearance of the hand-pulled surface decorations then coming
from Italy (and a few West Virginia factories). Viking's Tundra was
a pressed line.

Left: Viking Glass,
Epic line duck
#1317, 9³⁄₈" h.,
Persimmon, $26–38.
Right: one of the
whimsied ducks sold
at the Viking outlet
and never produced
in the line for the
catalog, 13¼" h.,
Bluenique, $40–55.

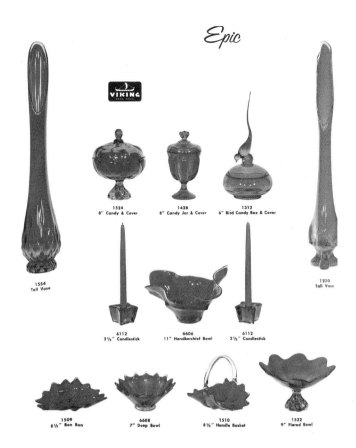

Viking Epic line items in Persimmon (orange). Noteworthy are the Epic #1512 swirl-base covered candy, #1312 bird covered candy box, #6606 handkerchief vase, and the Astra pattern #6112 candlesticks.

Viking Epic line #1312 covered candy boxes. Persimmon, 12¾" h. $45–55; Amber, 11½" h., $38–45.

Viking Glass company catalog, 1971. Epic line in green.

Viking Glass Epic line egret #1315. Left to right: Persimmon, 10¼", $18–28; Amber, $14–22; Ruby, $20–28; and Amber with exceptionally long (and fragile) neck, 13", $18–26.

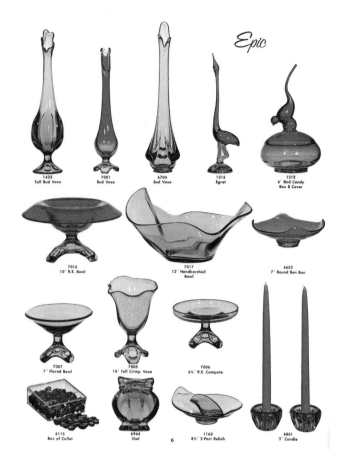

Viking Glass, Epic line, #7017 handkerchief bowl, 12", Amber, $30–40; Ruby, $48–60.

Viking Glass, Epic catalog page, 1971.

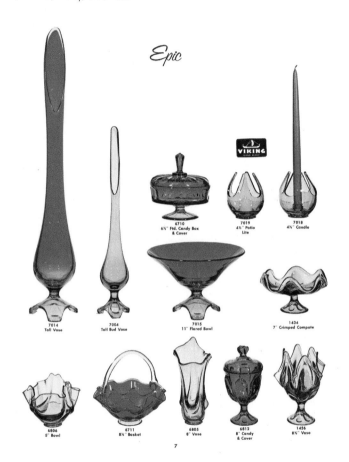

Viking Glass, Epic line catalog page, 1971. Amber and Persimmon colors.

Viking Glass, Epic line, "drape" candlesticks. Note that the earlier form had pattern only on the foot and not on the sides, and featured an arched, open three-point foot. This was reportedly difficult to produce and, in 1970, was altered to create the flat footed, pattern-sided version shown here in Green. As shown: Amber (less desirable color, more desirable form), $8–14 each; Green (more desirable color, less desirable form), $10–14.

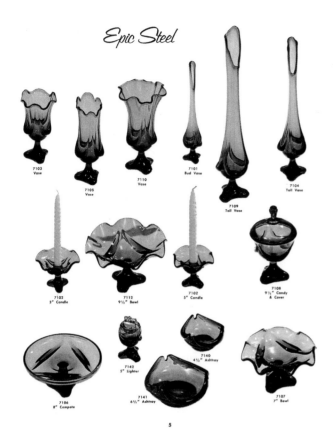

Epic Steel

Viking Glass, Epic line, drape pattern. Left to right: #7103 vase, $16–24; #7108 footed candy with lid, Amber, 9½", $14–26; #7108 footed candy, Steel, $18–28.

Viking Glass Epic "Steel" items as featured in the 1971 catalog. Note that Steel was slightly more blue than the earlier Charcoal, which was more gray. The forms, all Epic drape, feature the redesigned solid, flat foot version of the pattern.

Viking Scroll pattern #1900 was first mentioned in *Crockery & Glass Journal*, September, 1954. Bowls were made in 5", 6", 6 1/2", 10" and 11" sizes. The 6½" was often marketed with a clear glass insert for flower arranging and holding two candles. Left to right: Emerald Green $18–22; Honey $14–20; Amethyst $18–22 and Evergreen $18–22. Numerous other tableware pieces were made in Scroll.

Epic

Viking Glass, Epic line 1971 catalog page, all Bluenique, many being from the Epic "six–petal" line.

Viking Glass, Epic line, six-petal, #1409 candlesticks, Charcoal, 7¹/₈" d., $14–18 each.

Viking Glass, Epic line, #1222 candle vase. Introduced in 1957, the line was called Three Foil in early trade notices. Charcoal, 9–11" h., $22–28.

With Viking Glass is one element of this example of modern design gone mad. Here, married to a Mediterranean metal base of Rococo formality, the two types of design fail to connect. With one foot in the 18th century and one in the 19th century this piece is lost in time. The glass candy base is threaded and can be removed from the cast metal base. Not marketed by Viking but by an aftermarket company. $12–18. Paul Eastwood collection.

Viking Glass textured candle lamp. Viking took the mid–century idea of rough textured, abstract surface decoration to a new high with this deep patterned candle/votive. Honey, $8–14.

Viking Glass catalog cover, 1971. As the AMCM era drew to a close, Viking fell into the then-current fascination with mushroom—a psychedelic ending to the 1960s.

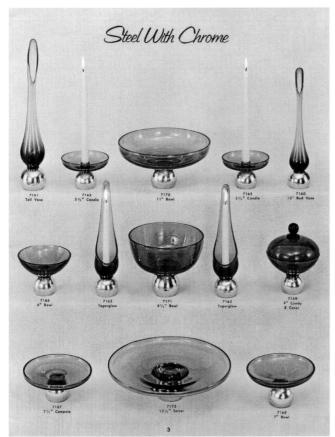

Viking Glass Steel With Chrome from its 1971 catalog. Note the sheer simplicity and lack of pattern or decoration on the glass. The line seems to have sold poorly and was not in the next year's catalog. The authors have seen only one piece of this ware over time.

Viking Glass Crystal With Chrome from the 1971 Viking catalog.

West Virginia Glass Specialty Company

Weston, West Virginia

1930–1987

West Virginia Glass Specialty Company opened in Weston, West Virginia, in 1930, and operated until production ceased in 1987. The large facility made mouth-blown, hand-formed glass, and, prior to 1940, a number of colors in glass. From 1940 until the closing, only colorless crystal was produced there. The factory produced tableware, barware, stemware, and giftware. The "Specialty" part of the name refers to the West Virginia Glass Specialty decorating shops, which turned out a diverse selection of hand painted, decaled, banded, sprayed, and otherwise embellished wares.

Two of the crystal lines that required special treatment and skilled glass workers were Whirlpool, a line of thin air-trapped forms, and Marine Ripple, an iridized crackle line. Both date from the 1950s. Crackle and air-trap glasses were popular mid-century treatments, and the Weston firm produced both.

West Virginia Glass Specialty introduced a line of air-traps in thin, mouth-blown crystal in 1953. The line was launched as Whirlpool.

West Virginia Glass Specialty footed colorless Whirlpool pitcher, circa 1953, 7⅞" h., $30–38. Collection of the West Virginia Museum of American Glass.

West Virginia Glass Specialty offered a new line called Marine Ripple, which featured an extra heavy crackle finish. Undated trade journal advertisement, circa early 1950s.

West Virginia Glass Specialty, Marine Ripple large rose/bubble ball #77, Iridescent, 8", $30–38.

West Virginia Glass Specialty, Blendo handmade pitcher, Lavender and Aqua. Pitcher, 11¼" h., $28–38; zombie tumblers, 6¾" h.,$4–8 each, .

West Virginia Glass Specialty, Blendo handmade pitcher with tumbler. Orange and Yellow. Tumbler, 6¾" h., $3–7 each; pitcher, 11¼" h., $28–32.

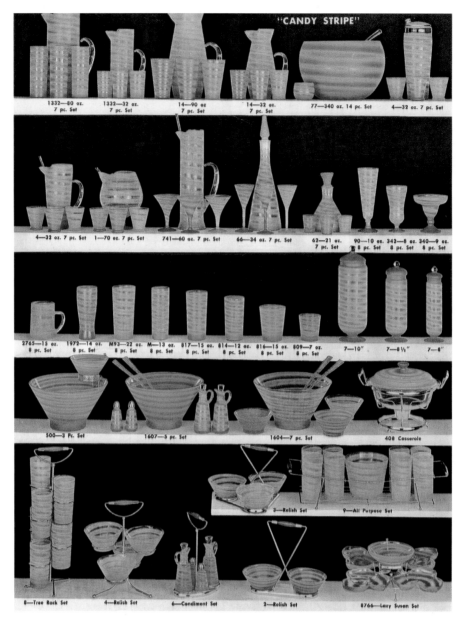

"CANDY STRIPE"

| 1332—80 oz. 7 pc. Set | 1332—32 oz. 7 pc. Set | 14—90 oz. 7 pc. Set | 14—32 oz. 7 pc. Set | 77—340 oz. 14 pc. Set | 4—32 oz. 7 pc. Set |

| 4—32 oz. 7 pc. Set | 1—70 oz. 7 pc. Set | 741—60 oz. 7 pc. Set | 66—34 oz. 7 pc. Set | 62—21 oz. 7 pc. Set | 90—10 oz. 8 pc. Set | 342—8 oz. 8 pc. Set | 340—9 oz. 8 pc. Set |

| 2765—15 oz. 8 pc. Set | 1972—14 oz. 8 pc. Set | M93—22 oz. 8 pc. Set | M—13 oz. 8 pc. Set | 817—15 oz. 8 pc. Set | 814—12 oz. 8 pc. Set | 816—15 oz. 8 pc. Set | 809—7 oz. 8 pc. Set | 7—10" | 7—8½" | 7—8" |

| 500—3 Pc. Set | 1607—5 pc. Set | 1604—7 pc. Set | 408 Casserole |

| 3—Relish Set | 9—All Purpose Set |

| 8—Tree Rack Set | 4—Relish Set | 6—Condiment Set | 2—Relish Set | 8766—Lazy Susan Set |

West Virginia Glass Specialty company catalog showing various decorations applied at factory. Note the use of wire holders and wooden handles on some sets. These were brightly colored, informal entertaining and dining sets.

West Virginia Glass Specialty #1607 "condiment set" in the decoration Candy Stripe. Original factory sample writing on glass.

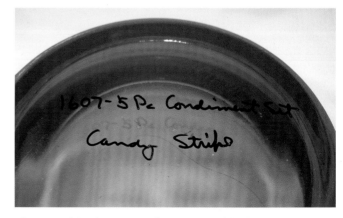

Close-up of the factory sample notation on the base of a large bowl. Collection of Museum of American Glass in West Virginia.

Designers of American

Mid-century Modern Glass

Winslow Anderson

Anderson (1917–2007) is well known for his Blenko designs and for his work at Lenox, where he was design director from 1953, when he left Blenko, until his retirement in 1980. A graduate of Alfred University Anderson was the first Blenko professional designer and created over 160 new designs for the firm in his six years there.

To Learn More:
www.blenkocollectors.com

Jascha Brojdo/ Georges Briard

The Ukranian born Jascha Brojdo rose to prominence as an American designer working in the 1950s–70s. The name Georges Briard was adopted to mark his commercial pieces. His numerous designs were produced first by M. Wille Company and later with Philip Stetson. Neither Brojo nor either of these firms manufactured hot glass, but worked in unison to place his art onto slumped forms. His glassware, often marked Georges Briard, was sold at high-end department stores and numerous other outlets. Jascha Brojdo died July 30, 2005, in New York City, at the age of 88.

Stan Fistick

Stan Fistick led Fenton Art Glass of Williamstown, West Virginia, into its first Mid-century Modern venture in 1953, when he designed the New World line.

A modernistic designer Stan Fistick was hired, in 1952, to bring contemporary design into the company's products. His first creation was a set of cookie canisters that proved difficult to make; thus, they were soon discontinued. Modern-style cased glass vases in Ruby and dark green were also produced, but they did not sell well and were discontinued at the end of the year. He forged ahead to design the New World shapes, but this pattern only enjoyed limited success and Fenton's experiment with contemporary style was put on hold. Fistick became disillusioned and moved on to academia. *See the Fenton chapter.*

Gay Fad

From her home in Ohio, Fran Taylor hand decorated small household metal objects (including waste bins) and glass pieces from 1938 until 1945. In 1945, Taylor opened Gay Fad Studios in Lancaster, Ohio. Until 1963 the firm was busy, and was one of the best known and most prolific glass decorating companies in the United States. The Gay Fad staff did extensive painting and decorating on glass "blanks" purchased from Hazel-Atlas, Anchor Hocking, West Virginia Glass Specialty, Federal Glass, and others. Some of the glass bears the mark of the glass producer. Fewer pieces bear any indication that it is Gay Fad's work on the blanks, though some pieces do bear a Gay Fad signature. One Gay Fad mark is a monogram like "G" and backward "F." The mark is commonly worked into the edge of the design.

Gay Fad juice glasses, signed. The right example is very Space Age– Atomic in design. Each $2–6.

Higgins Glass Studio

Michael Higgins, born 1908 in London, England, married Frances Stewart, born 1912 in Haddock, Georgia, in 1948, and so began a decades-long artistic collaborative. She completed a Master of Fine Arts degree at the Institute of Design in Chicago, where Michael taught. Their efforts to decorate clear, flat glass began early in their relationship and they began Higgins Glass Studio. In 1950, they added a staff person to assist them.

Their ware was formed by the labor-intensive process of fusing glass. The process creates a "glass sandwich." They created a design, either drawn with colored enamels or utilized pieces, quilt style, of smaller colored glass shapes. A second piece of enameled glass is laid on the first. The entire composition is then placed over a shaped mold and then heated. Heat causes the glass to "slump" over and into the shape provided by the mould. At the same time, the design is permanently fixed and fused between the two glass layers. Supplemental layers were at times added to give further texture, visual complexity, and color.

To create these objects, they worked as a team, taking shifts from their Chicago apartment, until entering a partnership with Dearborn Glass near Chicago in 1958. They worked at Dearborn Glass until moving on to do work for Haeger Pottery in 1964. When the Higginses left Haeger in 1966, they returned to working for themselves and acquired a location in Riverside, Illinois. Michael Higgins died in 1999; Frances Higgins in 2004. The Higgins Studio continues to operate at the time of this writing. Following the wish of the Higgins', Higgins Glass Studio is now under the ownership and direction of design associates Louise and Jonathan Wimmer.

To Learn More:
Johnson, Donald-Brian. *Higgins: Poetry in Glass.* Atglen, Pennsylvania: Schiffer Publishing, Ltd. 2005.

To Learn More:
McGrady, Donna & Kitty Hanson. *Gay Fad: Fran Taylor's Extraordinary Legacy, Volume 1–2.* Santa Fe Trading Post. 2011.

Gay Fad crystal pitcher with all–over decoration appears quite modern.

Gay Fad signature on the illustrated pitcher. Note that the literature for this describes the pattern as inspired by a Navajo Indian blanket design. This begs the question of using a traditional, historic design to create modern appealing objects.

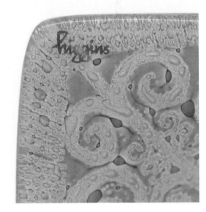

Higgins signature as it appears on the nearby plate/ tray.

Higgins square plate or tray, signed.

Michael Lax

Born in New York City (1929–1999) Michael Lax graduated from Alfred University in 1951. Lax created work for Dunbar Glass that earned him the Museum of Modern Art's Good Design award. He then developed the Festive line, produced by Duncan & Miller. In 1953–54 he was awarded a Fulbright scholarship and studied with Kaj Franck, a renowned Finnish designer of glass and ceramics. Upon his return to the U.S., Lax assisted Russel Wright in designs for ceramic dinnerware. In 1965, he established the Madison Avenue firm of Michael Lax Associates, Inc. He did design work into the 1980s, and is deemed one the most successful American industrial designers. (See the Fenton, Dunbar, and Duncan and Miller chapters.)

Peter Max

Peter Max was born in Germany in 1937. He became a popular American illustrator and graphic artist, incorporating psychedelic shapes and bold, bright color in his work. His early work appeared on posters that were found on the walls of college dorms all across America. Max became intrigued by new printing techniques that allowed four-color reproduction on product merchandise, including printing on glass. He spent a period of time in western Pennsylvania at the Houze Glass site, and the result was a series of wall hanging plaques or plates that today seem to capture the essence of the 1960s in America. (See the chapter on Houze glass for more.)

Peter Max design printed on a smoke glass decorative plate made at Houze Glass, circa 1962.

Fred Press

Fred Press (b. Boston, Massachusetts) was an American designer and artist whose product designs were granted a Good Design award by the Museum of Modern Art, New York. His designs on glassware reached popularity in the 1940–60s. Fred Press wares often incorporated glass in metal holders.

In May, 1957, Fred Press wrote an article titled, "What Will Be Tomorrow's Trends?" that appeared in *The Gift and Art Buyer*. In the introduction to the article, it noted that it was "By Fred Press, vice-president Rubel & Co. Decorative Accessories Inc., New York."

James Rosati

James Rosati (1911–1988) designed the Laguna line for Duncan and Miller glass of Washington, Pennsylvania, his home town. The line won a Good Design award from the Museum of Modern Art in 1953. Rosati had been involved with Robert May at Duncan on various lines before his 1953 Laguna creations. Rosati is best known for his abstract sculptures and teaching at Pratt Institute, Cooper Union, and Yale University.

Rubel & Co.

Rubel & Co. of New York City were factory representatives for various companies (glass and others) and manufacturers who had objects made specifically to their criteria. Both Paden City Glass and Fenton Art Glass in West Virginia made glass mid-century for Rubel. Paden City produced ware for Rubel until the glass factory closed in 1951. Fenton assumed making many of the same objects in the same color for Rubel late in 1951, and continued until 1954. Distinguishing the Rubel ware made by Paden City from that of Fenton is at times difficult, as often the same moulds and colors were utilized at both factories. Authors Carrie and Gerald Domitz discovered that pieces with black metal frame and wooden ball feet were made after Fenton began production for Rubel. Paden City glass pieces made for Rubel are held in glossy, copper metal frames.

In a 1957 trade journal article the author, Fred Press, was noted as "vice-president Rubel & Co. Decorative Accessories, New York." (See the entry for Fred Press.)

When Fenton Art Glass began to sell their assets, including their museum holdings and morgue, several items came into both public view and available for purchase that were identified as Rubel creations made at Fenton. The Museum of American Glass in West Virginia was successful in obtaining some of those Fenton for Rubel objects shown here.

To Learn More:
Domitz, Carrie and Gerald. *Fenton Made for Other Companies 1970–2005.* Paducah, Kentucky: Collector Books. 2005.

Raymor

Richards Morgenthau & Co. and Raymor were interconnected New York-based firms that worked and marketed modern-designed domestic products. Irving Richards, the company's founder, had links with Russel Wright that dated back to 1935, and the work of Raymor reflects that association. The company offered designs by many of the best known contemporary designers including Teague, Seibel, Eames, and Zeisel, as well as designs by Richards himself. As early as 1947, when Richards Morgenthau & Co. began, the firm manufactured lighting, ceramics, and glass from their factory in New Jersey.

Using a Ben Seibel design titled Raymor Modern, a glassware line was produced by Morgantown Glassware guild that included five forms in four colors. The colors were Gray, Green, Honey and Crystal. Examples of this line are uncommon. (See the entry for Ben Seibel.)

Utilizing the production capacity of Duncan and Miller Glass Co. Raymor Connoisseur was another of the Raymor-designed lines and a product exclusively marketed by them.

Raymor influenced public opinion with their advertising slogan, "Modern is Good." Today, Raymor is remembered for design and imports, and Richards Morgenthau & Co. is remembered for sales, marketing, and distribution.

Dick Schnake

Schnake, a resident of New Martinsville, West Virginia, with no formal design background, designed the line Astra for Viking Glass of New Martinsville. Astra was first produced in late 1960.

Ben Seibel

Seibel was born in 1918, in Newark, New Jersey. Early studies in architecture at Columbia were interrupted by World War II. After being discharged, he studied industrial design at Pratt Institute, beginning in 1945. Prior to completing his academic work he launched his own studio, and worked until his death at age 65 in 1985. His body of work has been described as "prolific and varied" and ranges from furniture and lighting to dinnerware and glass.

In glass, Seibel designed the Raymor Connoisseur line made by Duncan and Miller as a line exclusively distributed by Richards Morgenthau & Co. of New York City. He designed the Raymor Modern Glassware line for Raymor (affiliated with Richards Morgenthau) that was produced by Morgantown Glassware Guild. He designed Pebble Beach and a number of other popular, plain lines for Fostoria in the 1960s.

To Learn More:
Racheter, Richard G. *Tableware Designs of Ben Seibel 1940s–1980s.* Atglen, Pennsylvania: Schiffer Publishing, Ltd. 2003.

Dorothy Thorpe

Dorothy Carpenter Thorpe was born in Utah in 1901 and graduated from Latter Day Saints University and the University of Utah before settling in Glendale, California. From her California studio she designed full tableware ensembles, accessories, and linens to complement them. Her creations were sold under her own name by large department stores like Marshall Field of Chicago and others across the U.S. She used glass made by Heisey, by Cambridge, and, extensively, by West Virginia Glass Specialty.

Dorothy Thorpe glass is usually marked; the signature is a sand-carved backward "D" followed by a larger "T" and then a second letter "D." She often outsourced the work on her glass to craftsmen in the United States and Mexico. In a letter dated October 22, 1945, to glass researcher J. Stanley Brothers, Thorpe discussed a line she created in 1936 for S & G Gump Company of Honolulu, saying, "We used the flora and fauna of the islands for inspiration for the decoration of glassware and table linens and did bowls, plates, trays, picture frames, bar glasses, vases and complete table settings. Some of the subjects used were fern, spider lily, Poinciana, bread fruit, sugar cane, bird-of-paradise, magnolia, api leaf, li leaf, philodendron leaves, palm aria, mountain ginger, gardenia, orchids, fish, seaweed, lapa cloth designs and many others." Her words convey the diversity of decoration and form that her glass creations addressed.

In the same letter, she added, "To my knowledge we were the first ones in this part of the world to employ sand carving as a medium of decoration for table and giftware. I feel that it all came about through inspiration. Each of our designs is original and is usually drawn from life. Before the war, I worked in Sweden and other parts of Europe to have original glass blanks made. Several American factories are making our own shapes for us."

Most of Thorpe's designs were created for, marketed by, and sold under the name of her company. One example is Hydrangea, a stemware line with elaborate sculptured floral stem, made by Heisey for her company.

The designs were predominately oversized flora and fauna sand-blasted deeply into the crystal, or simpler decoration of wide silver bands. As much as anything else, it is the scale of her work, the sheer size and proportions, that set it apart from prior glass designs and make it a possible AMCM product. Thorpe died in 1989.

To Learn More:
Edan, Hughes, "Artists in California, 1786–1940." *American Women: The Standard Biographical Dictionary of Notable Women.* Volume III (1939-40) Los Angeles, California: American Publications, Inc. 1939.

Dorothy Thorpe advertisement appearing in the August 1956 issue of *Giftwares.* The forms and decoration are, indeed, modern in their appeal.

Dorothy Thorpe leaf decoration on large hurricane globes. It is unlikely that these wooden bases were original to the glass or period.

Russel Wright

Wright was born April 3, 1904, in Lebanon, Ohio. He attended Princeton and then apprenticed in New York City with successful industrial and theater designer Norman Geddes. Wright designed everything during his career. From spun aluminum to furniture, extensive patterns of ceramic tableware to less expansive lines of glassware, he tried them all. In the 1950s and into the 1960s, Wright created lines of glassware.

Wright-designed lines include those made by Bartlett Collins (Eclipse), Imperial Glass (Pinch, Flair, and Twist), Old Morgantown (American Modern), and Paden City Glass (Snow Glass).

To Learn More:
Keller, Joe and David Ross. *Russel Wright: Dinnerware, Pottery & More.* Atglen, Pennsylvania: Schiffer Publishing, Ltd. 2000

Dorothy Thorpe "tear–drop" stems in the pattern Coronation. Trade journal date unknown

Eva Zeisel

Eva Striker Zeisel was born in Budapest, Hungary in 1906. At age 17 she entered the Hungarian Royal Academy of Fine Arts as a painter. She shortly chose to work with more practical materials, and became an apprentice in ceramics. Before her marriage and immigration to America, Zeisel was engaged by German ceramic manufacturers and later by Russian ceramics firms. Today she is best known for her work as an American industrial designer.

In 1946, Zeisel was given her first one-woman show, "Eva Zeisel: Designer for Industry," at the Museum of Modern Art in New York City.

Eva Zeisel designed extensively for both pottery/china and glass manufacturers in the mid-years of the twentieth century. Her first glass designs came in 1952, when she launched a line called Silhouette glass to complement her Halcraft line for Hall China Company of East Liverpool, Ohio. It was marketed by Sun-Glo studios and made by Bryce Brothers. The line remained illustrated in Bryce literature until 1958. The Bryce 1965 price list shows Silhouette as being possibly still available, and solicits buyer inquiries. It is possible other Bryce lines were Zeizel designs, but no proof connecting her to specific designs has been found to date.

She came to work for Heisey Glass of Newark, Ohio. Glass scholar Tom Felt noted in the *Heisey News* in 1998 that in "December, 1953, an advertisement appeared on the back cover of *Crockery and Glass Journal* announcing that Mrs. Zeisel had been appointed as art director for A.H. Heisey. It must be remembered that, by 1953, Heisey was already suffering from the economic difficulties that would eventually lead to the factory's closing four years later and it is clear, from the advertising copy, that they were aware of the need to find new markets if they were to survive." The Zeisel designs did not, however, provide the needed new market shares. If their availability today is any indication, the Zeisel designs were very modest sellers at best.

For her Town and Country pattern, she won one of the Good Design awards from the Museum of Modern Art. While at Heisey, she created four shape lines introduced in 1954: #6009A Roundelay, #6007A Crystal Buds, #6006 Hour Glass, and #1637A Town and Country (produced until 1957).

She created a number of decorations for Heisey in a relatively short time. Etchings #3523B Steed, #524B Classic, #525B Chintz, #526B Pennsylvania Dutch and #527B Ponies (all on the Buds line) were her creations. No known examples of any of these have been found, but they appear on a company pricelist. Her other designs, that were not necessarily on shapes she designed, include #520B Leaf, #521B Scroll, and #522B Cocktail party.

She is known to have created designs for Federal Glass as well: it is believed those came after her time at Heisey, circa early 1960s.

She died December 30, 2011, well the past the century mark.

To Learn More:

Cudd, Viola. *Heisey Glassware*. Privately published. 1969.

Felt, Tom. "Spotlight On Heisey Designers: Eva Zeisel." *Heisey News*. December 1998.

Eva Zeisel design for Heisey Glass, the pattern is Town and Country. See the Heisey entry for more information.

Eva Zeisel design for Heisey Glass. The decoration appeared on a line titled Cocktail Party. Draft of October 21, 2013.